[kra_]
[koa_]

[reign_of_x]

NEW MUTANTS BY VITA AYALA VOL. 1. Contains material originally published in magazine form as NEW MUTANTS (2019) #14-18. First printing 2021. ISBN 978-1-302-92787-5. Published by MARVEL WORLDWIDE, INC., a subsidiary of MARVEL ENTERTAINMENT, LLC. OFFICE OF PUBLICATION: 1290 Avenue of the Americas, New York, NY 10104. © 2021 MARVEL No similarity between any of the names, characters, persons, and/or institutions in this magazine with those of any living or dead person or institution is intended, and any such similarity which may exist is purely coincidental. **Printed in Canada.** KEVIN FEIGE, Chief Creative Officer; DAN BUCKLEY, President, Marvel Entertainment; JOE QUESADA, EVP & Creative Director; DAVID BOGART, Associate Publisher & SVP of Talent Affairs; TOM BREVOORT, VP, Executive Editor; NICK LOWE, Executive Editor, VP of Content, Digital Publishing; DAVID GABRIEL, VP of Print & Digital Publishing; JEFF YOUNGQUIST, VP of Production & Special Projects; ALEX MORALES, Director of Publishing Operations; DAN EDINGTON, Managing Editor; RICKEY PURDIN, Director of Talent Relations; JENNIFER GRÜNWALD, Senior Editor, Special Projects; SUSAN CRESPI, Production Manager; STAN LEE, Chairman Emeritus. For information regarding advertising in Marvel Comics or on Marvel.com, please contact Vit DeBellis, Custom Solutions & Integrated Advertising Manager, at vdebellis@marvel.com. For Marvel subscription inquiries, please call 888-511-5480. **Manufactured between 6/11/2021 and 7/13/2021 by SOLISCO PRINTERS, SCOTT, QC, CANADA.**

10 9 8 7 6 5 4 3 2 1

Writer:	Vita Ayala
Artist:	Rod Reis
Letterer:	VC's Travis Lanham
Cover Art:	Rod Reis (#14-15)
	& Christian Ward (#16-18)

Head of X:	Jonathan Hickman
Design:	Tom Muller
Assistant Editor:	Annalise Bissa
Editor:	Jordan D. White

Collection Editor:	Jennifer Grünwald
Assistant Editor:	Daniel Kirchhoffer
Assistant Managing Editor:	Maia Loy
Assistant Managing Editor:	Lisa Montalbano
VP Production & Special Projects:	Jeff Youngquist
SVP Print, Sales & Marketing:	David Gabriel
Editor in Chief:	C.B. Cebulski

NEW
MUTANT
NEW
MUTANT
NEW
MUTANT
NEW
MUTANT

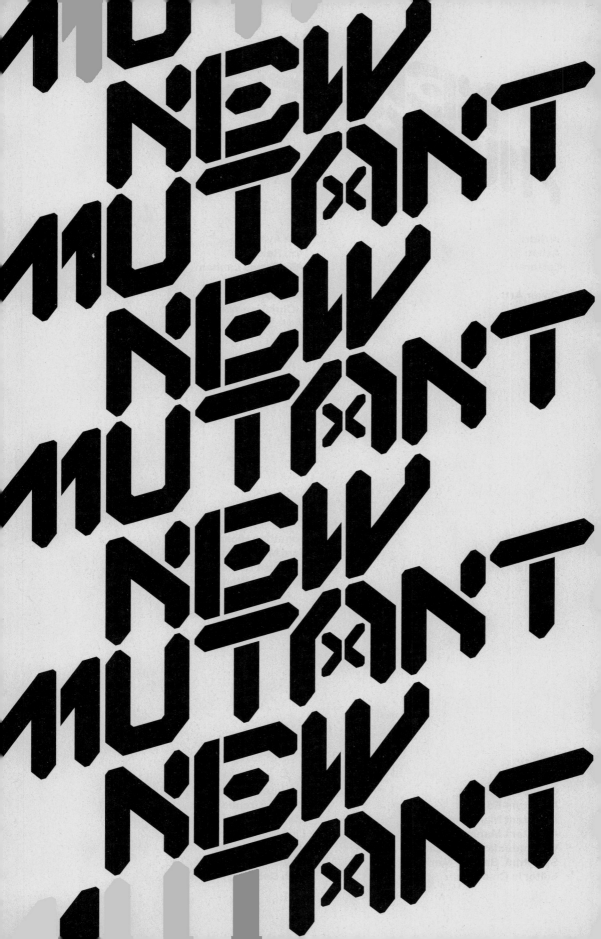

NEW MUTANTS
NEW MUTANTS
NEW MUTANTS
NEW MUTANTS

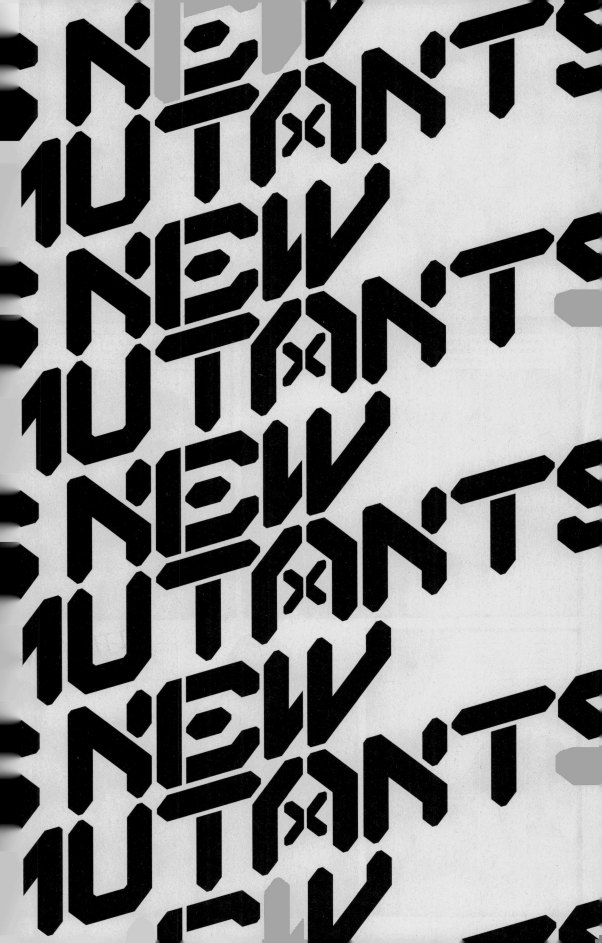

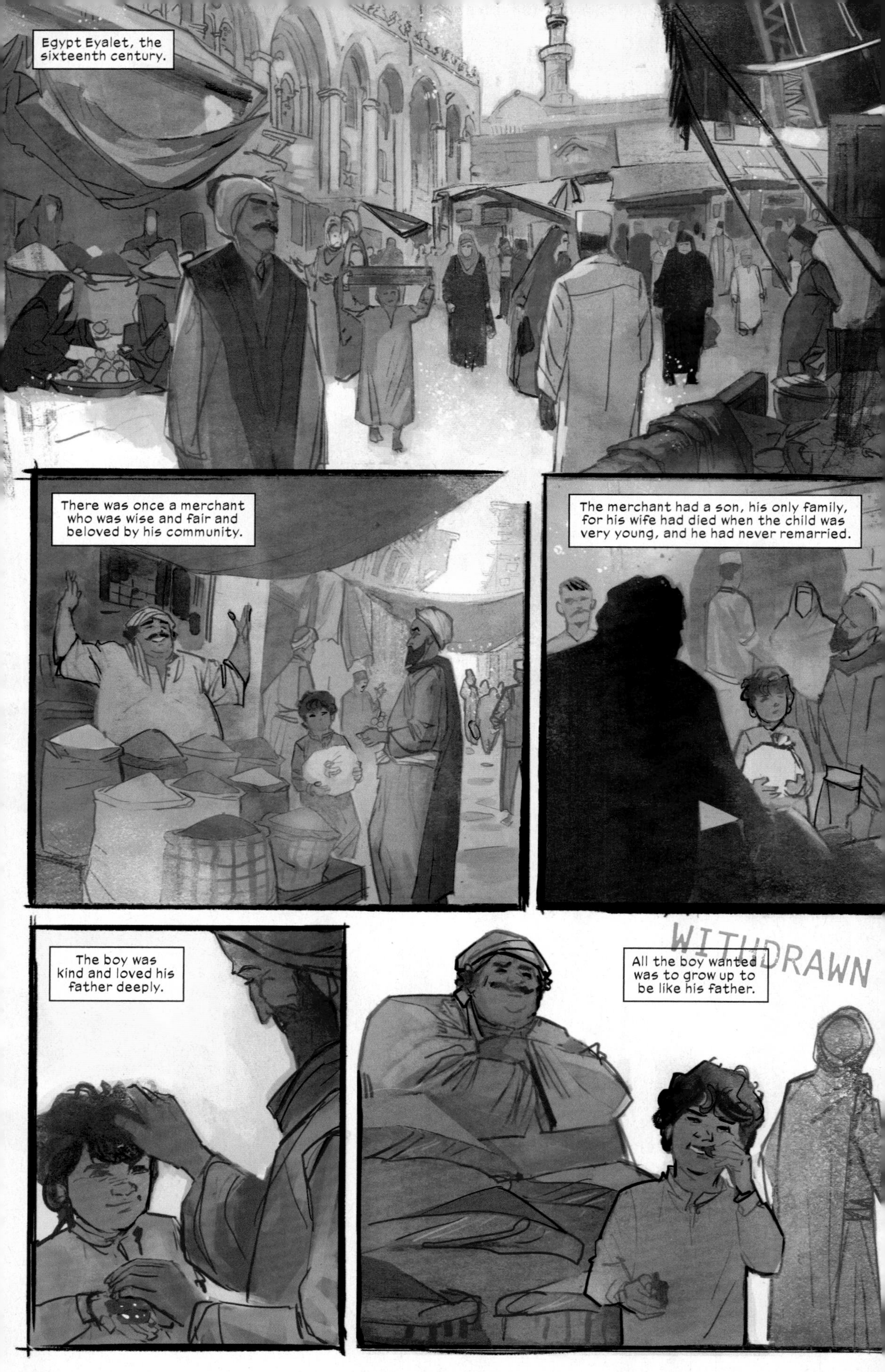
Egypt Eyalet, the sixteenth century.
There was once a merchant who was wise and fair and beloved by his community.
The merchant had a son, his only family, for his wife had died when the child was very young, and he had never remarried.
The boy was kind and loved his father deeply.
All the boy wanted was to grow up to be like his father.

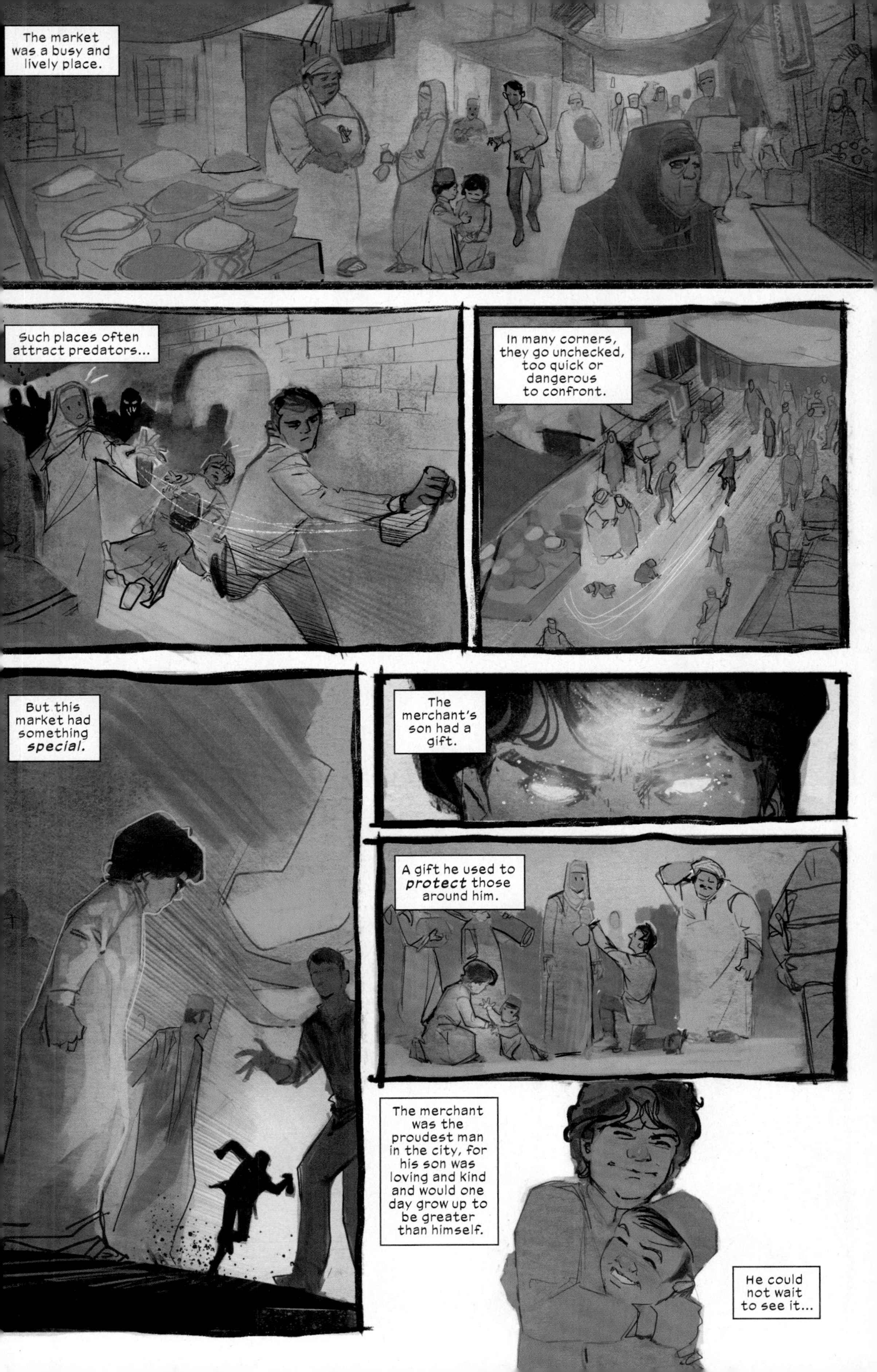

The market was a busy and lively place.
Such places often attract predators...
In many corners, they go unchecked, too quick or dangerous to confront.
But this market had something *special.*
The merchant's son had a gift.
A gift he used to *protect* those around him.
The merchant was the proudest man in the city, for his son was loving and kind and would one day grow up to be greater than himself.
He could not wait to see it...

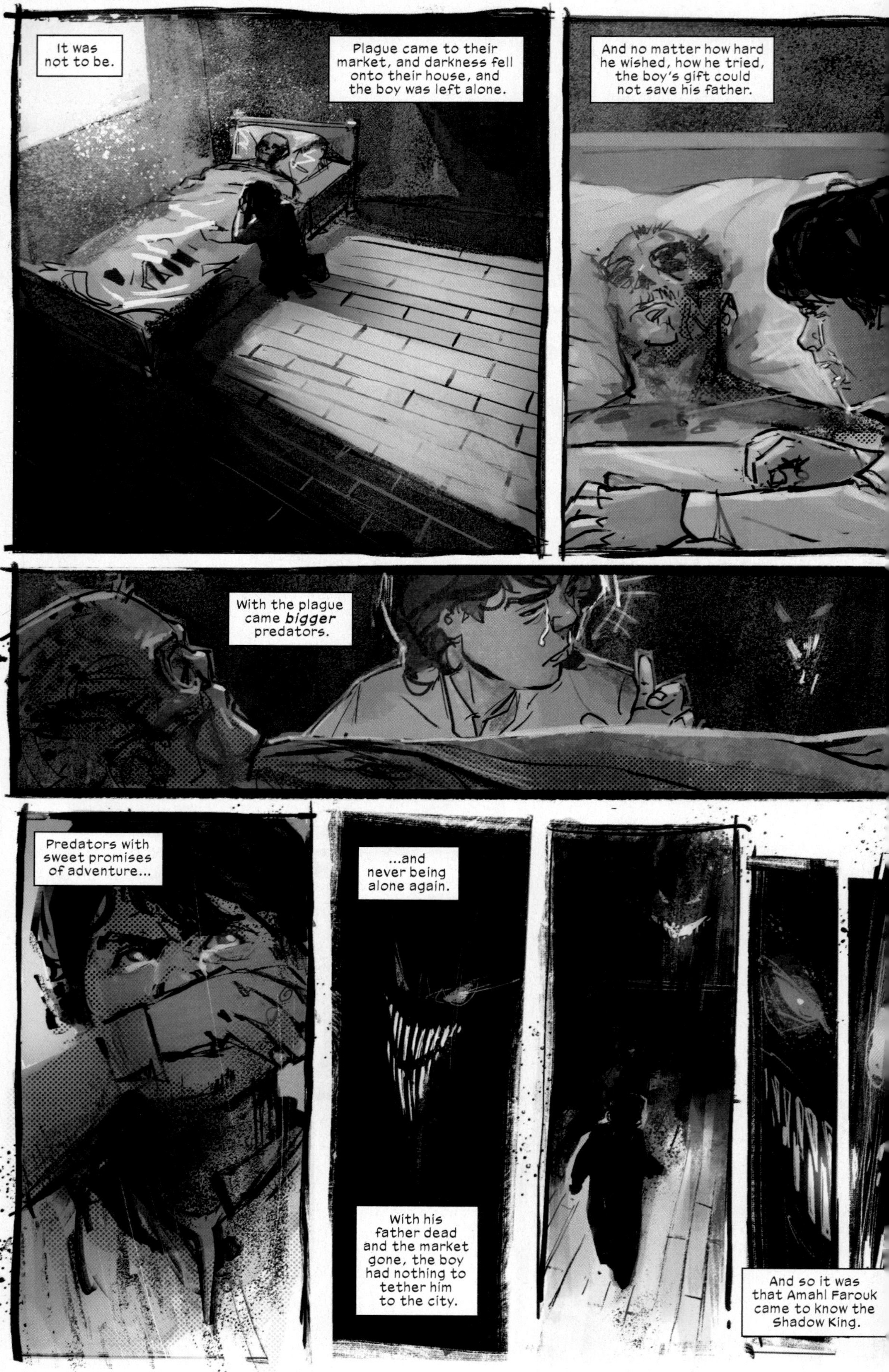

It was not to be.
Plague came to their market, and darkness fell onto their house, and the boy was left alone.
And no matter how hard he wished, how he tried, the boy's gift could not save his father.
With the plague came *bigger* predators.
Predators with sweet promises of adventure...
...and never being alone again.
With his father dead and the market gone, the boy had nothing to tether him to the city.
And so it was that Amahl Farouk came to know the Shadow King.

⸭⸭⸭⸭⸭⸭⸭⸭⸭⸭⸭⸭⸭⸭⸭

SYNERGY

On the island-nation of Krakoa, the good work continues: building a society where every mutant can find their place to belong.

And on the island-nation of Krakoa...the NEW MUTANTS aren't so sure. Belonging is hard enough -- even when you aren't a teenager and don't have mutant powers, and when everyone who knows what they're doing isn't busy running a country.

Youth of Krakoa, rise up! Time to figure it out for ourselves.

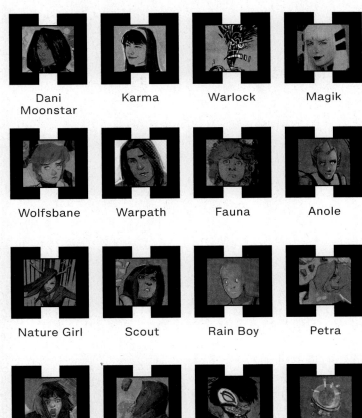

Dani Moonstar   Karma   Warlock   Magik

Wolfsbane   Warpath   Fauna   Anole

Nature Girl   Scout   Rain Boy   Petra

Sprite   Dust   Cosmar   No-Girl

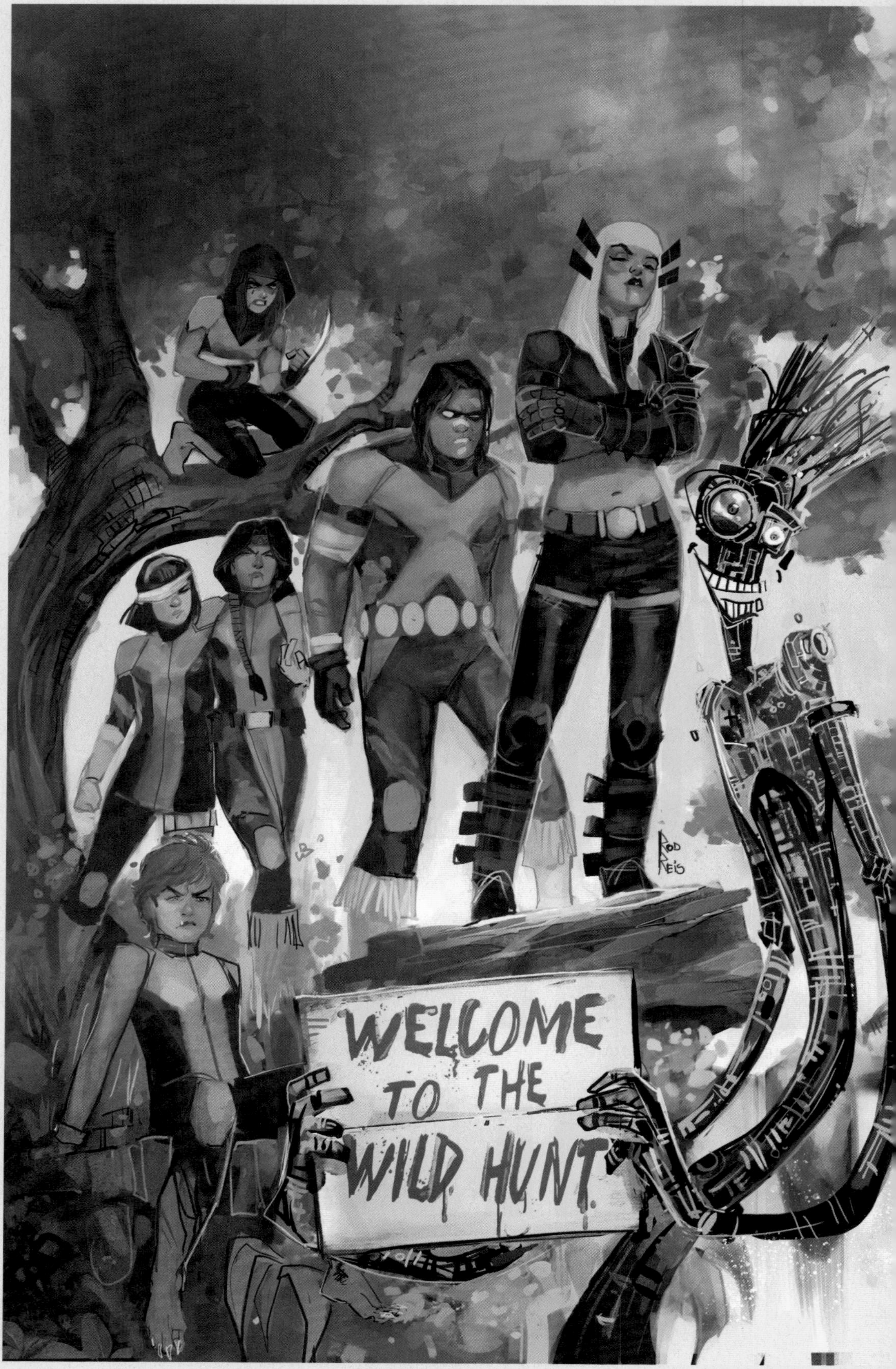
WELCOME TO THE WILD HUNT
ROD REIS

Welcome to the Wild Hunt

RE: PETITION TO QUIET COUNCIL REGARDING THE RESIDENTS OF THE AKADEMOS HABITAT

We, the undersigned, would like to bring the below to the attention of the Quiet Council, in the hopes that structural changes will be instituted to help address what is happening.

In the last few weeks, we have noticed the younger mutants in the habitat (and, we assume, in other habitats) have an abundance of unstructured time, leading to:

- boredom and depression
- lack of interest in furthering the understanding and refining of their powers
- lack of engagement with any sort of education (no impetus to be self-directed)
- lack of interest in building community beyond small in-groups
- more and more cases of troublemaking and general nuisances

Attached you will find a number of documented cases of the above, including numerous fights, attempts of self-harm, accidental damage to property/other mutants and more.

We understand that the business of nation-making is priority right now, but there are a lot of young mutants at loose ends falling through the cracks. There are vital needs that go beyond food and shelter, and we believe there should be a group dedicated to making sure younger mutants have those needs met.

Sincerely,

Danielle Moonstar   *Rahne Sinclair*

James Proudstar   *Xi'an Coy Manh*

Magik

As you may well guess, issues such as these are near and dear to my heart. And it seems that all of you are very invested as well -- in both your nation and your community. I thank you for not only bringing this to the attention of the Quiet Council, but also volunteering to be a solution. We look forward to seeing how you help guide and teach the youth of Krakoa.

Please let us know if there are any resources you will need.

With gratitude and admiration,

Professor X

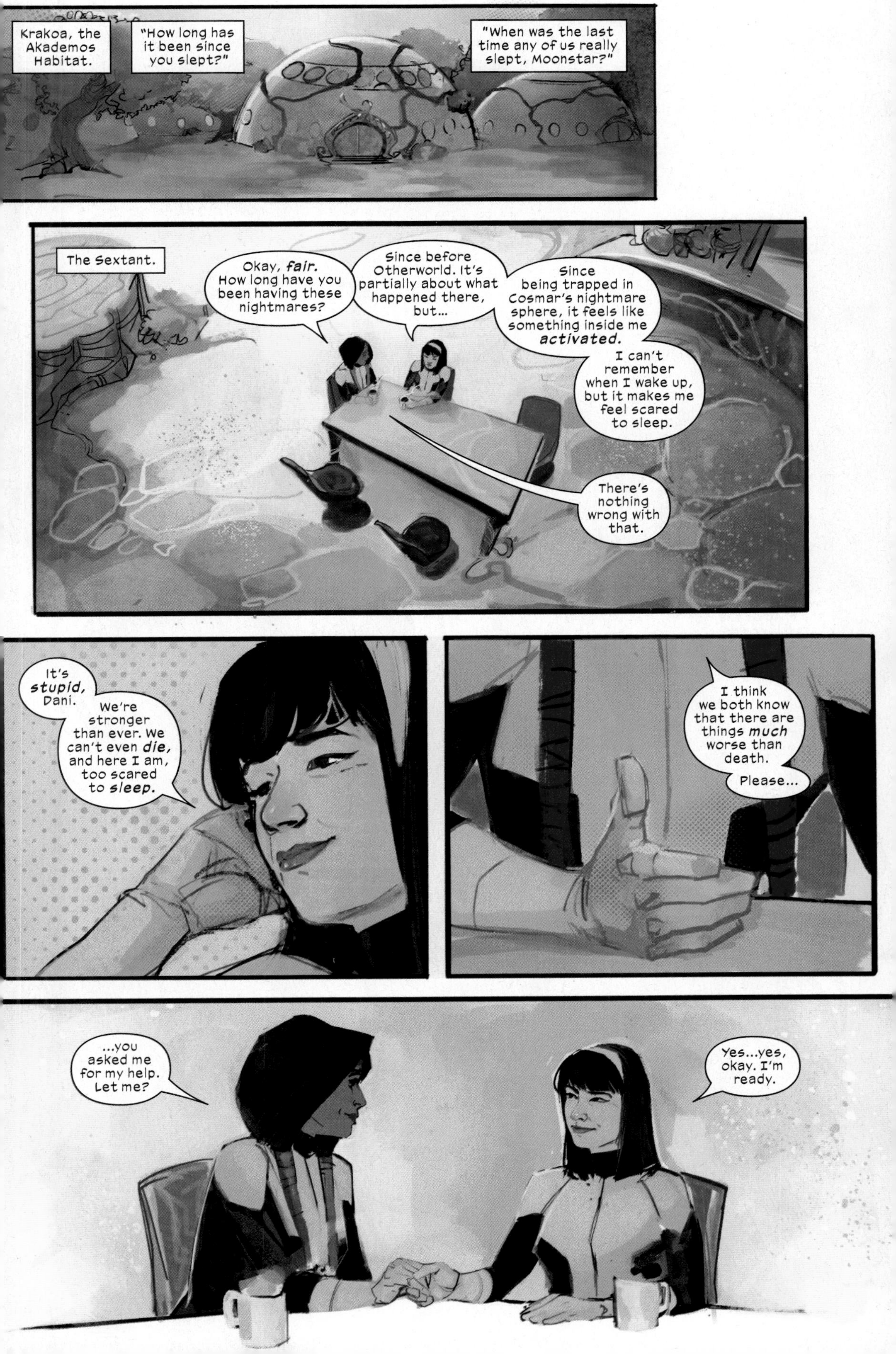
Krakoa, the Akademos Habitat.
"How long has it been since you slept?"
"When was the last time any of us really slept, Moonstar?"
The Sextant.
Okay, *fair.* How long have you been having these nightmares?
Since before Otherworld. It's partially about what happened there, but...
Since being trapped in Cosmar's nightmare sphere, it feels like something inside me *activated.*
I can't remember when I wake up, but it makes me feel scared to sleep.
There's nothing wrong with that.
It's *stupid,* Dani.
We're stronger than ever. We can't even *die,* and here I am, too scared to *sleep.*
I think we both know that there are things *much* worse than death.
Please...
...you asked me for my help. Let me?
Yes...yes, okay. I'm ready.

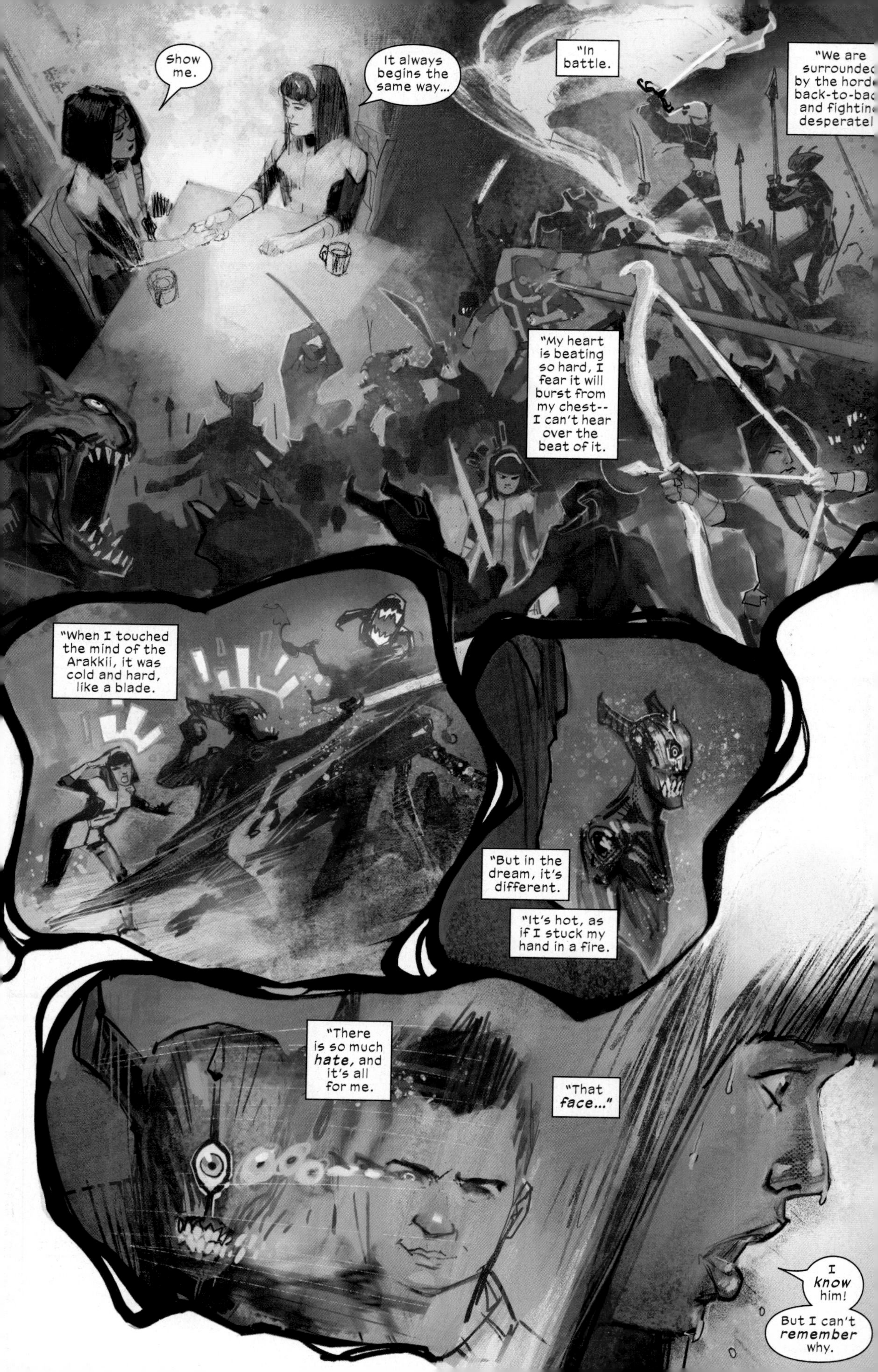
Show me.
It always begins the same way...
"In battle.
"We are surrounded by the horde back-to-back and fighting desperately.
"My heart is beating so hard, I fear it will burst from my chest-- I can't hear over the beat of it.
"When I touched the mind of the Arakkii, it was cold and hard, like a blade.
"But in the dream, it's different.
"It's hot, as if I stuck my hand in a fire.
"There is so much *hate,* and it's all for me.
"That *face...*"
I *know* him!
But I can't *remember* why.

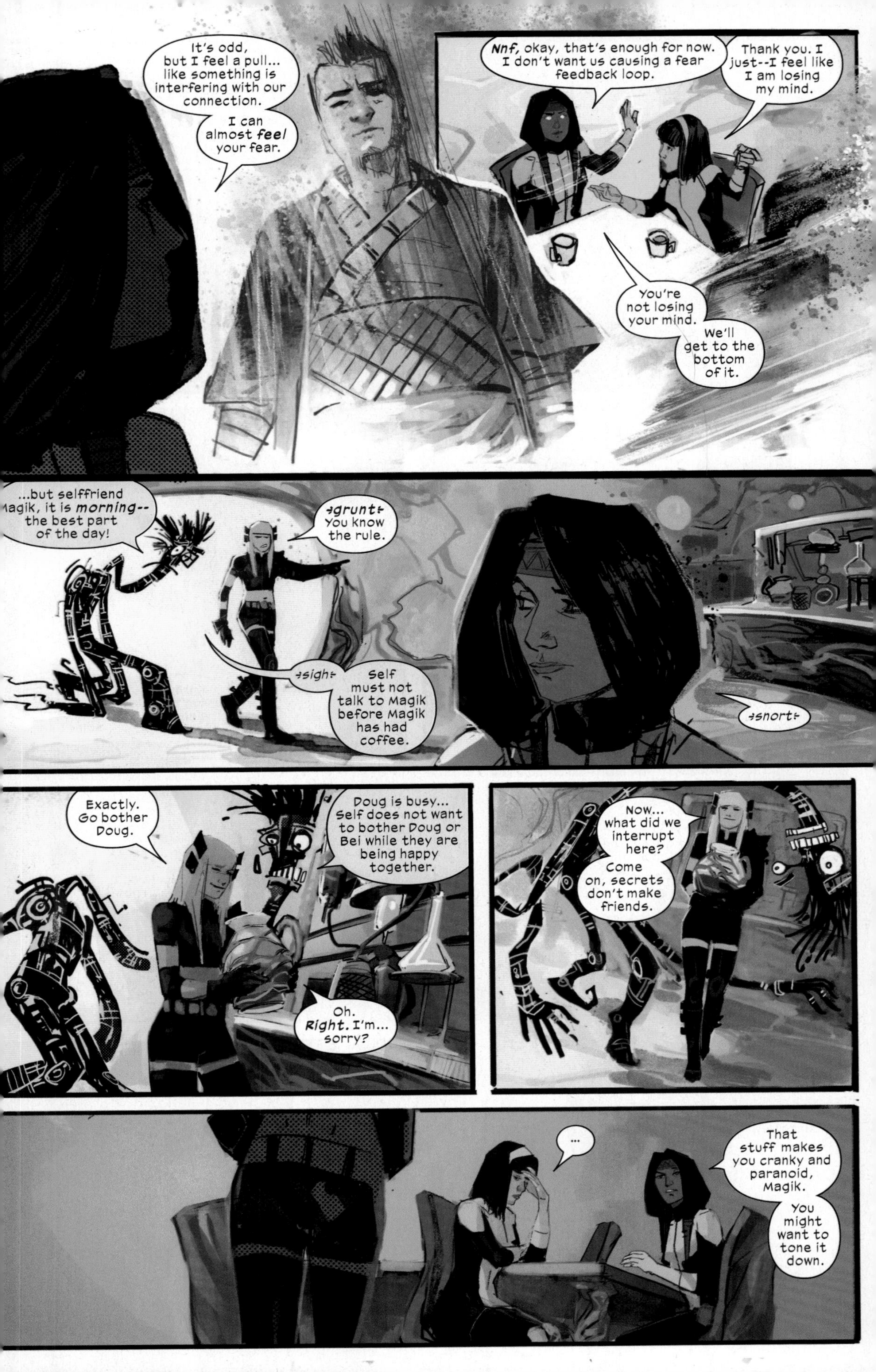
It's odd, but I feel a pull... like something is interfering with our connection.
I can almost *feel* your fear.
Nnf, okay, that's enough for now. I don't want us causing a fear feedback loop.
Thank you. I just--I feel like I am losing my mind.
You're not losing your mind.
We'll get to the bottom of it.
...but selffriend Magik, it is *morning*-- the best part of the day!
grunt You know the rule.
sigh
Self must not talk to Magik before Magik has had coffee.
snort
Exactly. Go bother Doug.
Doug is busy... Self does not want to bother Doug or Bei while they are being happy together.
Oh. *Right.* I'm... sorry?
Now... what did we interrupt here?
Come on, secrets don't make friends.
...
That stuff makes you cranky and paranoid, Magik.
You might want to tone it down.

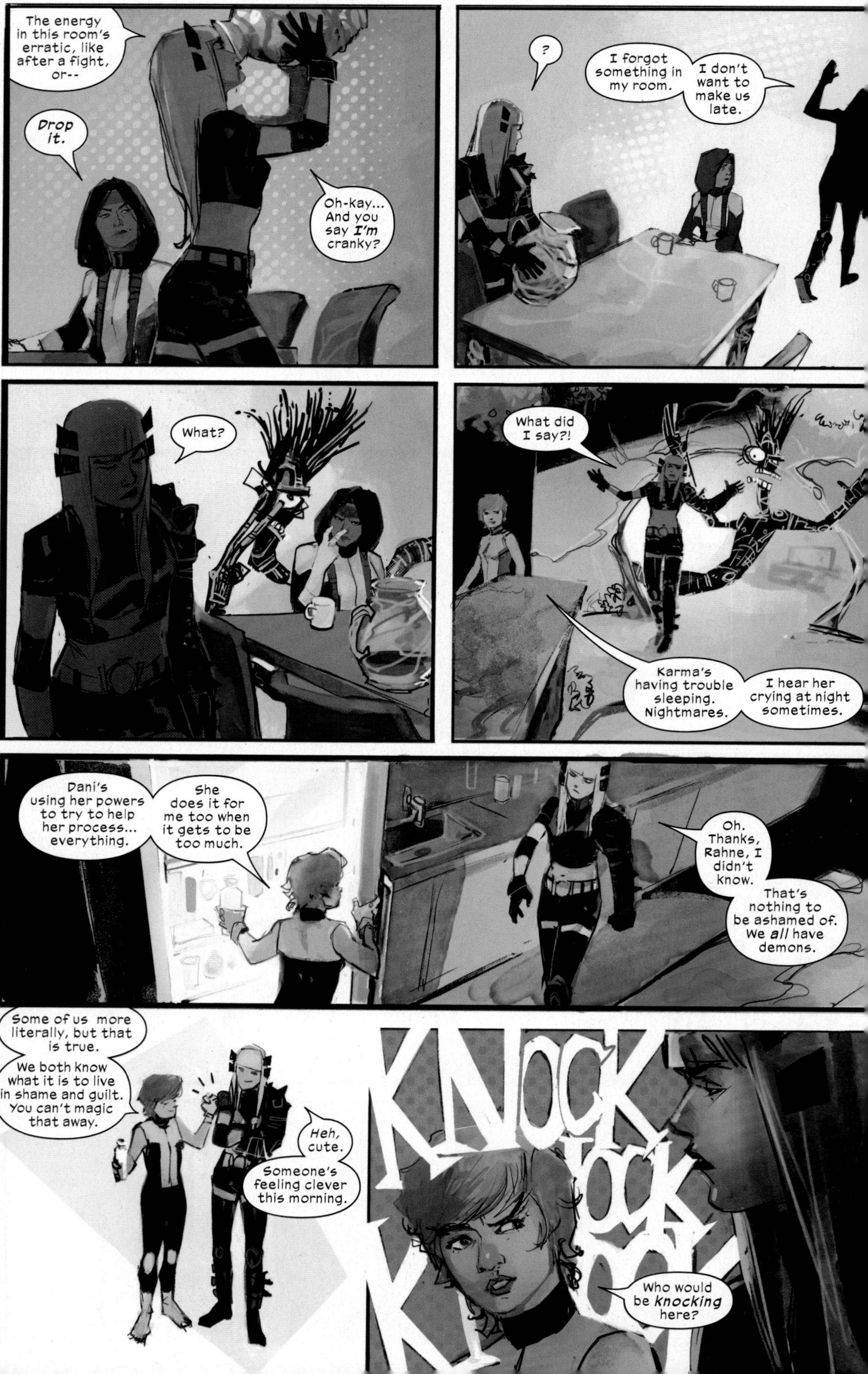
The energy in this room's erratic, like after a fight, or--
Drop it.
Oh-kay... And you say I'm cranky?
?
I forgot something in my room.
I don't want to make us late.
What?
What did I say?!
Karma's having trouble sleeping. Nightmares.
I hear her crying at night sometimes.
Dani's using her powers to try to help her process... everything.
She does it for me too when it gets to be too much.
Oh. Thanks, Rahne, I didn't know.
That's nothing to be ashamed of. We all have demons.
Some of us more literally, but that is true.
We both know what it is to live in shame and guilt. You can't magic that away.
Heh, cute.
Someone's feeling clever this morning.
KNOCK KNOCK
Who would be knocking here?

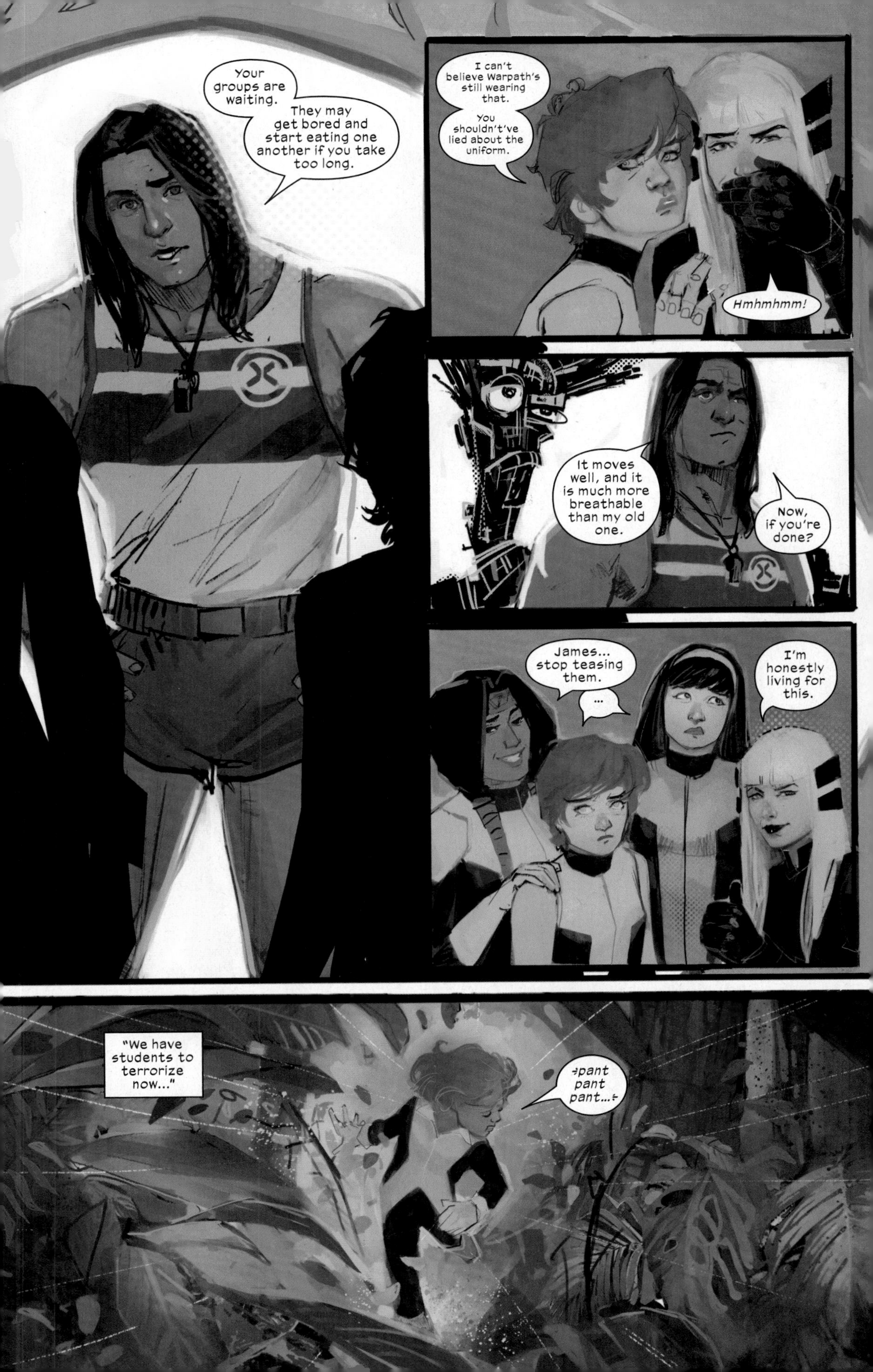
Your groups are waiting.
They may get bored and start eating one another if you take too long.
I can't believe Warpath's still wearing that.
You shouldn't've lied about the uniform.
Hmhmhmm!
It moves well, and it is much more breathable than my old one.
Now, if you're done?
James... stop teasing them.
...
I'm honestly living for this.
"We have students to terrorize now..."
pant pant pant...

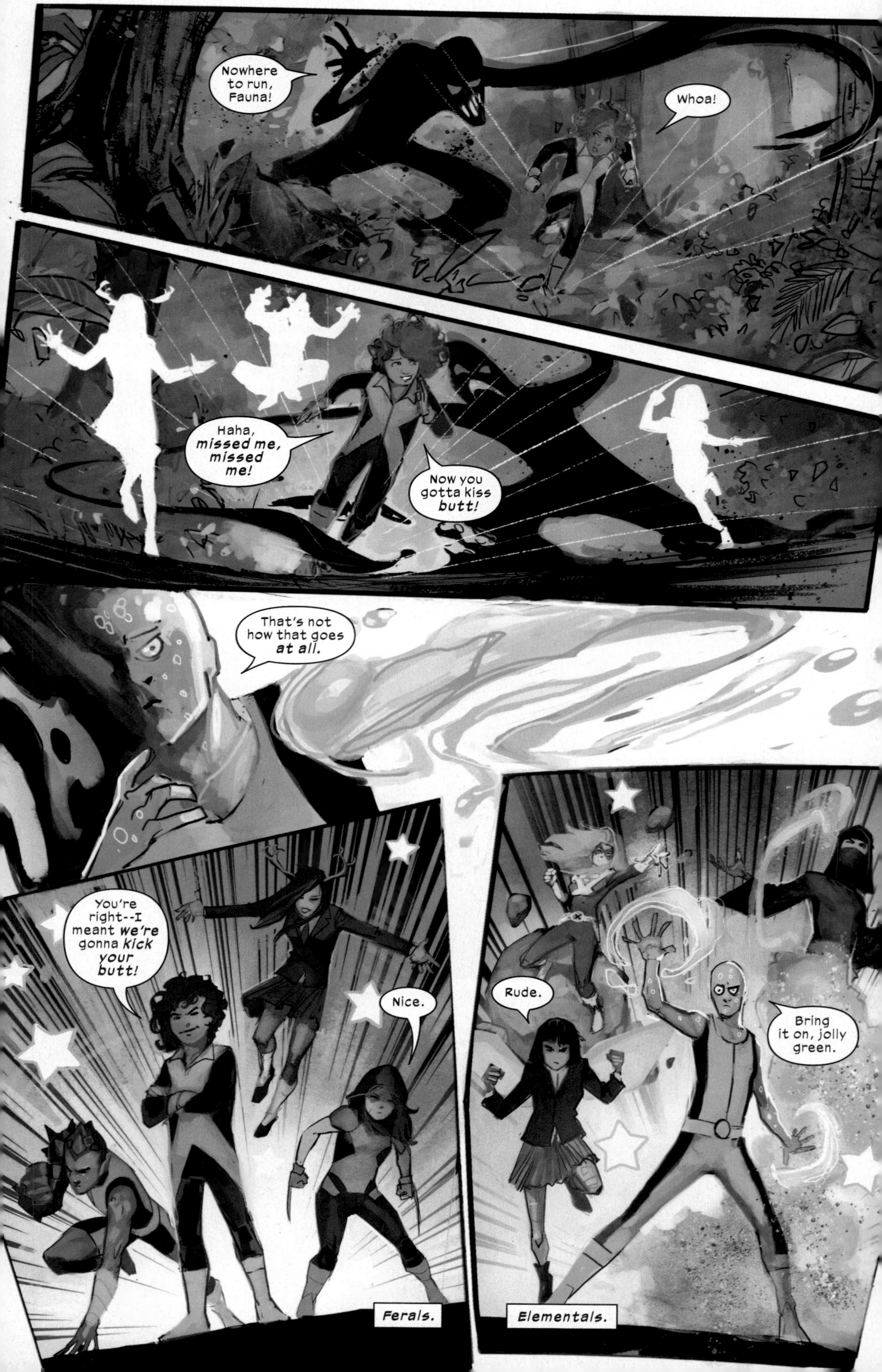
Nowhere to run, Fauna!
Whoa!
Haha, missed me, missed me!
Now you gotta kiss butt!
That's not how that goes at all.
You're right--I meant we're gonna kick your butt!
Nice.
Rude.
Bring it on, jolly green.
Ferals.
Elementals.

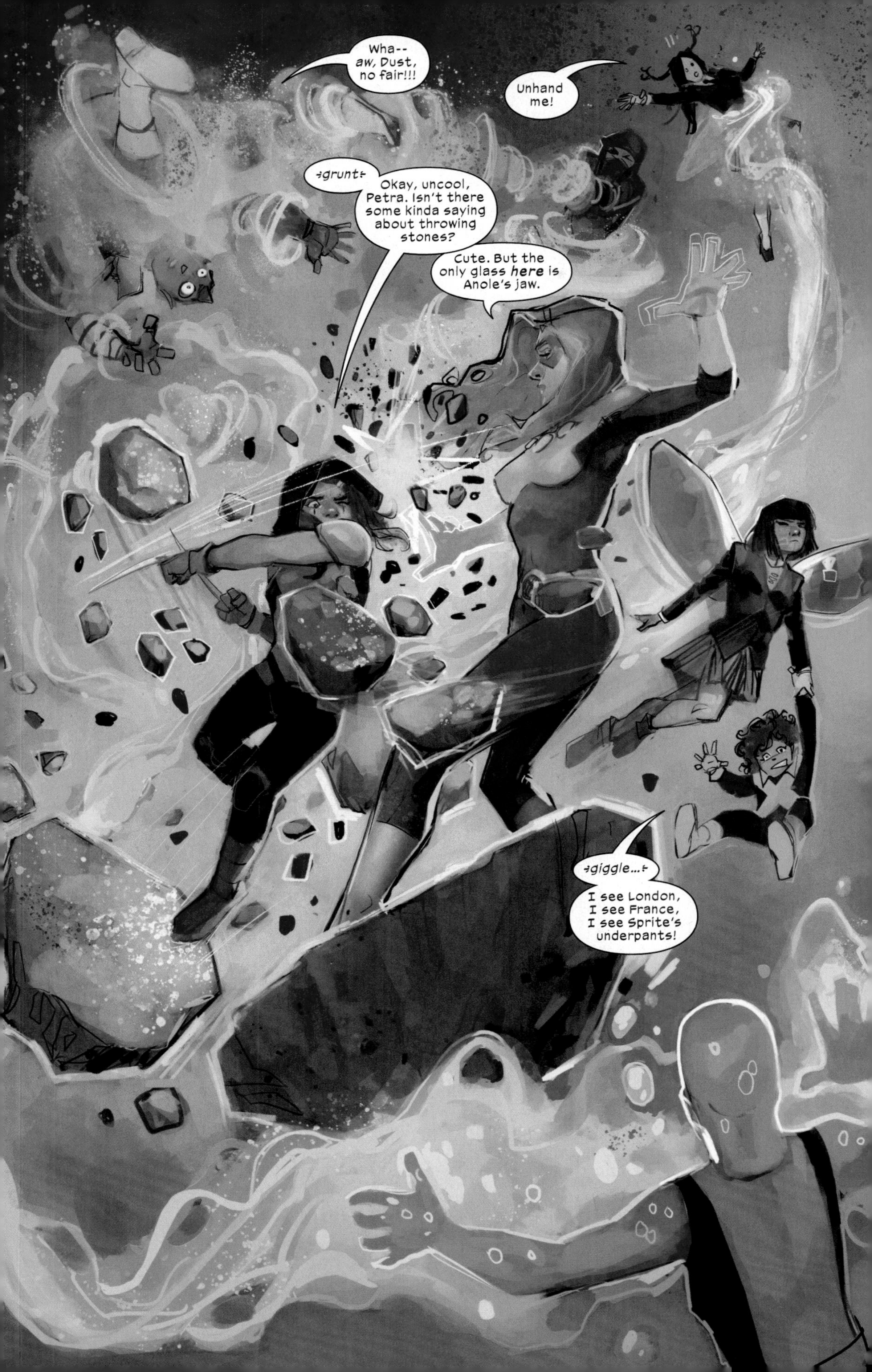
Wha-- aw, Dust, no fair!!!
Unhand me!
-grunt-
Okay, uncool, Petra. Isn't there some kinda saying about throwing stones?
Cute. But the only glass *here* is Anole's jaw.
-giggle...-
I see London, I see France, I see Sprite's underpants!

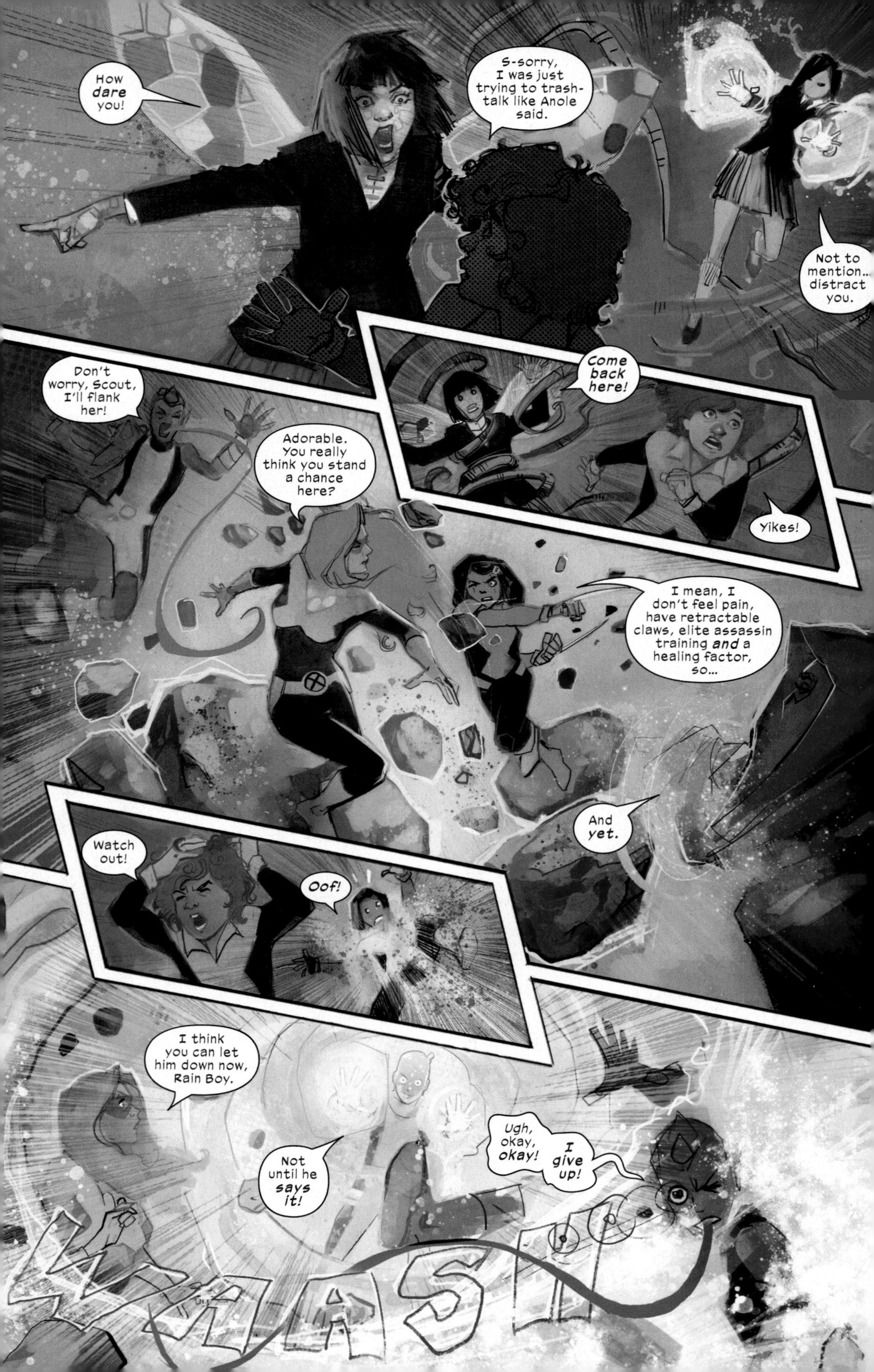
How dare you!
S-sorry, I was just trying to trash-talk like Anole said.
Not to mention... distract you.
Don't worry, Scout, I'll flank her!
Come back here!
Yikes!
Adorable. You really think you stand a chance here?
I mean, I don't feel pain, have retractable claws, elite assassin training and a healing factor, so...
And yet.
Watch out!
Oof!
I think you can let him down now, Rain Boy.
Not until he says it!
Ugh, okay, okay!
I give up!
WHASH

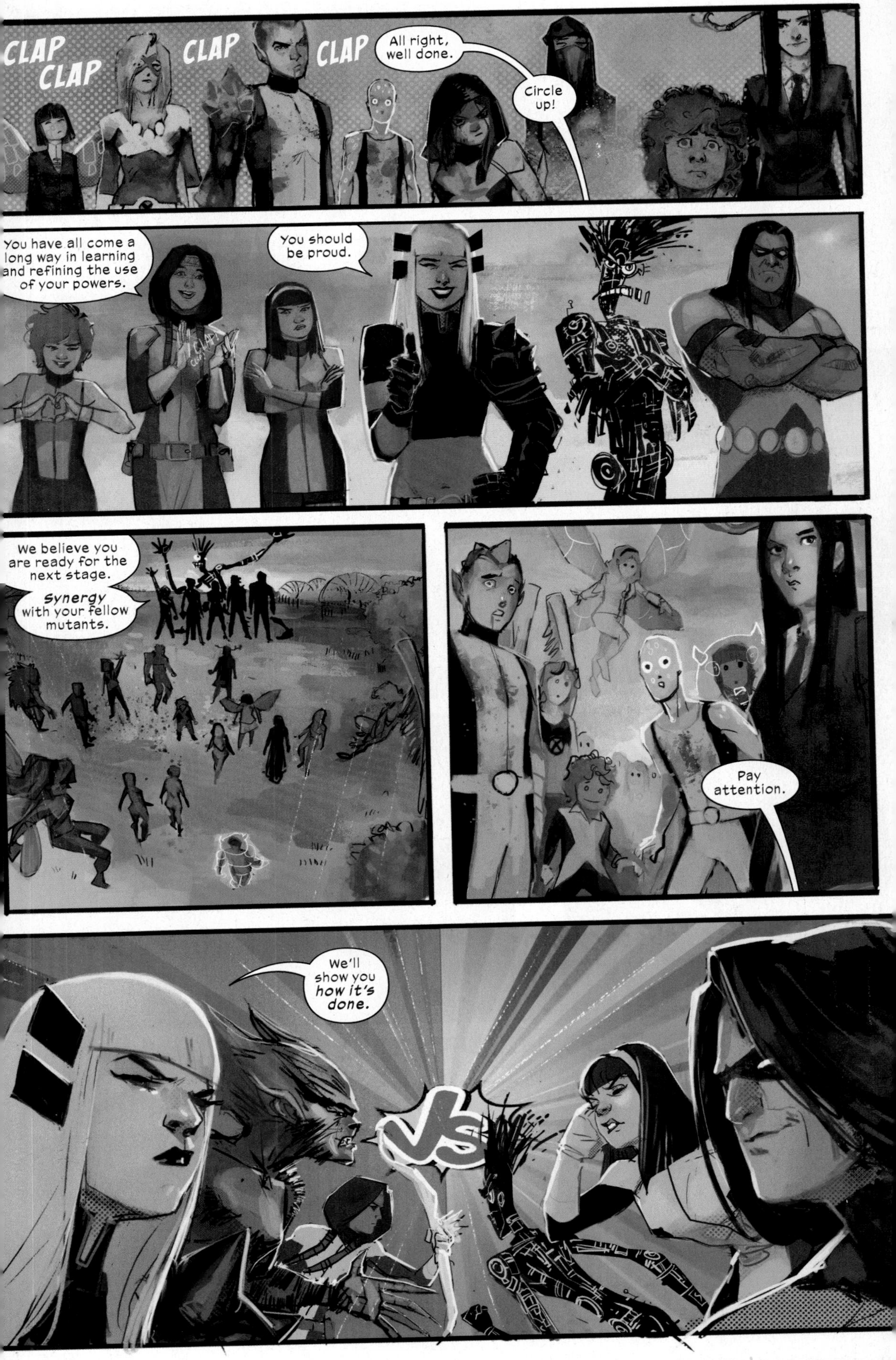
CLAP CLAP
CLAP
CLAP
All right, well done.
Circle up!
You have all come a long way in learning and refining the use of your powers.
CLAP CLAP
You should be proud.
We believe you are ready for the next stage.
Synergy with your fellow mutants.
Pay attention.
We'll show you *how it's done.*
VS

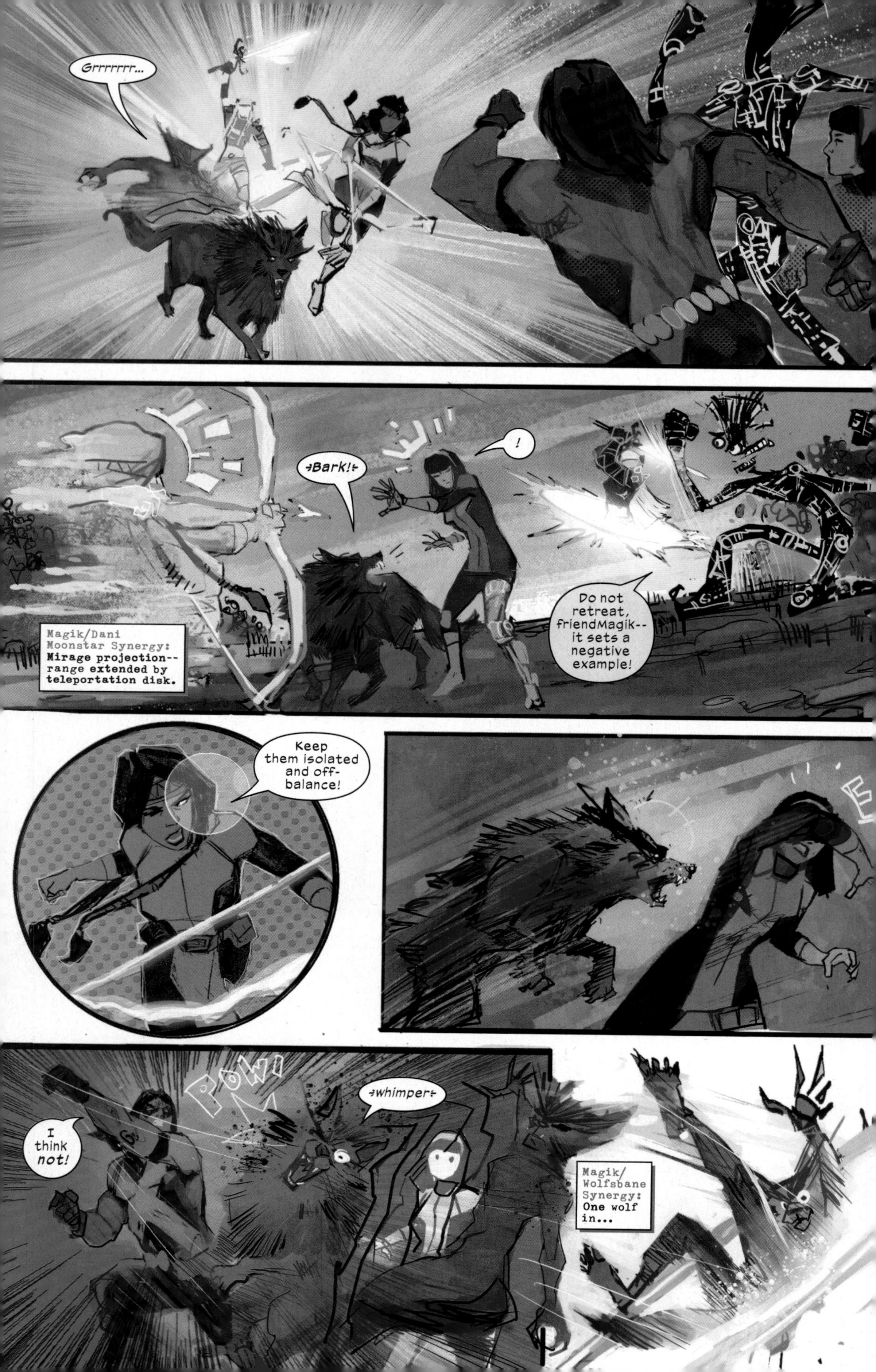
Grrrrrrr...
⇢Bark!⇠
!
Do not retreat, friendMagik--it sets a negative example!
Magik/Dani Moonstar Synergy: Mirage projection--range extended by teleportation disk.
Keep them isolated and off-balance!
I think not!
POW!
⇢whimper⇠
Magik/Wolfsbane Synergy: One wolf in...

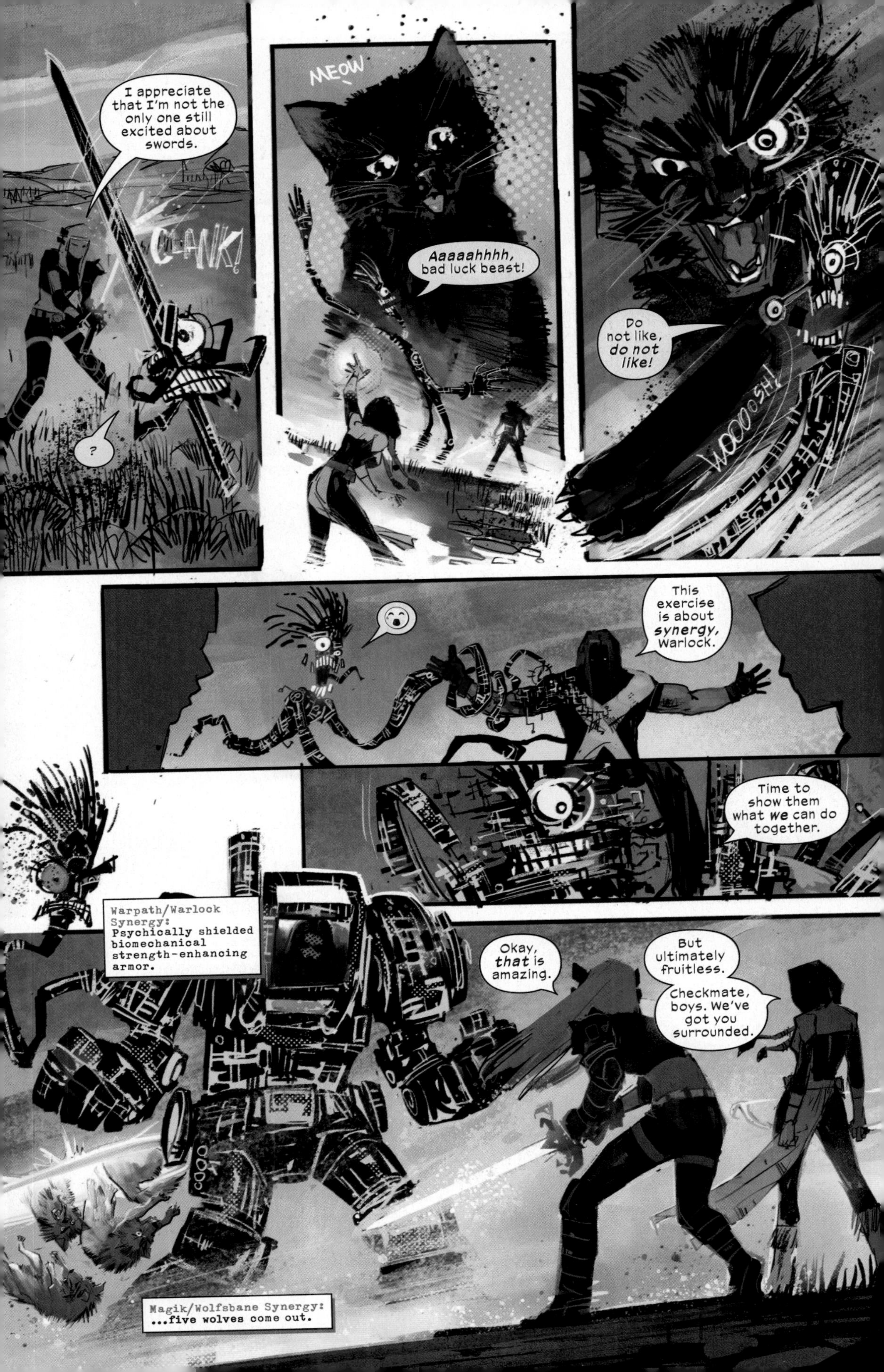
I appreciate that I'm not the only one still excited about swords.
CLANK!
?
MEOW
Aaaaahhhh, bad luck beast!
Do not like, do not like!
WOOOOOSH!
This exercise is about synergy, Warlock.
Time to show them what we can do together.
Warpath/Warlock Synergy: Psychically shielded biomechanical strength-enhancing armor.
Okay, that is amazing.
But ultimately fruitless.
Checkmate, boys. We've got you surrounded.
Magik/Wolfsbane Synergy: ...five wolves come out.

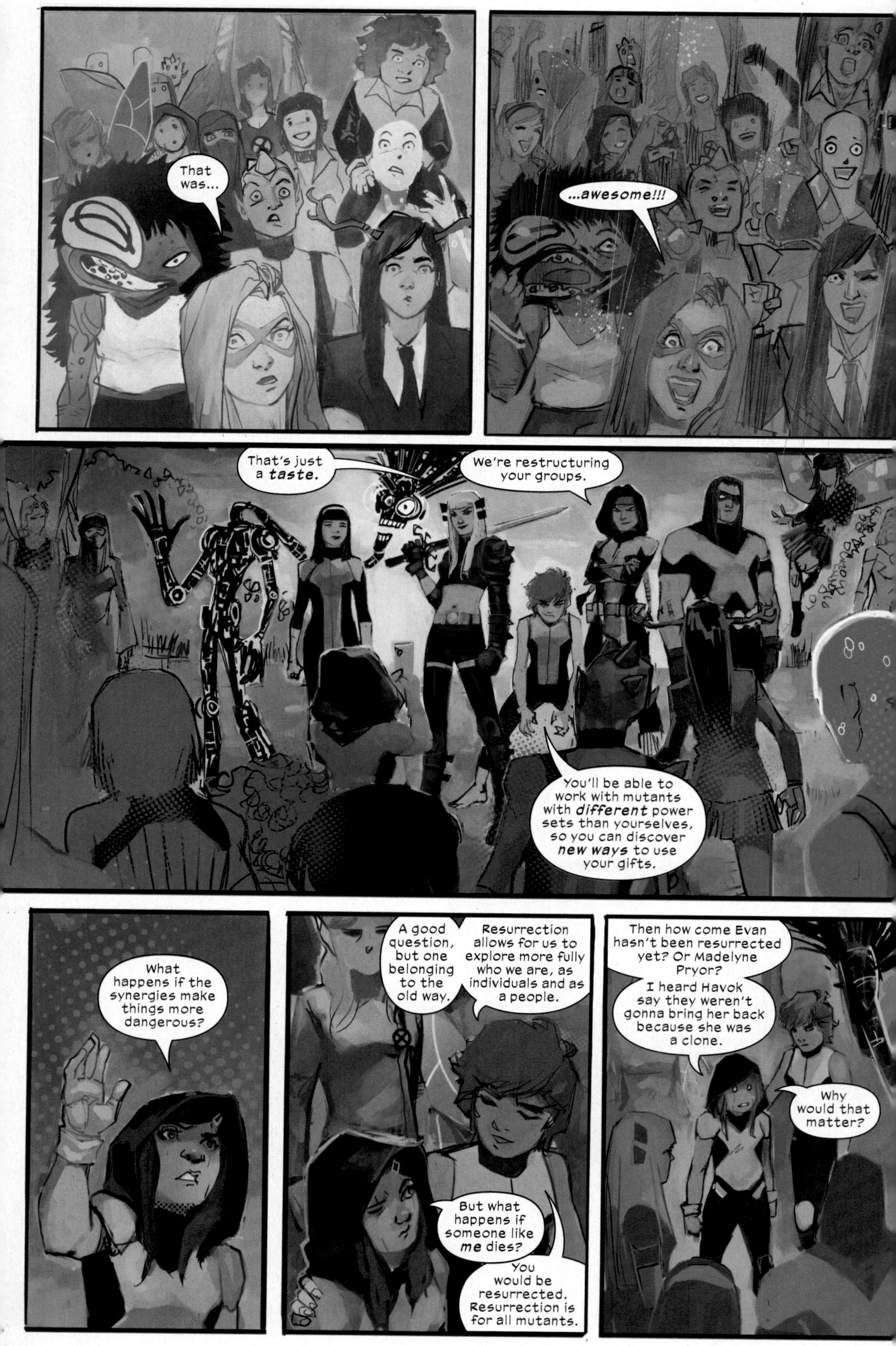
That was...
...awesome!!!
That's just a *taste.*
We're restructuring your groups.
You'll be able to work with mutants with *different* power sets than yourselves, so you can discover *new ways* to use your gifts.
What happens if the synergies make things more dangerous?
A good question, but one belonging to the old way.
Resurrection allows for us to explore more fully who we are, as individuals and as a people.
But what happens if someone like *me* dies?
You would be resurrected. Resurrection is for all mutants.
Then how come Evan hasn't been resurrected yet? Or Madelyne Pryor?
I heard Havok say they weren't gonna bring her back because she was a clone.
Why would that matter?

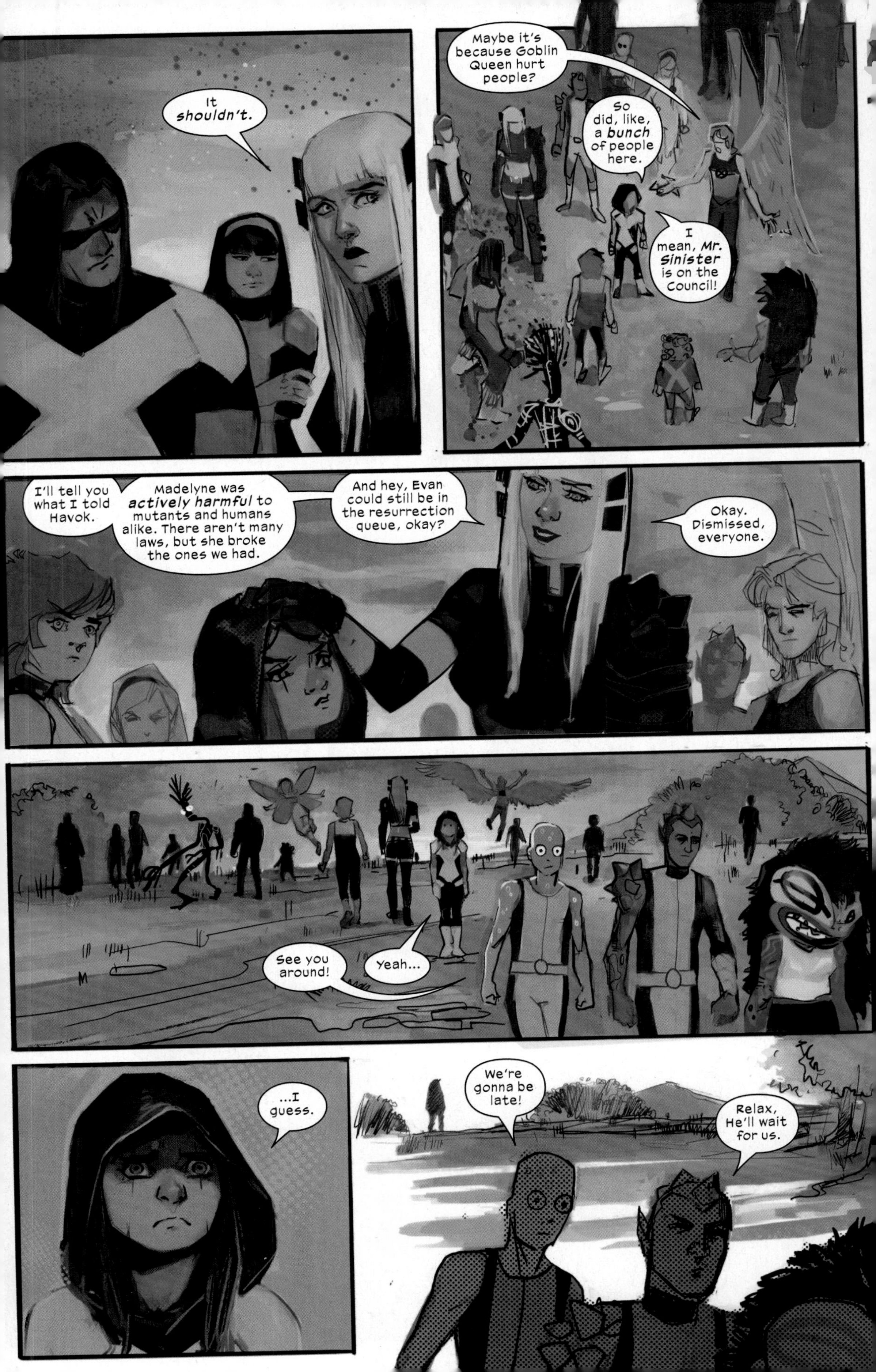

It shouldn't.
Maybe it's because Goblin Queen hurt people?
So did, like, a bunch of people here.
I mean, Mr. Sinister is on the Council!
I'll tell you what I told Havok.
Madelyne was actively harmful to mutants and humans alike. There aren't many laws, but she broke the ones we had.
And hey, Evan could still be in the resurrection queue, okay?
Okay. Dismissed, everyone.
See you around!
Yeah...
...I guess.
We're gonna be late!
Relax, He'll wait for us.

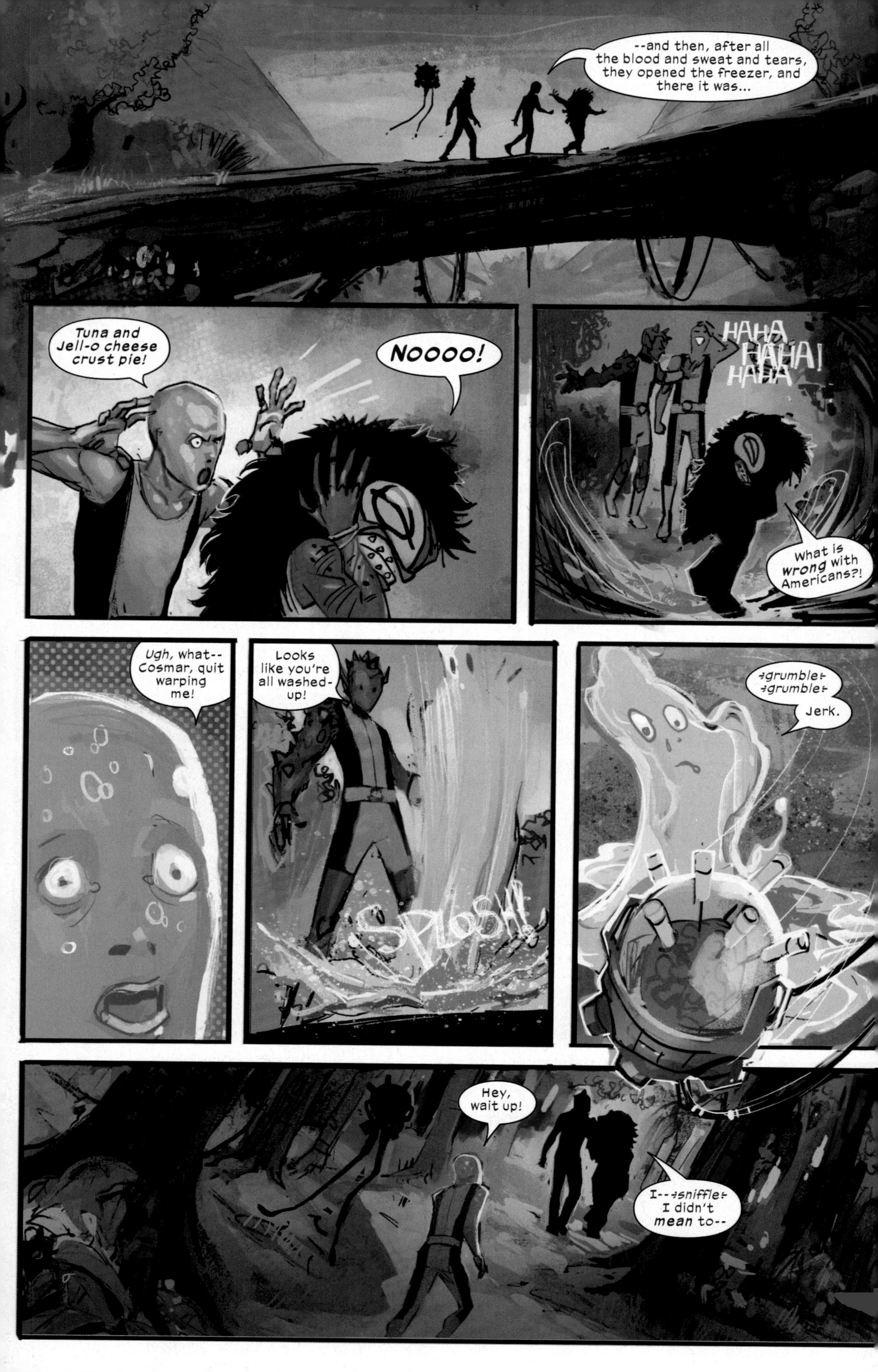
--and then, after all the blood and sweat and tears, they opened the freezer, and there it was...
Tuna and Jell-o cheese crust pie!
NOOOO!
HAHA HAHA! HAHA
What is *wrong* with Americans?!
Ugh, what--Cosmar, quit warping me!
Looks like you're all washed-up!
SPLOSH!
-grumble- -grumble- Jerk.
Hey, wait up!
I-- -sniffle- I didn't *mean* to--

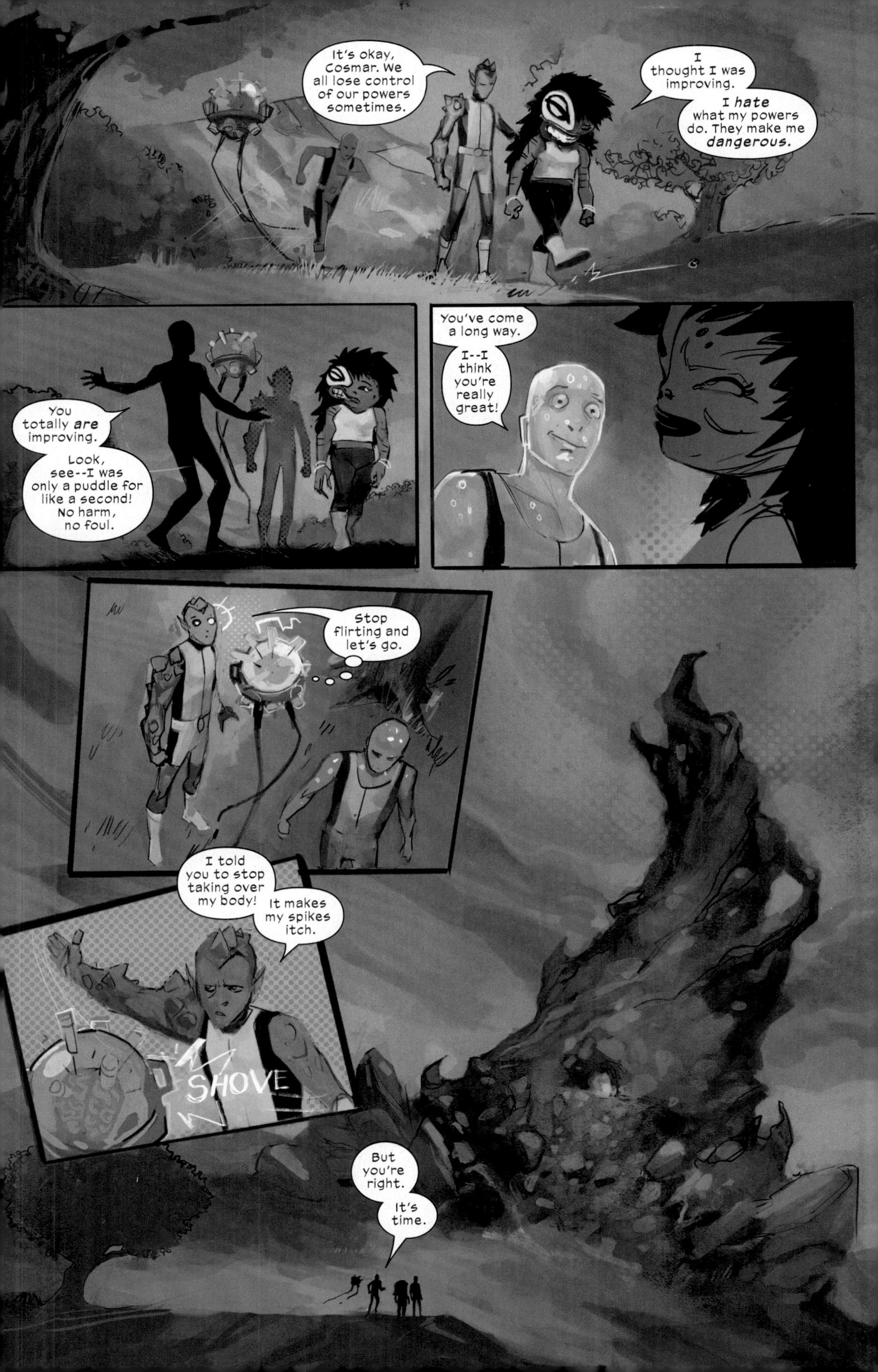
It's okay, Cosmar. We all lose control of our powers sometimes.
I thought I was improving.
I *hate* what my powers do. They make me *dangerous.*
You totally *are* improving.
Look, see--I was only a puddle for like a second! No harm, no foul.
You've come a long way.
I--I think you're really great!
Stop flirting and let's go.
I told you to stop taking over my body!
It makes my spikes itch.
SHOVE
But you're right.
It's time.

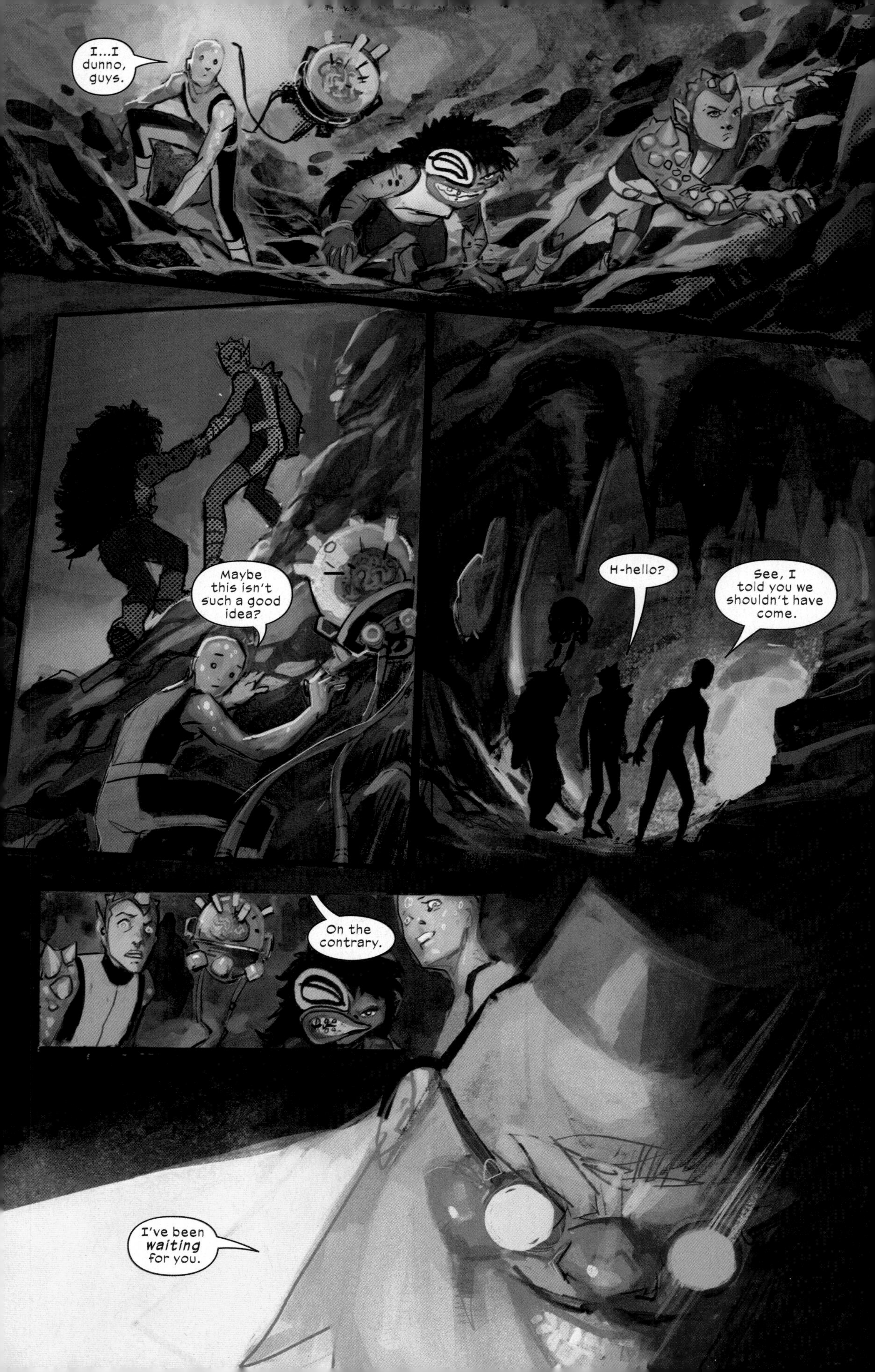
I...I dunno, guys.
Maybe this isn't such a good idea?
H-hello?
See, I told you we shouldn't have come.
On the contrary.
I've been *waiting* for you.

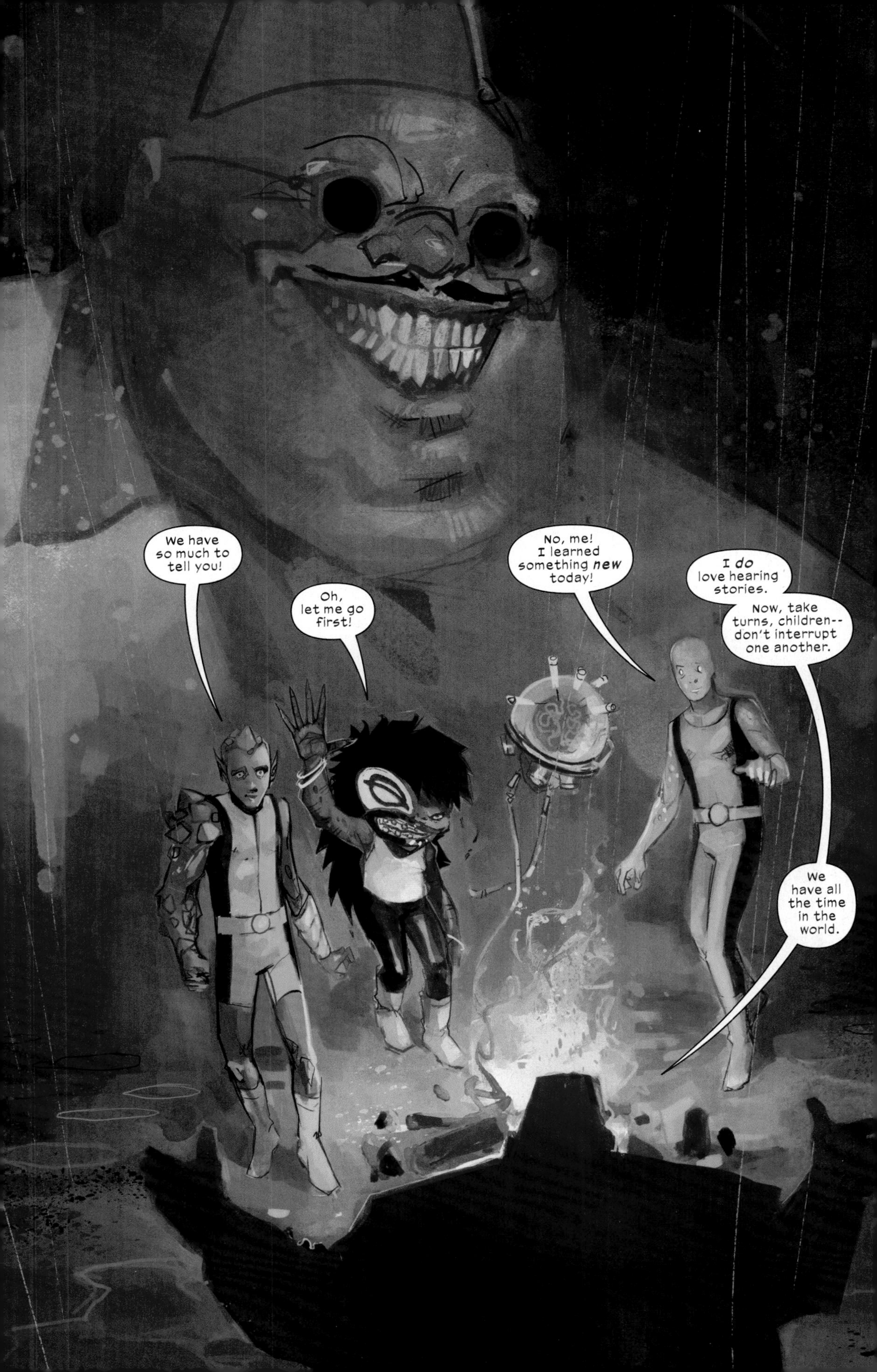
We have so much to tell you!
Oh, let me go first!
No, me! I learned something *new* today!
I *do* love hearing stories.
Now, take turns, children--don't interrupt one another.
We have all the time in the world.

Proudstar,

I would say sorry for getting you into this mess, but honestly, it would be a lie. I know you didn't sign up to be any sort of teacher when you joined the X-Men, and, now more than ever, it seems like what Krakoa should need of you is your physical prowess, but there is more to you than that. You are a man who has stood tall and protected his people when he himself lost so much.

Part of what we are doing now is not just strengthening bodies and powers, but building up the minds and spirits of these younger mutants. You are a good man, a good friend and a role model and, thus, should lead by example.

I am asking all of us to start keeping journals. We need to dig deep, to know ourselves well, so we can give guidance and confidence to these kids. You can keep the journal on whatever feels right to you, and don't ever have to show it to anyone. It is a tool for you.

I'm including a list of prompt questions (some of them are hokey, I know, but they are jumping off points, not SAT questions).

Strength and peace to you, my friend,

Moonstar

PROMPTS

How do you view the world and others? Do you think of yourself as optimistic or pessimistic?

What are five songs that move you? For each song, write about what speaks to you. What do they make you feel when you hear them?

When is the last time you did something for someone else? What was it and how did it make you feel?

Write down all the compliments you can think of that you've received.

Write about something that is currently frustrating to you.

Who are the people in your life that make you feel the most like you can be yourself around, and what do they do to make you feel that way?

To you, what makes someone a good friend?

What are some silver linings in hard lessons that you've learned?

Write about an incredibly difficult choice you've had to make in your life.

What are small changes you can make to your routine to help improve it? What commitments can you make to care for yourself?

I deserve to be happy because _____

What does love mean to you? What roles do love and affection play in your life?

If you could go back in time and talk to your younger self, what would you tell them?

Write about your one of your most treasured memories.

Write a letter of forgiveness to yourself.

[reign_of_x]

[kra_]
[koa_]

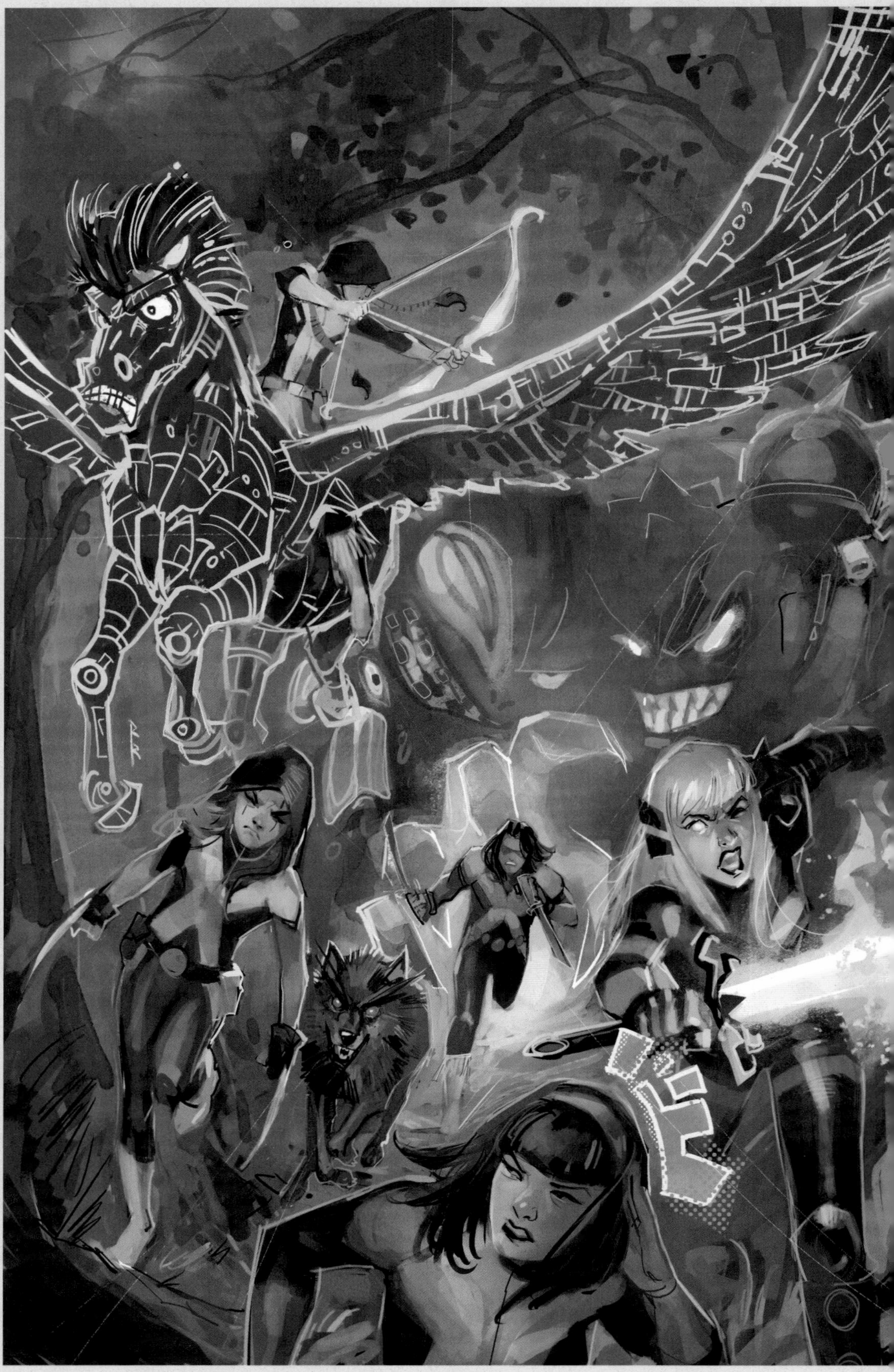

The Kids Ain't Alright

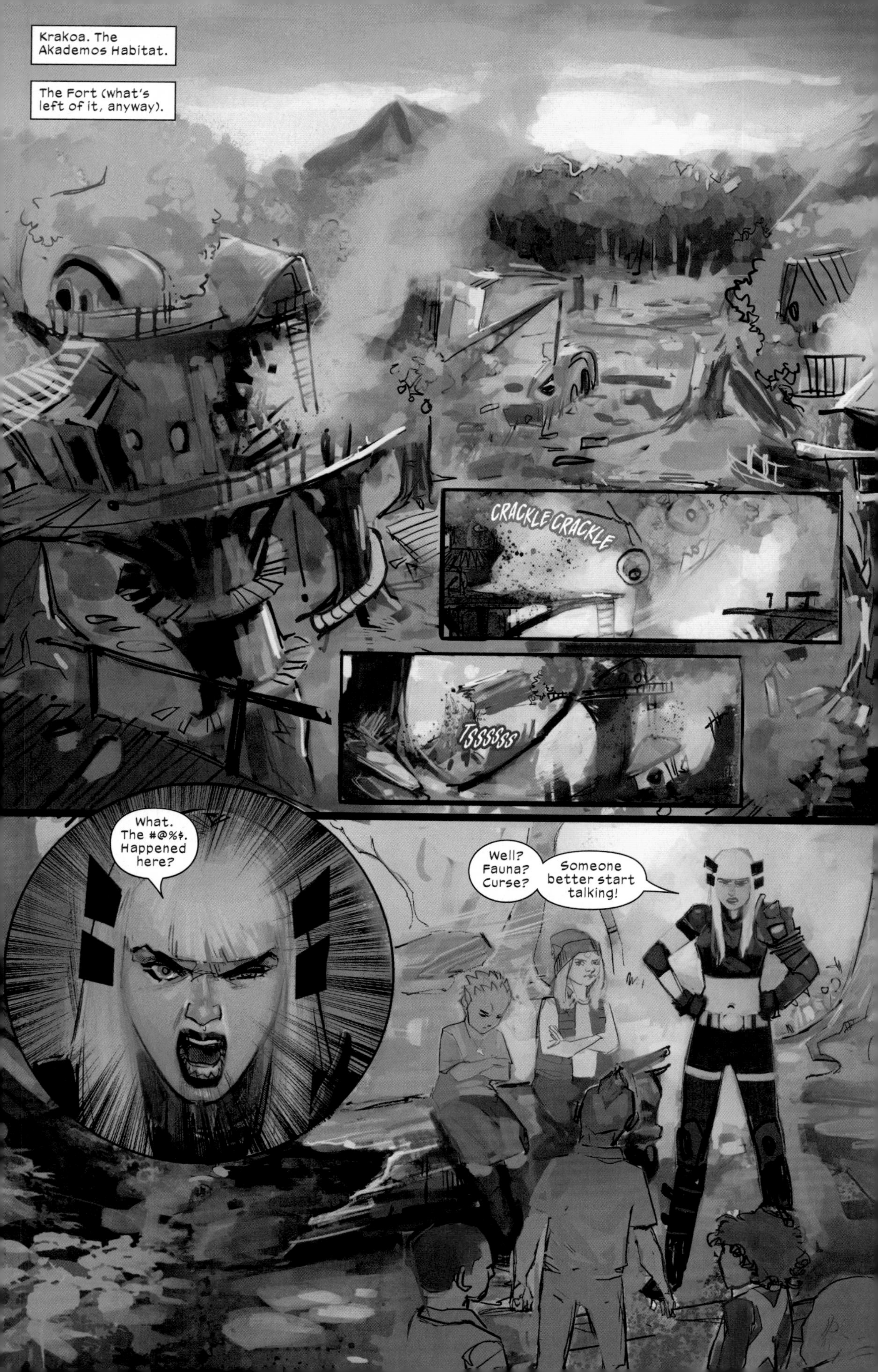
Krakoa. The Akademos Habitat.
The Fort (what's left of it, anyway).
CRACKLE CRACKLE
TSSSSSS
What. The #@%$. Happened here?
Well? Fauna? Curse?
Someone better start talking!

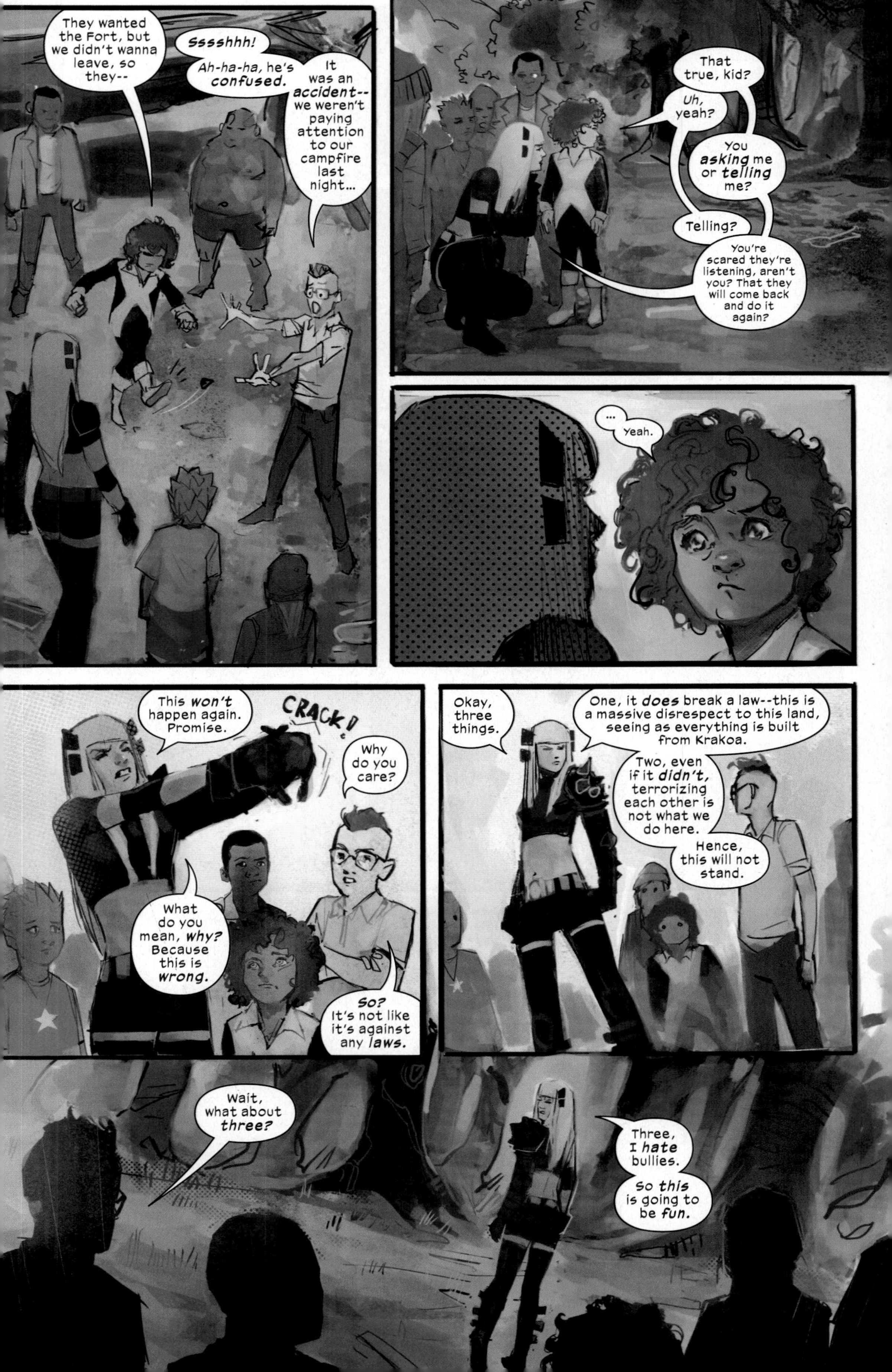
They wanted the Fort, but we didn't wanna leave, so they--
Sssshhh!
Ah-ha-ha, he's confused.
It was an accident--we weren't paying attention to our campfire last night...
That true, kid?
Uh, yeah?
You asking me or telling me?
Telling?
You're scared they're listening, aren't you? That they will come back and do it again?
... Yeah.
This won't happen again. Promise.
CRACK!
Why do you care?
What do you mean, why? Because this is wrong.
So? It's not like it's against any laws.
Okay, three things.
One, it does break a law--this is a massive disrespect to this land, seeing as everything is built from Krakoa.
Two, even if it didn't, terrorizing each other is not what we do here.
Hence, this will not stand.
Wait, what about three?
Three, I hate bullies.
So this is going to be fun.

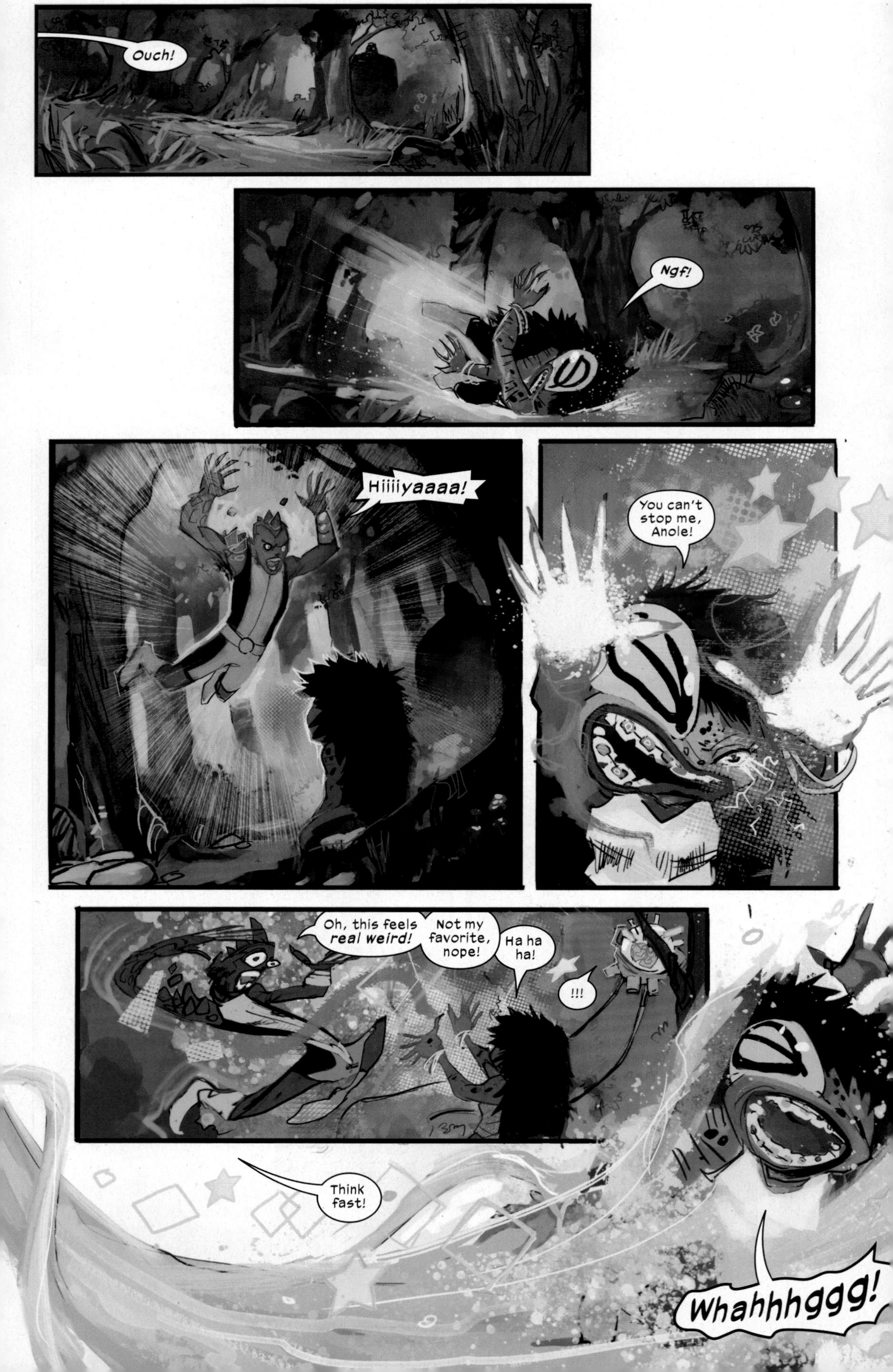
Ouch!
Ngf!
Hiiiiyaaaa!
You can't stop me, Anole!
Oh, this feels *real weird!*
Not my favorite, nope!
Ha ha ha!
!!!
Think fast!
Whahhhggg!

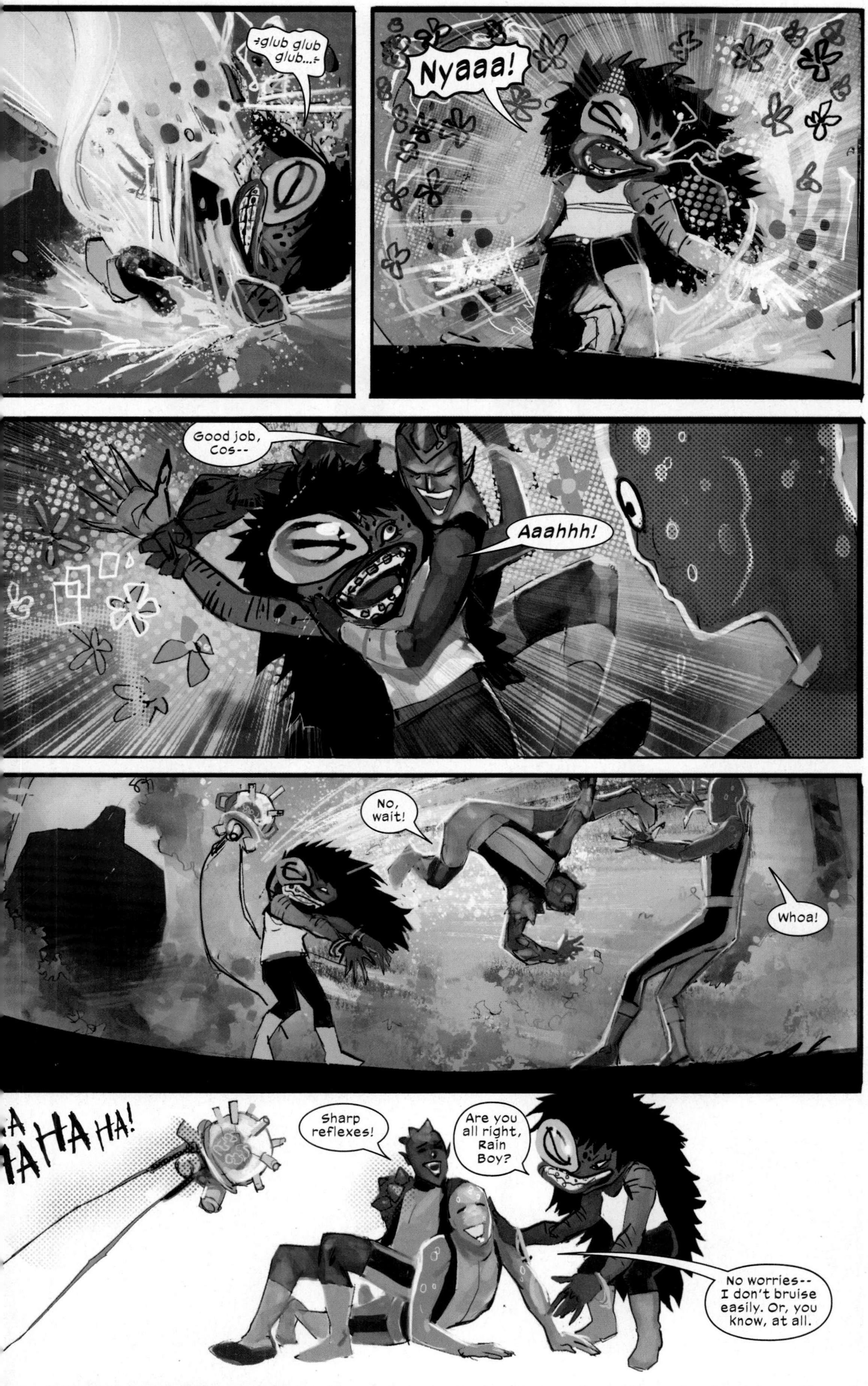

≈glub glub glub...≈
Nyaaa!
Good job, Cos--
Aaahhh!
No, wait!
Whoa!
HAHAHA!
Sharp reflexes!
Are you all right, Rain Boy?
No worries-- I don't bruise easily. Or, you know, at all.

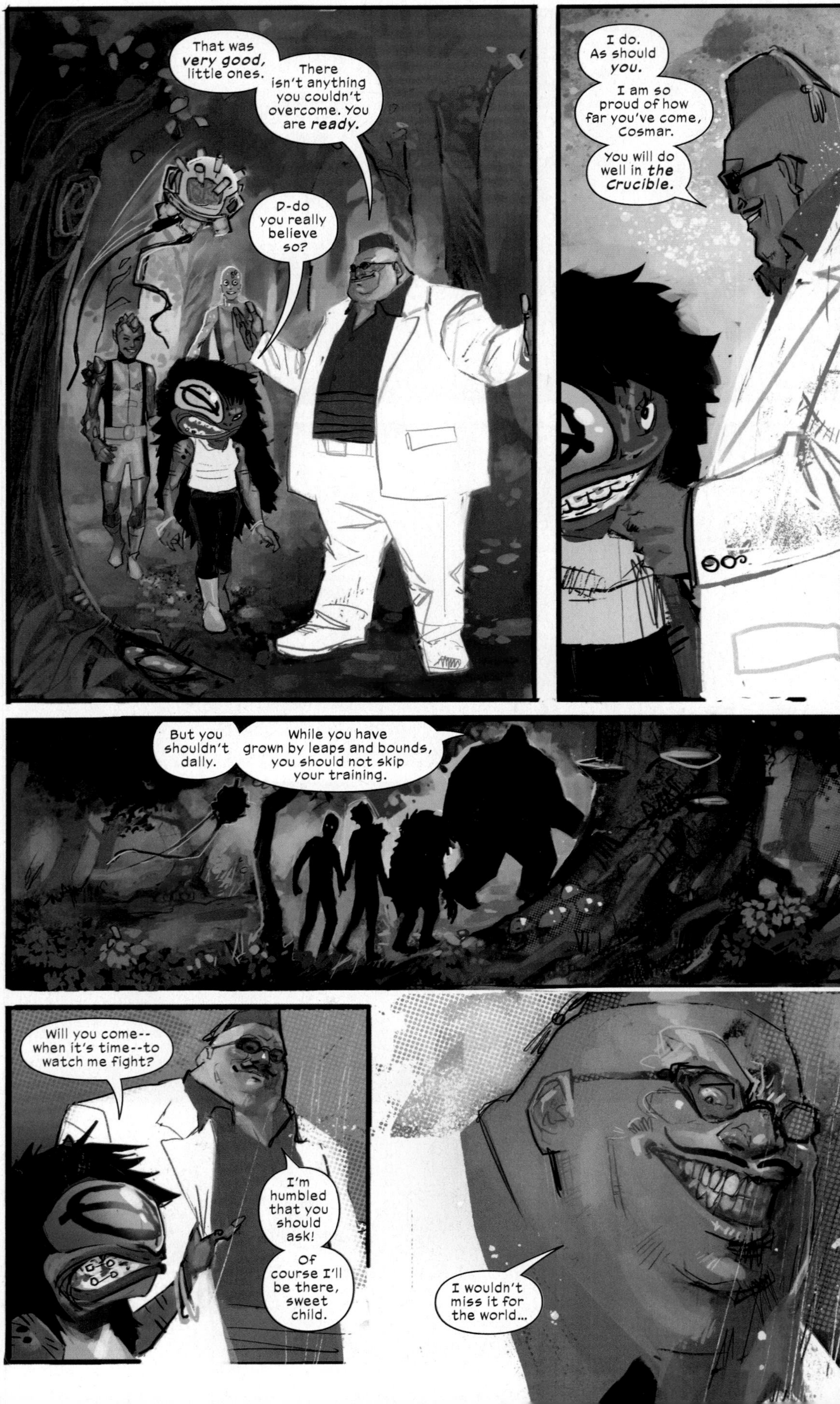
That was *very good*, little ones.
There isn't anything you couldn't overcome. You are *ready*.
D-do you really believe so?
I do. As should *you*.
I am so proud of how far you've come, Cosmar.
You will do well in *the Crucible*.
But you shouldn't dally.
While you have grown by leaps and bounds, you should not skip your training.
Will you come-- when it's time--to watch me fight?
I'm humbled that you should ask!
Of course I'll be there, sweet child.
I wouldn't miss it for the world...

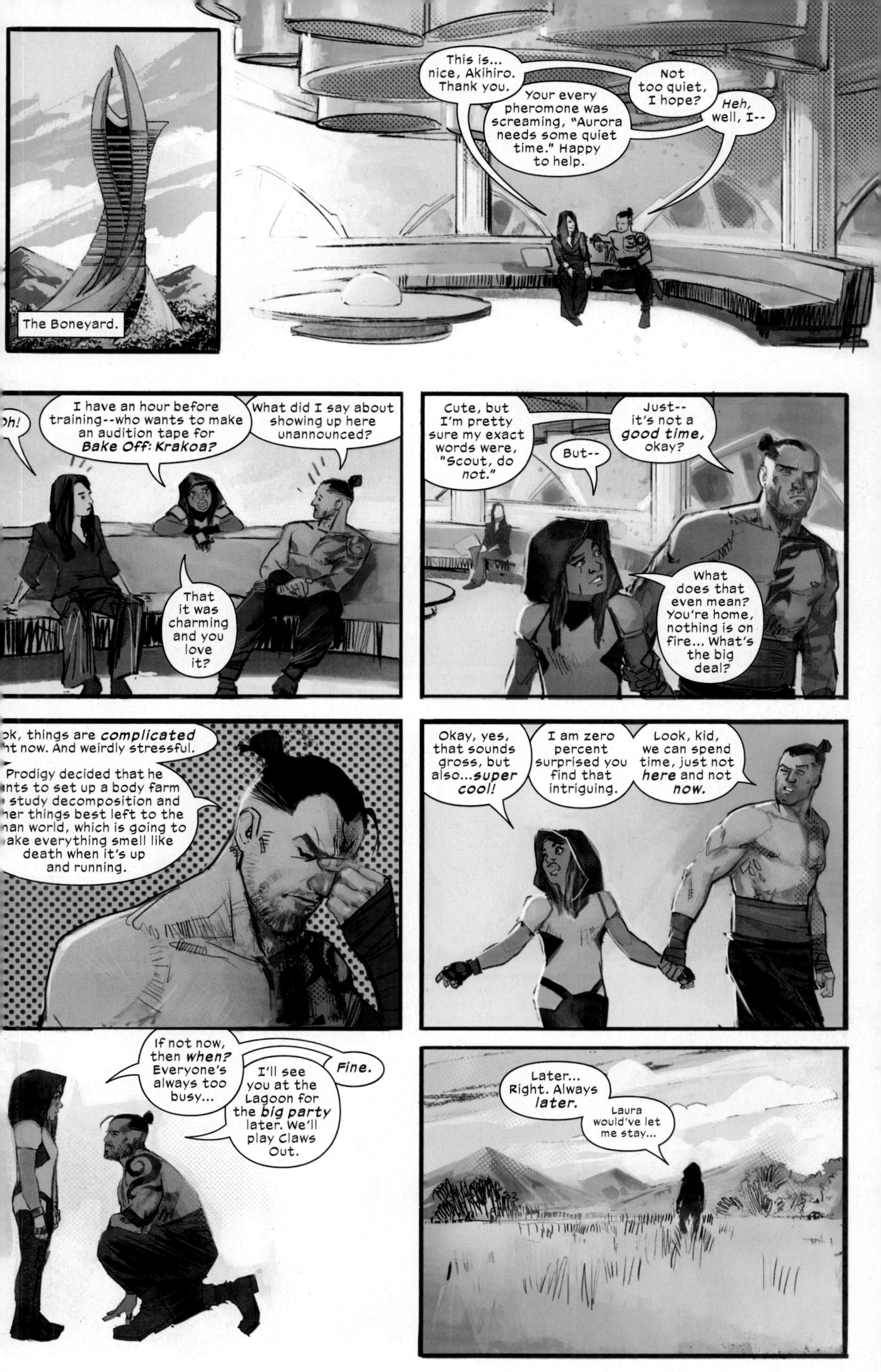

The Boneyard.
This is... nice, Akihiro. Thank you.
Your every pheromone was screaming, "Aurora needs some quiet time." Happy to help.
Not too quiet, I hope?
Heh, well, I--
Oh!
I have an hour before training--who wants to make an audition tape for Bake Off: Krakoa?
What did I say about showing up here unannounced?
That it was charming and you love it?
Cute, but I'm pretty sure my exact words were, "Scout, do not."
But--
Just-- it's not a good time, okay?
What does that even mean? You're home, nothing is on fire... What's the big deal?
ook, things are complicated
ht now. And weirdly stressful.
Prodigy decided that he
ants to set up a body farm
study decomposition and
her things best left to the
nan world, which is going to
ake everything smell like
death when it's up
and running.
Okay, yes, that sounds gross, but also...super cool!
I am zero percent surprised you find that intriguing.
Look, kid, we can spend time, just not here and not now.
If not now, then when? Everyone's always too busy...
Fine.
I'll see you at the Lagoon for the big party later. We'll play Claws Out.
Later... Right. Always later.
Laura would've let me stay...

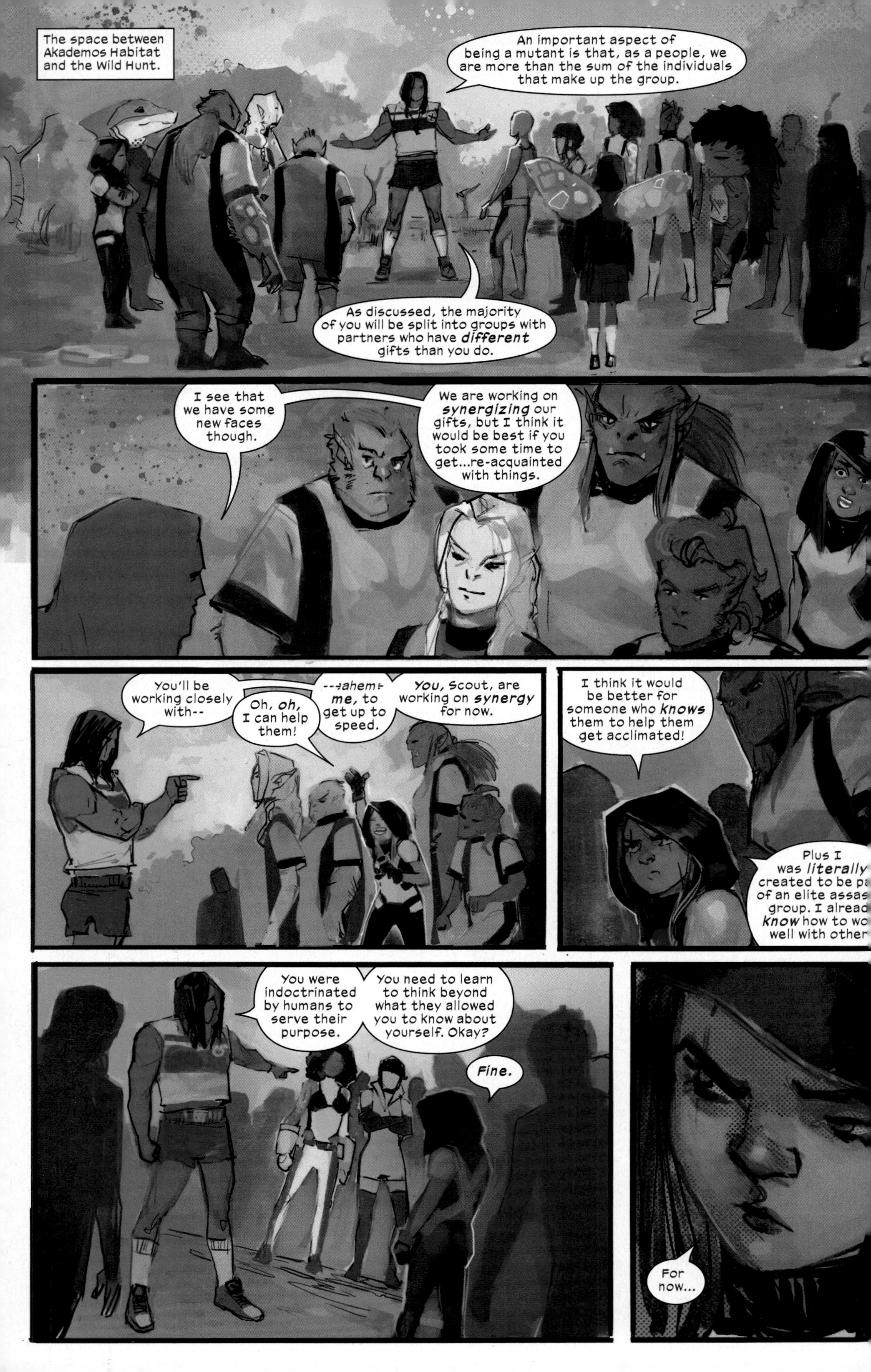

The space between Akademos Habitat and the Wild Hunt.
An important aspect of being a mutant is that, as a people, we are more than the sum of the individuals that make up the group.
As discussed, the majority of you will be split into groups with partners who have *different* gifts than you do.
I see that we have some new faces though.
We are working on *synergizing* our gifts, but I think it would be best if you took some time to get...re-acquainted with things.
You'll be working closely with--
Oh, *oh,* I can help them!
--*ahem*-- *me,* to get up to speed.
You, Scout, are working on *synergy* for now.
I think it would be better for someone who *knows* them to help them get acclimated!
Plus I was *literally* created to be pa of an elite assas group. I alread *know* how to wo well with other
You were indoctrinated by humans to serve their purpose.
You need to learn to think beyond what they allowed you to know about yourself. Okay?
Fine.
For now...

...raining assessment: spatial awareness.

Rain Boy/ Shark Girl Synergy: **Carcharodon Cyclone.**

...raining assessment: agility.

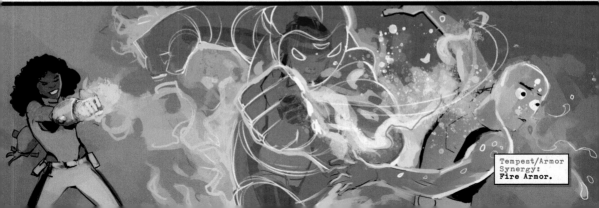

Tempest/Armor Synergy: **Fire Armor.**

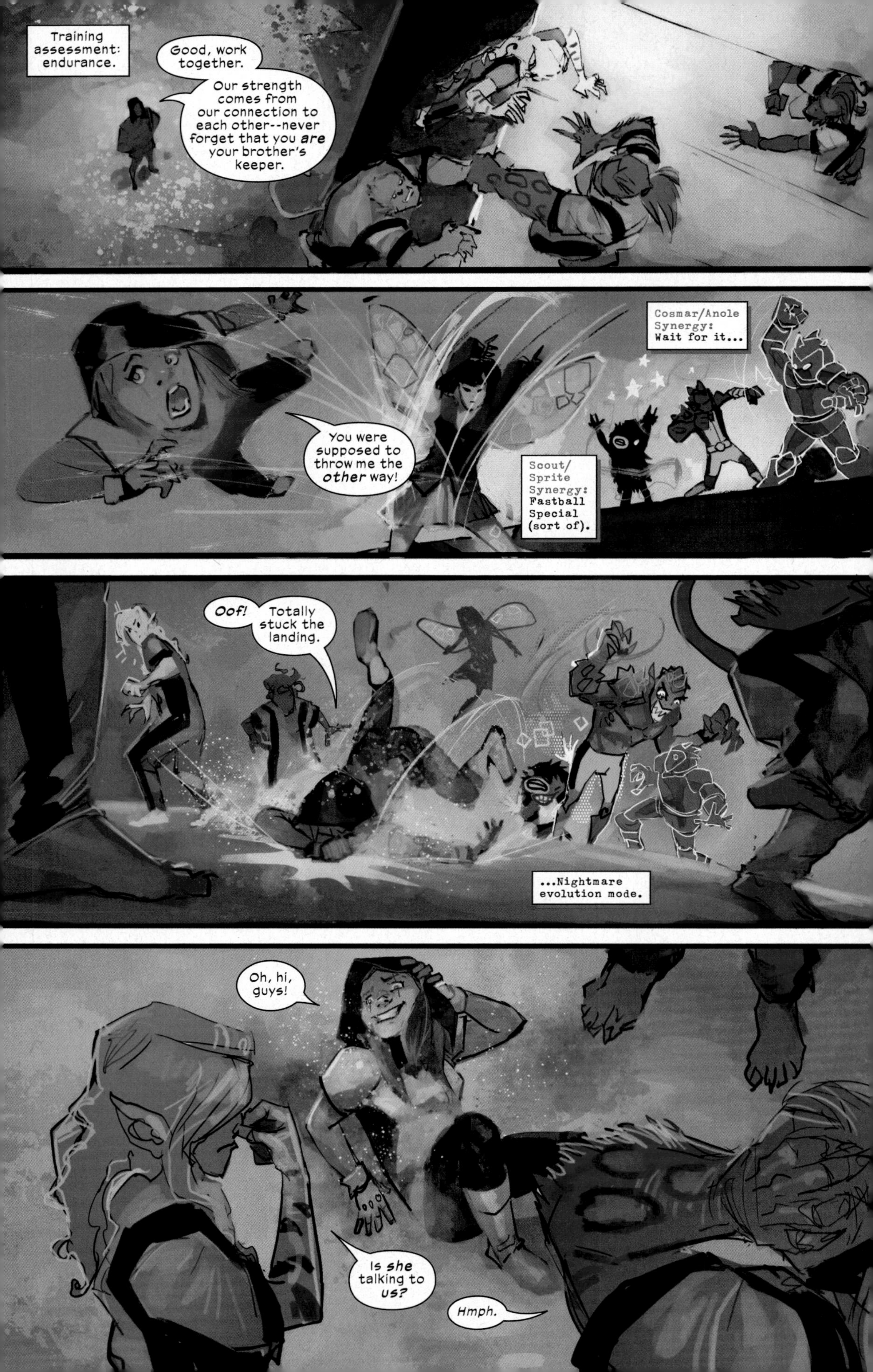
Training assessment: endurance.
Good, work together.
Our strength comes from our connection to each other--never forget that you *are* your brother's keeper.
Cosmar/Anole Synergy: Wait for it...
You were supposed to throw me the *other* way!
Scout/Sprite Synergy: Fastball Special (sort of).
Oof!
Totally stuck the landing.
...Nightmare evolution mode.
Oh, hi, guys!
Is *she* talking to *us?*
Hmph.

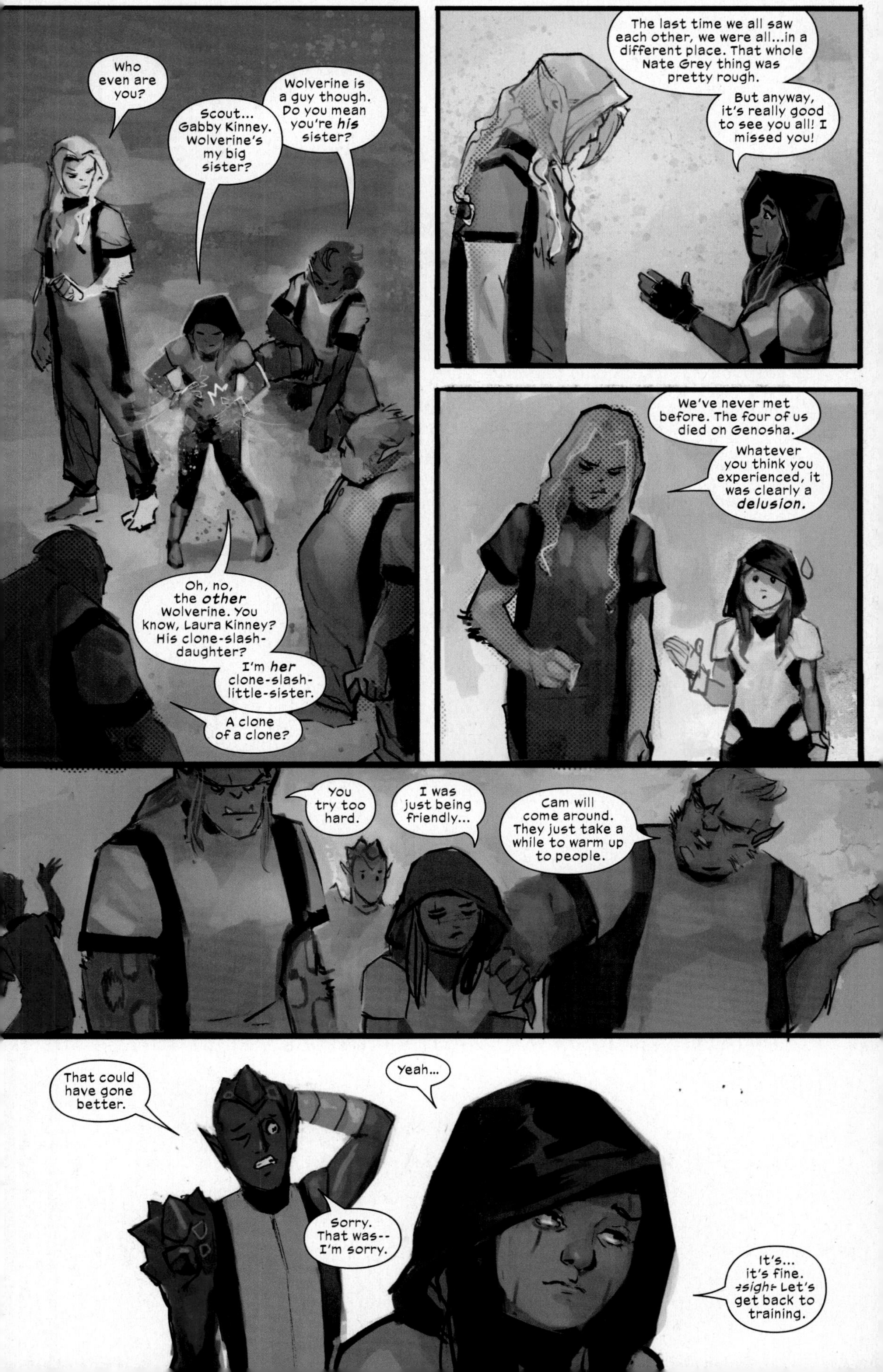
Who even are you?
Scout... Gabby Kinney. Wolverine's my big sister?
Wolverine is a guy though. Do you mean you're *his* sister?
Oh, no, the *other* Wolverine. You know, Laura Kinney? His clone-slash-daughter?
I'm *her* clone-slash-little-sister.
A clone of a clone?
The last time we all saw each other, we were all...in a different place. That whole Nate Grey thing was pretty rough.
But anyway, it's really good to see you all! I missed you!
We've never met before. The four of us died on Genosha.
Whatever you think you experienced, it was clearly a *delusion.*
You try too hard.
I was just being friendly...
Cam will come around. They just take a while to warm up to people.
That could have gone better.
Yeah...
Sorry. That was-- I'm sorry.
It's... it's fine. *sigh* Let's get back to training.

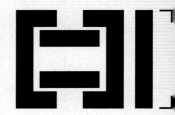

RE: RESURRECTION REQUEST

Wolfsbane,

Look, there is no jumping the queue for anyone unless the Council decrees it, and I won't break rules even for you--BUT, that being said, I looked into seeing when Tier was slated to be resurrected so I could tell you, and he isn't in the queue.

I'm not sure what this means, so I've tapped X-Factor to look into it for you. They're pretty swamped right now, so you may have to follow up with them.

You know I care about you, and I want you to be happy. I wish I could help more.

If you need anything that isn't bending rules, don't hesitate to call on me.

Take care of yourself, Rahne.

Elixir

—

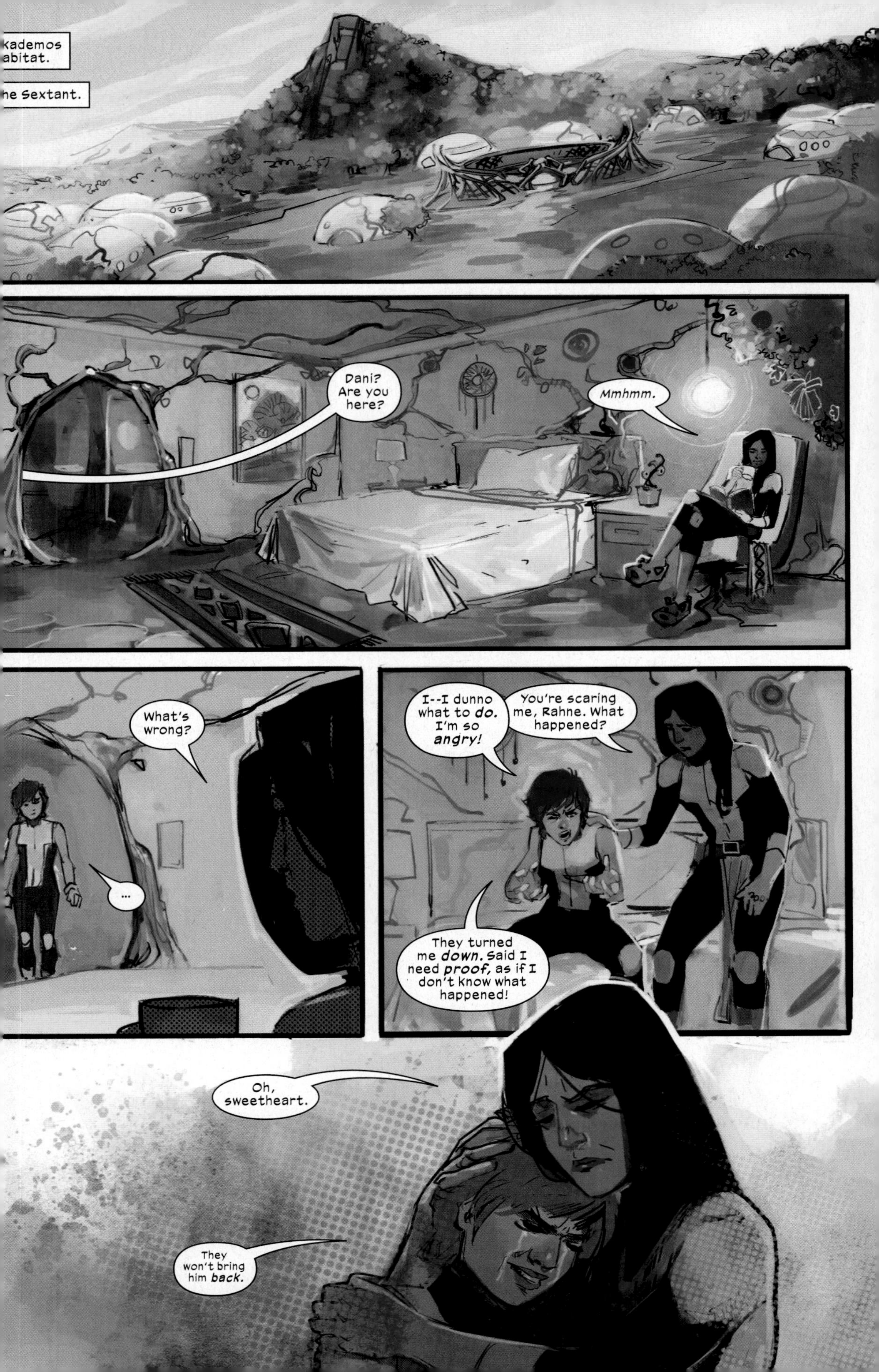
kademos
abitat.
he Sextant.
Dani? Are you here?
Mmhmm.
What's wrong?
...
I--I dunno what to do. I'm so angry!
You're scaring me, Rahne. What happened?
They turned me down. Said I need proof, as if I don't know what happened!
Oh, sweetheart.
They won't bring him back.

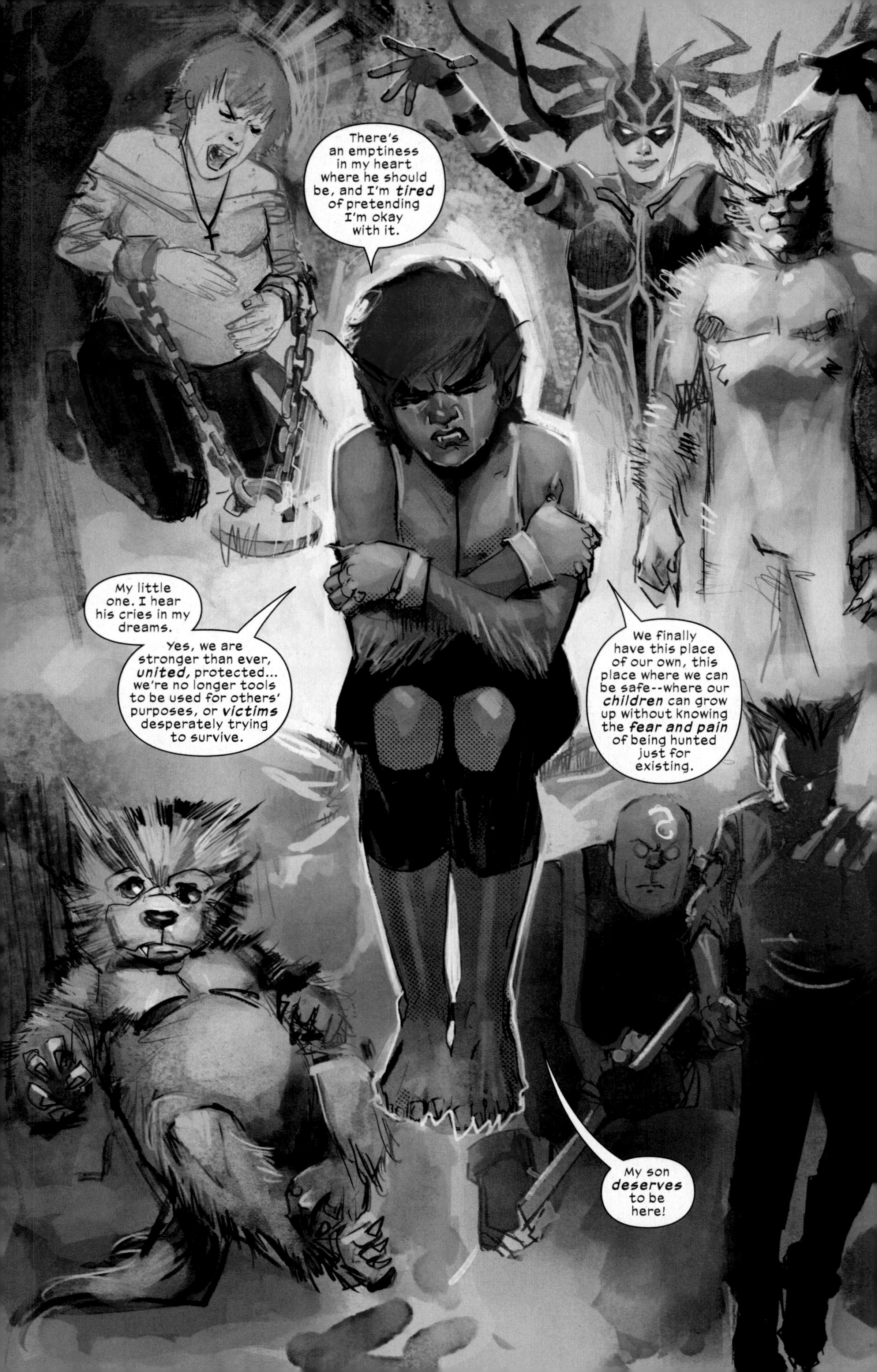
There's an emptiness in my heart where he should be, and I'm *tired* of pretending I'm okay with it.
My little one. I hear his cries in my dreams.
Yes, we are stronger than ever, *united,* protected... we're no longer tools to be used for others' purposes, or *victims* desperately trying to survive.
We finally have this place of our own, this place where we can be safe--where our *children* can grow up without knowing the *fear and pain* of being hunted just for existing.
My son *deserves* to be here!

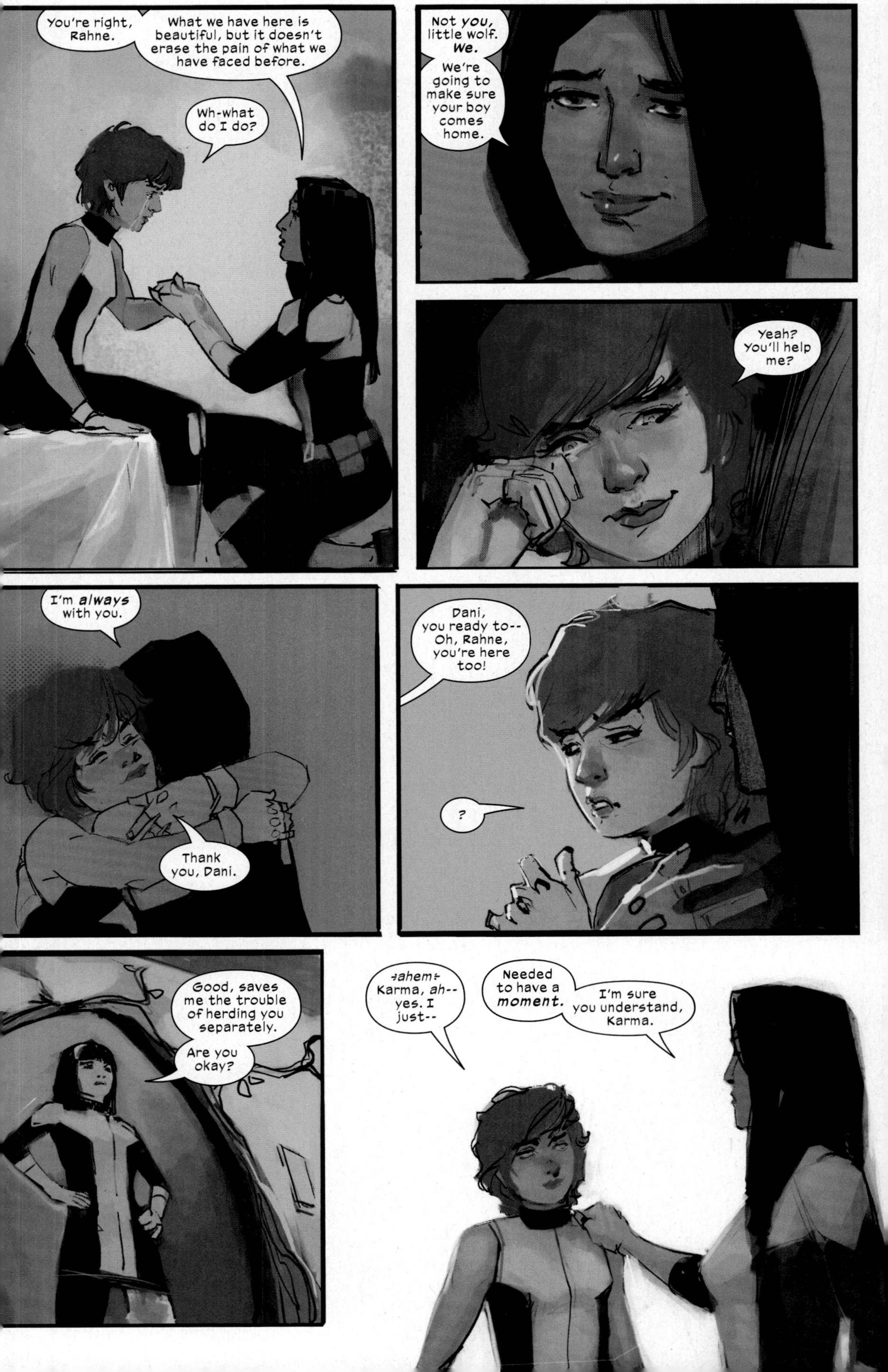
You're right, Rahne.
What we have here is beautiful, but it doesn't erase the pain of what we have faced before.
Wh-what do I do?
Not *you*, little wolf. ***We.***
We're going to make sure your boy comes home.
Yeah? You'll help me?
I'm ***always*** with you.
Thank you, Dani.
Dani, you ready to-- Oh, Rahne, you're here too!
?
Good, saves me the trouble of herding you separately.
Are you okay?
=ahem= Karma, *ah*-- yes. I just--
Needed to have a ***moment.***
I'm sure you understand, Karma.

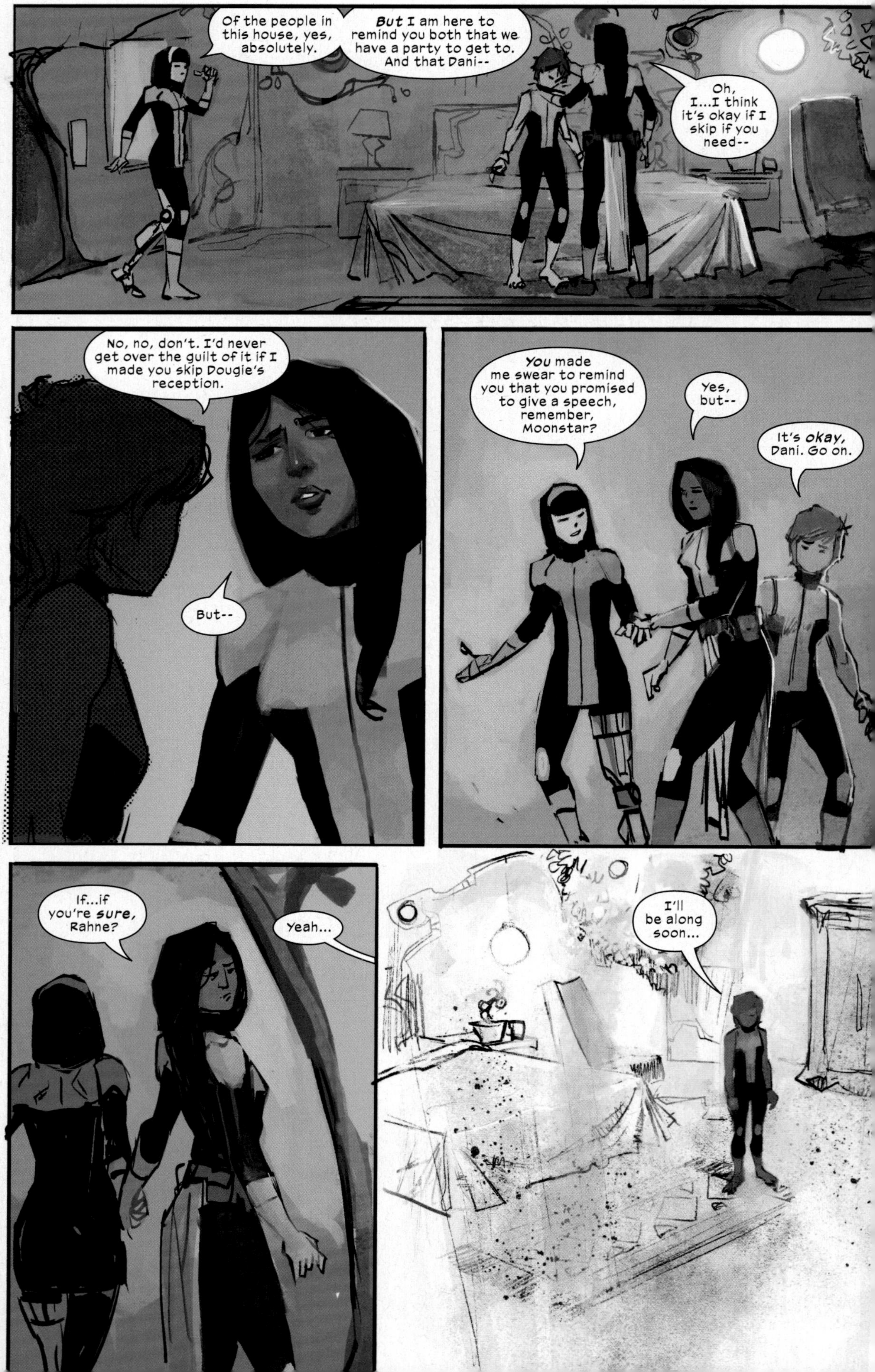
Of the people in this house, yes, absolutely.
But I am here to remind you both that we have a party to get to. And that Dani--
Oh, I...I think it's okay if I skip if you need--
No, no, don't. I'd never get over the guilt of it if I made you skip Dougie's reception.
But--
You made me swear to remind you that you promised to give a speech, remember, Moonstar?
Yes, but--
It's *okay,* Dani. Go on.
If...if you're *sure,* Rahne?
Yeah...
I'll be along soon...

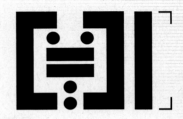

THE JOURNALS OF AMAHL FAROUK

The Shadow tells me that he can teach me to fully control my gifts -- so that I might be able to help people. In exchange, I allow him to ride my soul, so that he can experience the world, so that he might know it. He watches as I eat and drink, as I play in the sun. He says it gives him joy.

He tells me that there are a million worlds like ours, each more strange and wonderful. That there are infinite possibilities, all lined up next to each other, just out of reach, and that he will take me there when I am ready.

I wish my father could see them too.

—

The Shadow asks me to use my gifts more each day, and each day I feel stronger. He tells me we are alike, that our gifts complement each other's -- he, a traveler of worlds, and me, and traveler of minds. With him, I will see things others could never imagine. With him, I will never be alone.

I know that father would be proud of how much I am learning, of the good I will do when I am stronger enough.

—

Sometimes I wake up in places that I do not remember going. The Shadow says we are growing.

He asks me to use my gifts to compel others to behave as they should. He says that if we keep people from doing wrong, it is better than punishing them for a mistake we could have prevented. We are our brother's keepers, we must use our gifts to shepherd him.

I think my father would understand. I wish I could hear his voice now, telling me he loves me.

—

Joy follows us wherever we go. Men clap me on the back and tell me they admire my prowess, and women swoon and give me their gifts. The people love us, we protect them from themselves and they bring us tribute.

We are always together now, I am never alone.

My mind is a haze, the more he rides my soul, the less real things feel.

I cannot remember the face of my father. It is my only regret. But the Shadow assures me that he is smiling, and that when I meet him again on the other side, he will hold me close and tell me he is proud.

—

Our power grows, and with it, we will shape and rule this world from the shadows. We will be King.

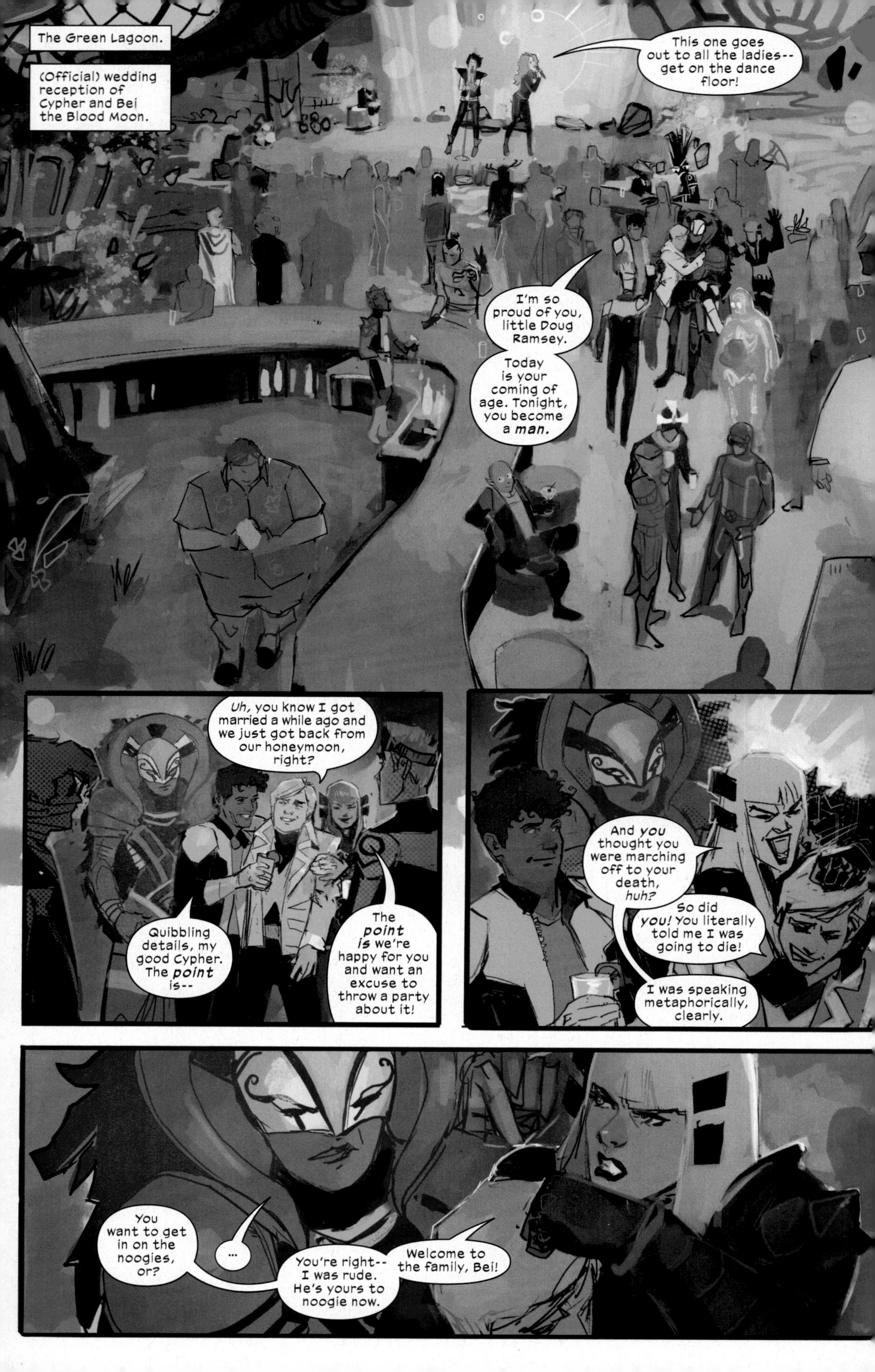

The Green Lagoon.
(Official) wedding reception of Cypher and Bei the Blood Moon.
This one goes out to all the ladies-- get on the dance floor!
I'm so proud of you, little Doug Ramsey.
Today is your coming of age. Tonight, you become a *man.*
Uh, you know I got married a while ago and we just got back from our honeymoon, right?
Quibbling details, my good Cypher. The *point* is--
The *point is* we're happy for you and want an excuse to throw a party about it!
And *you* thought you were marching off to your death, *huh?*
So did *you!* You literally told me I was going to die!
I was speaking metaphorically, clearly.
You want to get in on the noogies, or?
...
You're right-- I was rude. He's yours to noogie now.
Welcome to the family, Bei!

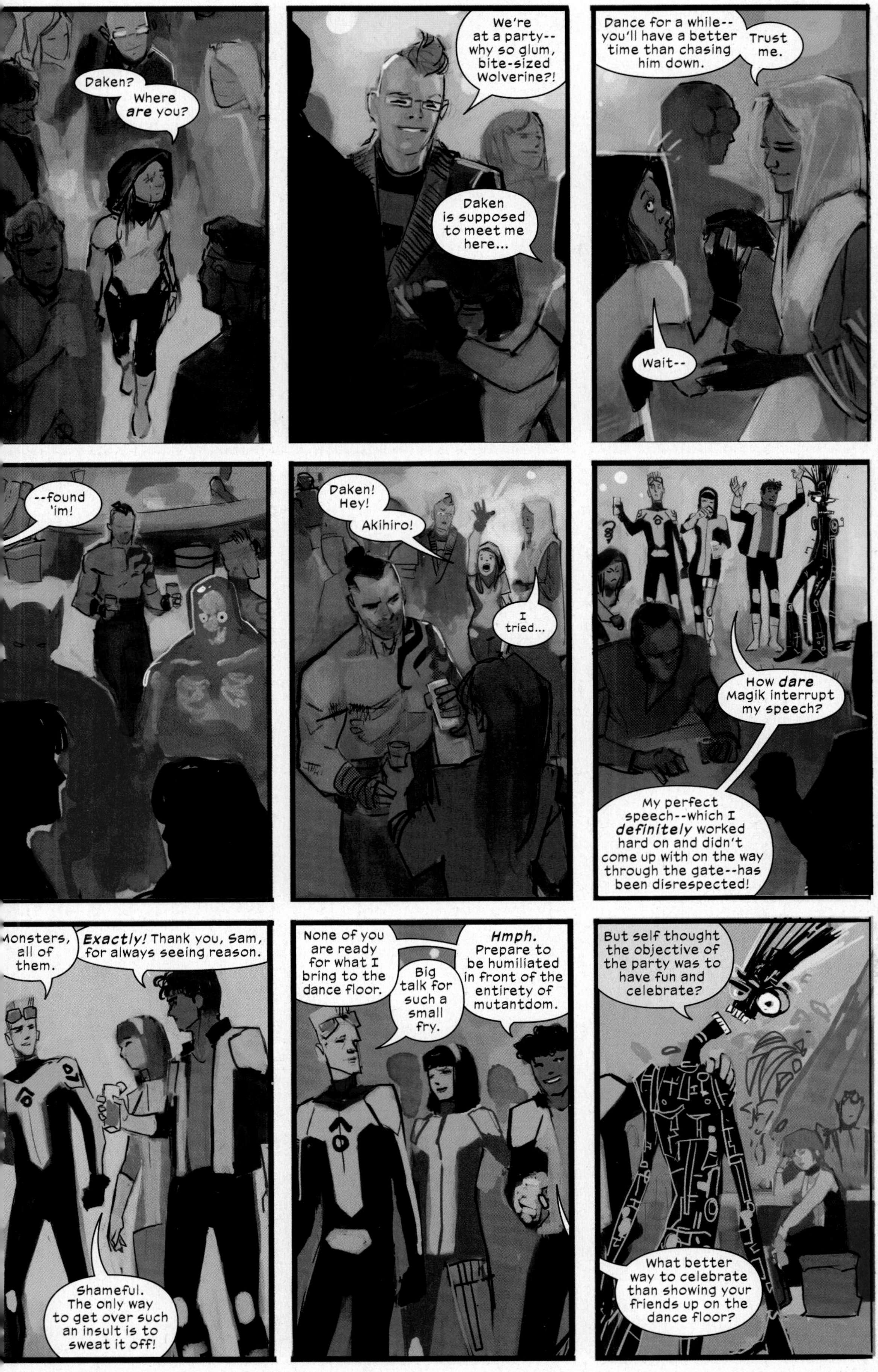

Daken? Where *are* you?
We're at a party--why so glum, bite-sized Wolverine?!
Daken is supposed to meet me here...
Dance for a while--you'll have a better time than chasing him down.
Trust me.
Wait--
--found 'im!
Daken! Hey!
Akihiro!
I tried...
How *dare* Magik interrupt my speech?
My perfect speech--which I *definitely* worked hard on and didn't come up with on the way through the gate--has been disrespected!
Monsters, all of them.
Exactly! Thank you, Sam, for always seeing reason.
Shameful. The only way to get over such an insult is to sweat it off!
None of you are ready for what I bring to the dance floor.
Big talk for such a small fry.
Hmph. Prepare to be humiliated in front of the entirety of mutantdom.
But self thought the objective of the party was to have fun and celebrate?
What better way to celebrate than showing your friends up on the dance floor?

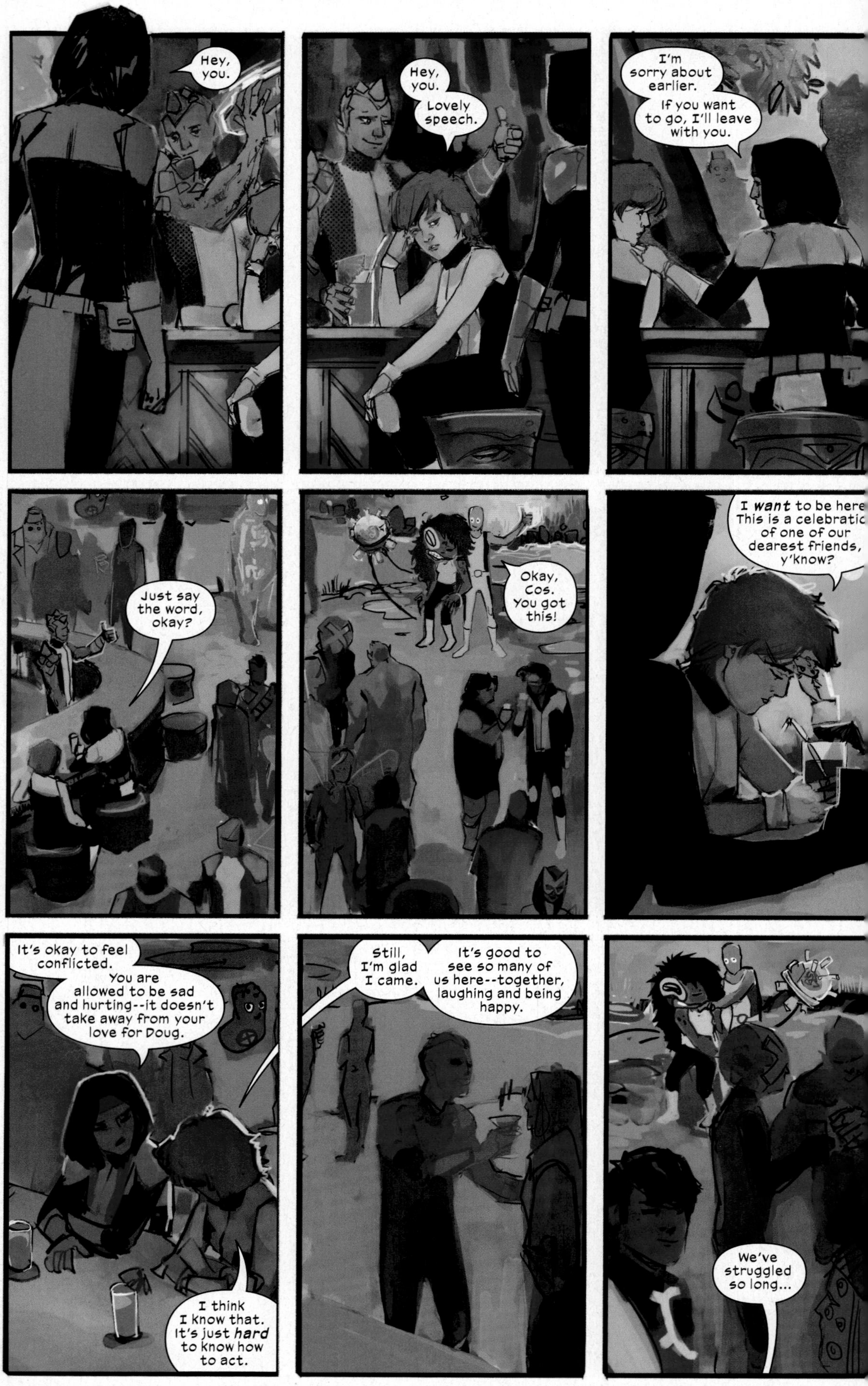
Hey, you.
Hey, you.
Lovely speech.
I'm sorry about earlier.
If you want to go, I'll leave with you.
Just say the word, okay?
Okay, Cos. You got this!
I *want* to be here
This is a celebratic
of one of our dearest friends, y'know?
It's okay to feel conflicted.
You are allowed to be sad and hurting--it doesn't take away from your love for Doug.
I think I know that. It's just *hard* to know how to act.
Still, I'm glad I came.
It's good to see so many of us here--together, laughing and being happy.
We've struggled so long...

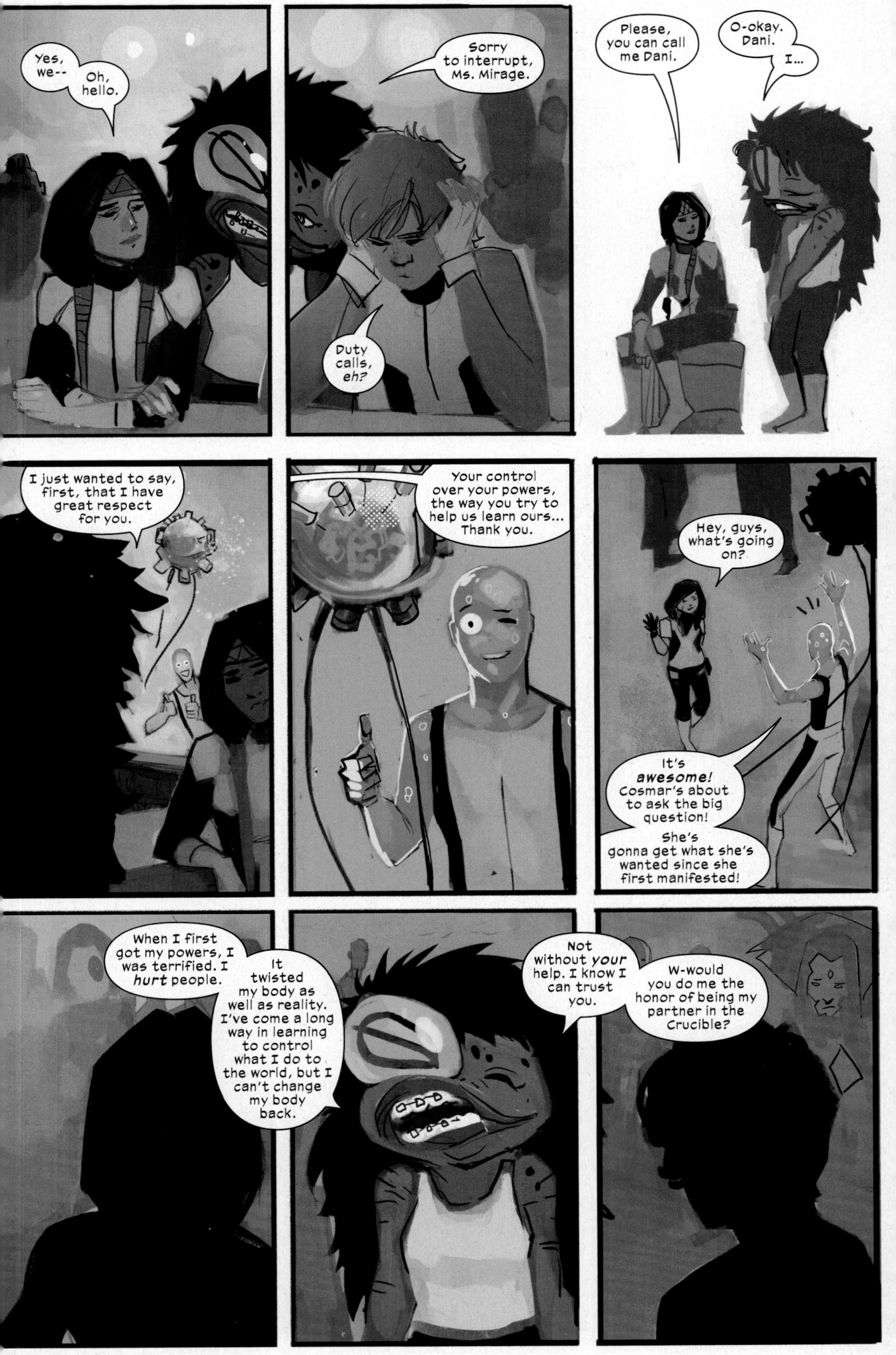
Yes, we--
Oh, hello.
Sorry to interrupt, Ms. Mirage.
Duty calls, *eh?*
Please, you can call me Dani.
O-okay. Dani. I...
I just wanted to say, first, that I have great respect for you.
Your control over your powers, the way you try to help us learn ours... Thank you.
Hey, guys, what's going on?
It's *awesome!* Cosmar's about to ask the big question!
She's gonna get what she's wanted since she first manifested!
When I first got my powers, I was terrified. I *hurt* people.
It twisted my body as well as reality. I've come a long way in learning to control what I do to the world, but I can't change my body back.
Not without *your* help. I know I can trust you.
W-would you do me the honor of being my partner in the Crucible?

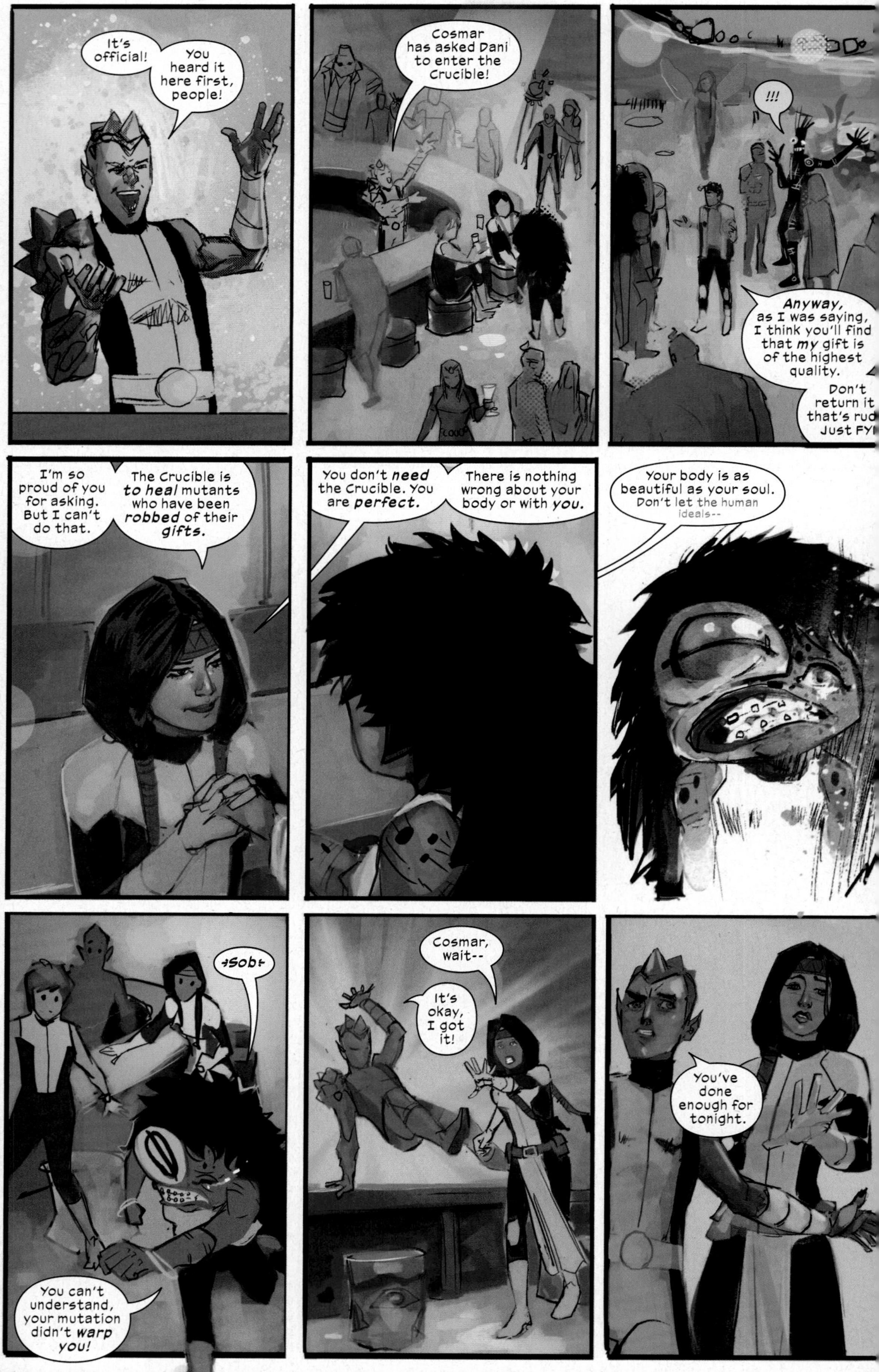
It's official!
You heard it here first, people!
Cosmar has asked Dani to enter the Crucible!
!!!
Anyway, as I was saying, I think you'll find that my gift is of the highest quality.
Don't return it that's rud Just FYI
I'm so proud of you for asking. But I can't do that.
The Crucible is to heal mutants who have been robbed of their gifts.
You don't need the Crucible. You are perfect.
There is nothing wrong about your body or with you.
Your body is as beautiful as your soul. Don't let the human ideals--
Sob
You can't understand, your mutation didn't warp you!
Cosmar, wait--
It's okay, I got it!
You've done enough for tonight.

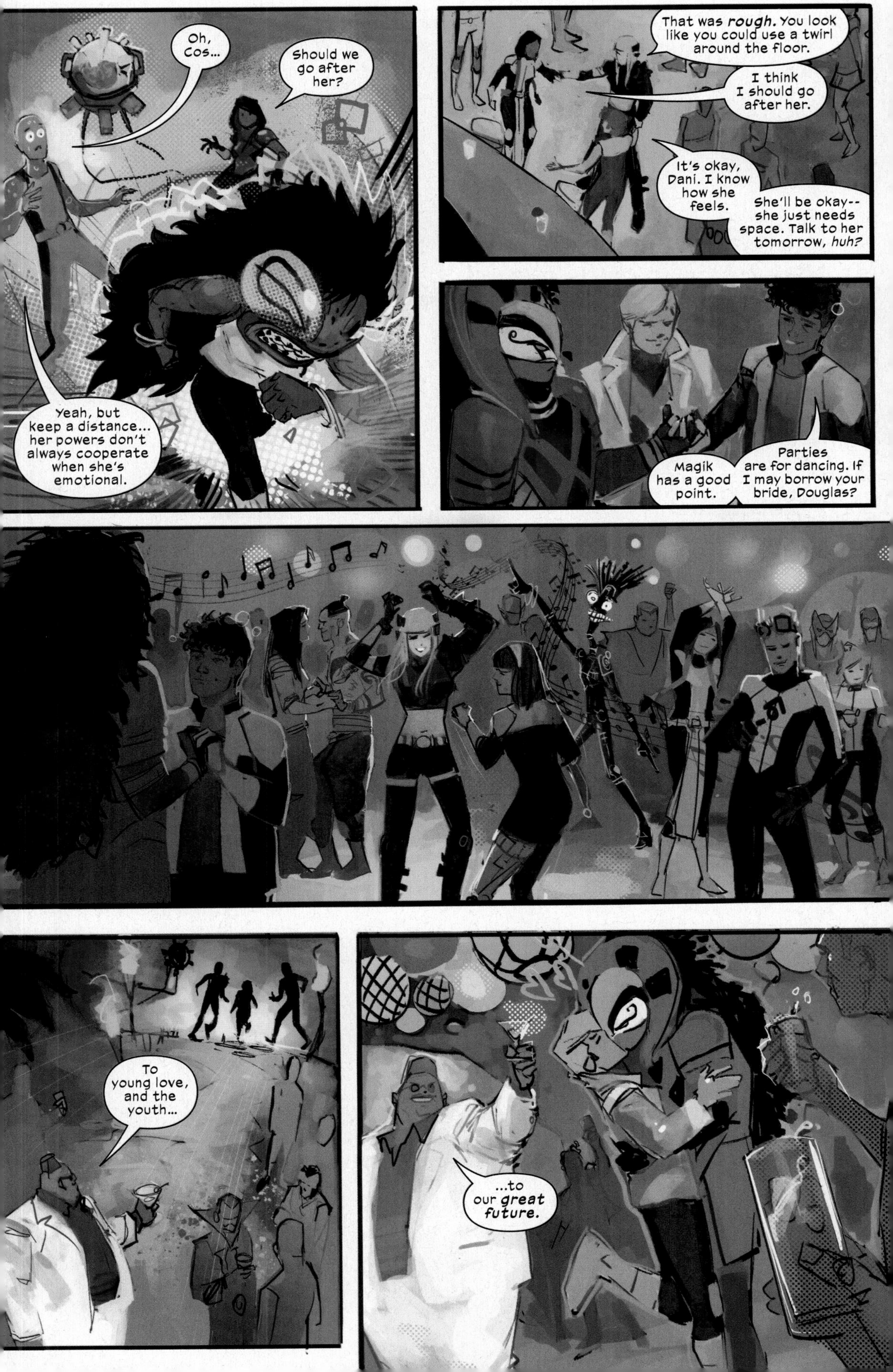
Oh, Cos...
Should we go after her?
Yeah, but keep a distance... her powers don't always cooperate when she's emotional.
That was *rough.* You look like you could use a twirl around the floor.
I think I should go after her.
It's okay, Dani. I know how she feels.
She'll be okay-- she just needs space. Talk to her tomorrow, *huh?*
Magik has a good point.
Parties are for dancing. If I may borrow your bride, Douglas?
To young love, and the youth...
...to our *great* future.

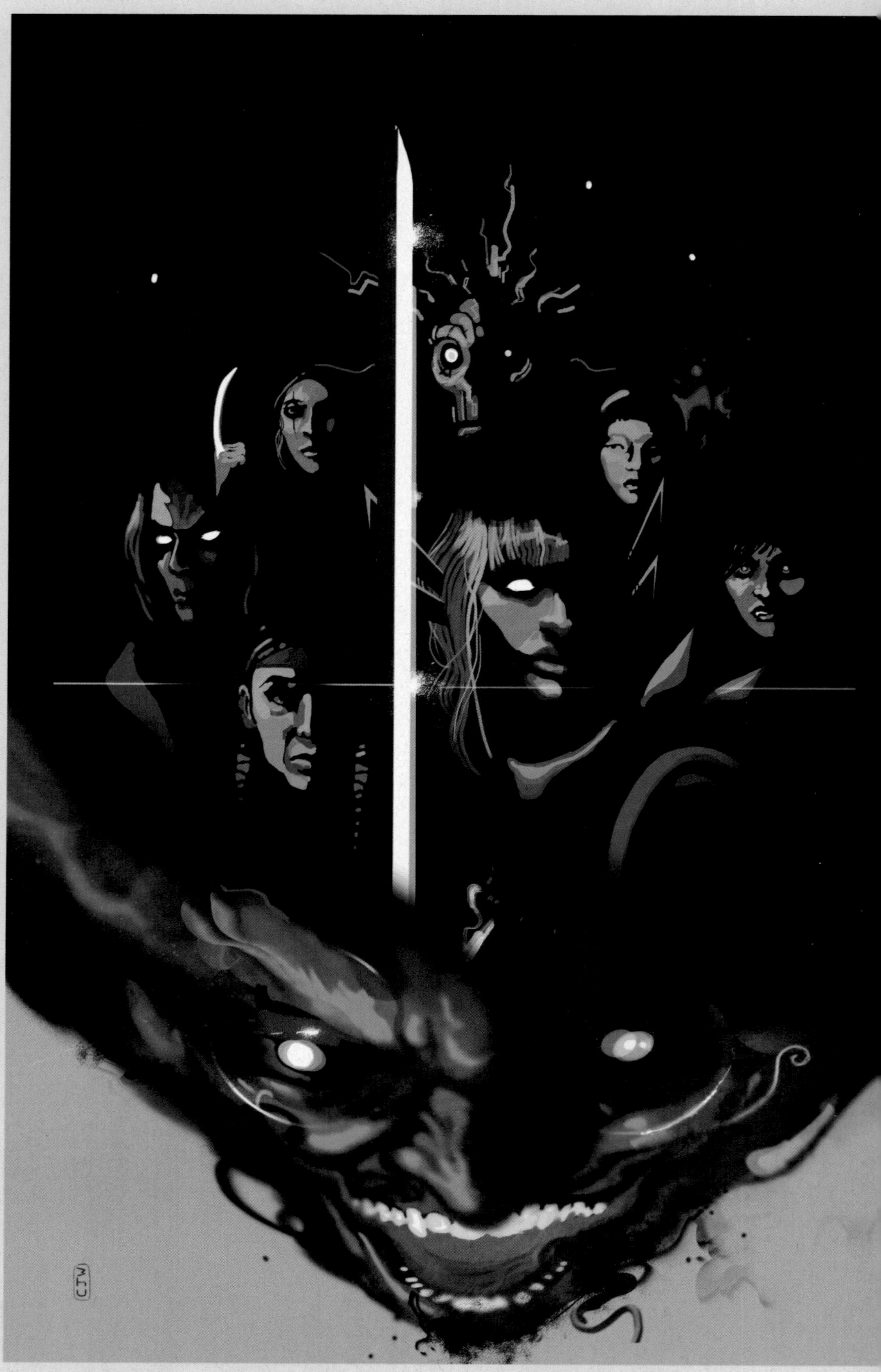

One Step Behind

[kra_]
[koa_]

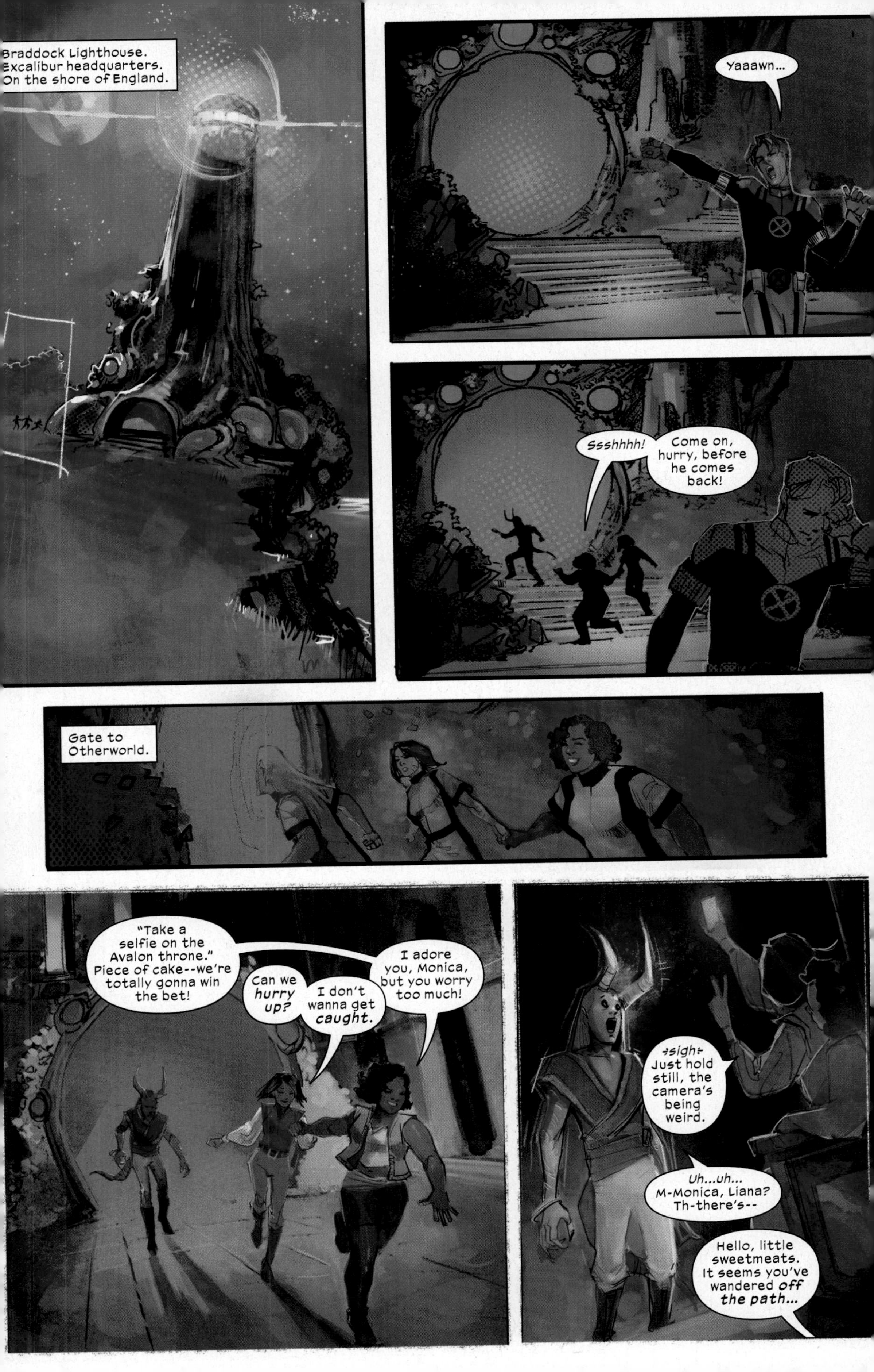

Braddock Lighthouse. Excalibur headquarters. On the shore of England.
Yaaawn...
Ssshhhh!
Come on, hurry, before he comes back!
Gate to Otherworld.
"Take a selfie on the Avalon throne." Piece of cake--we're totally gonna win the bet!
Can we *hurry up?*
I don't wanna get *caught.*
I adore you, Monica, but you worry too much!
sigh Just hold still, the camera's being weird.
Uh...uh... M-Monica, Liana? Th-there's--
Hello, little sweetmeats. It seems you've wandered *off the path...*

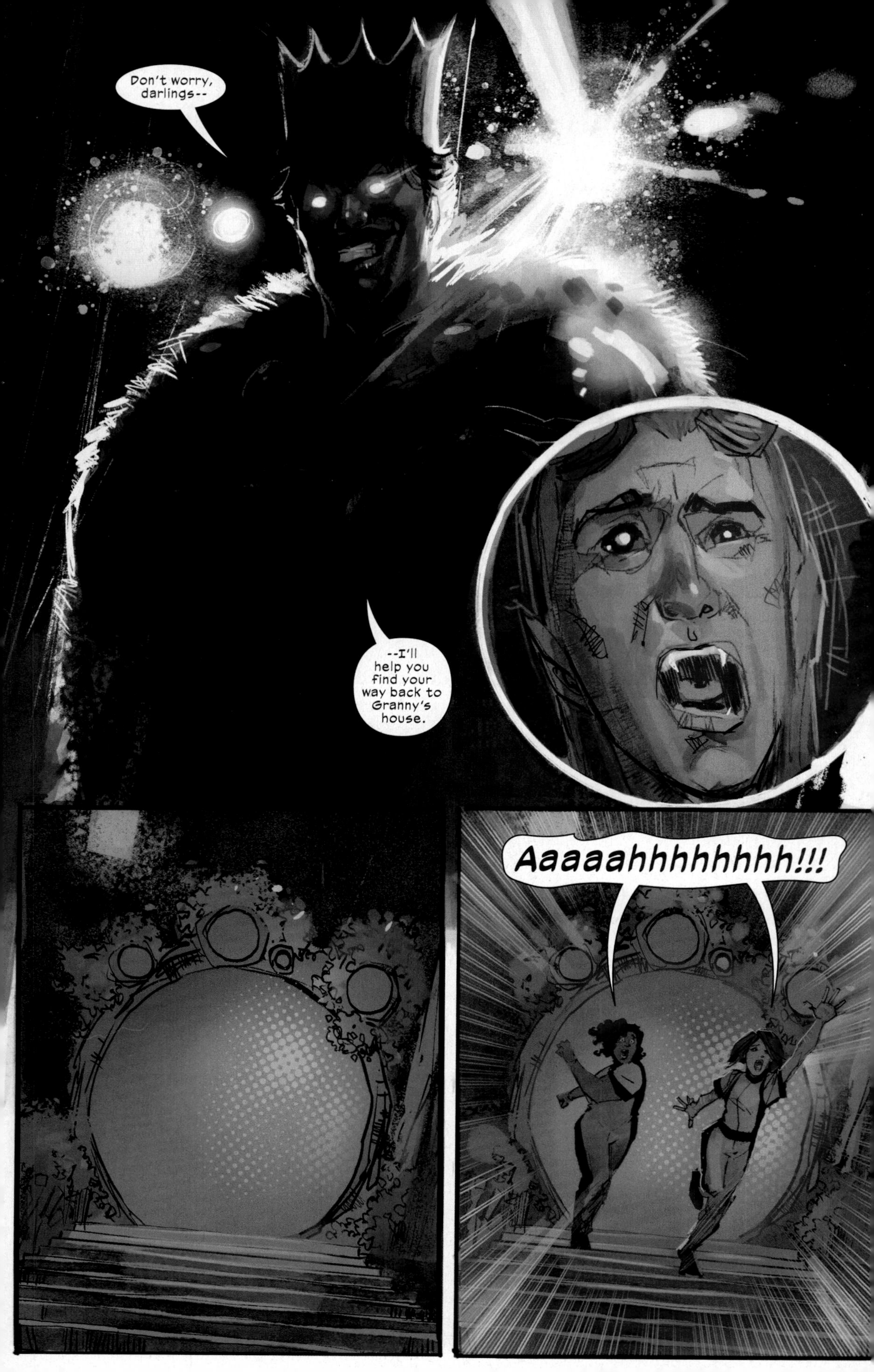
Don't worry, darlings--
--I'll help you find your way back to Granny's house.
Aaaaahhhhhhhh!!!

WARPATH JOURNAL, ENTRY 001

Pretty sure Moonstar got these questions out of a self-help book, but she's right: If we're going to guide, then we have to be willing to be led.

I doubt this will end up being useful, but I lose nothing by participating -- giving it a chance.

How do you view yourself?

With a mirror or other reflective surfaces. Sometimes in photos.

How do you view the world and others?

Generally with my eyes, but most of my other senses come into play. Sound and touch particularly help me get a sense of my environment.

Are you optimistic or pessimistic?

I think I misunderstood the last few questions, but since I used a pen, I'll press forward.

Being optimistic leaves you vulnerable to danger (internal and external). Being pessimistic cuts you off from possibilities. Neither is useful. Better to be a realist, to take things as they come and make any plans based on what you have observed.

Now let me circle back to the first two questions.

I view myself as a man who will do what needs to be done. I am a man who, even before Xavier's fancy machine, did not fear his own death, if it was what was needed. I am a man who hopes to help those that come after to do more than survive -- they deserve to thrive, more so because we didn't have the option.

The world supports and sustains life. It is an intricate, interconnected system of creation and destruction. Of balance. That is obvious.

Some people know how to be in harmony with the Earth's balance and some do not. It is unfortunate that the latter are able to exert their power so efficiently. That's where men like me come into the picture.

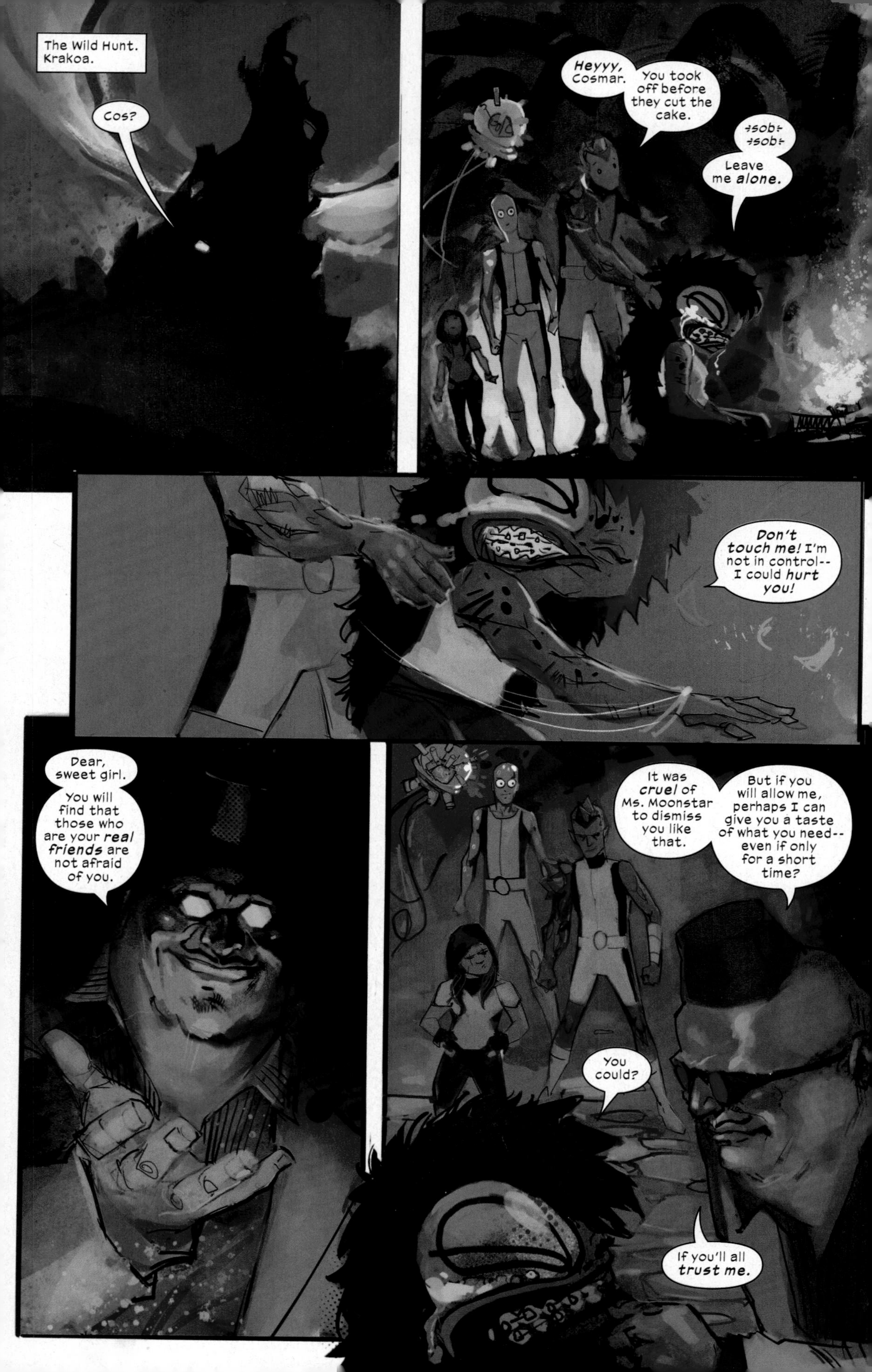
The Wild Hunt.
Krakoa.
Cos?
Heyyy, Cosmar.
You took off before they cut the cake.
~sob~
~sob~
Leave me alone.
Don't touch me! I'm not in control-- I could hurt you!
Dear, sweet girl.
You will find that those who are your real friends are not afraid of you.
It was cruel of Ms. Moonstar to dismiss you like that.
But if you will allow me, perhaps I can give you a taste of what you need--even if only for a short time?
You could?
If you'll all trust me.

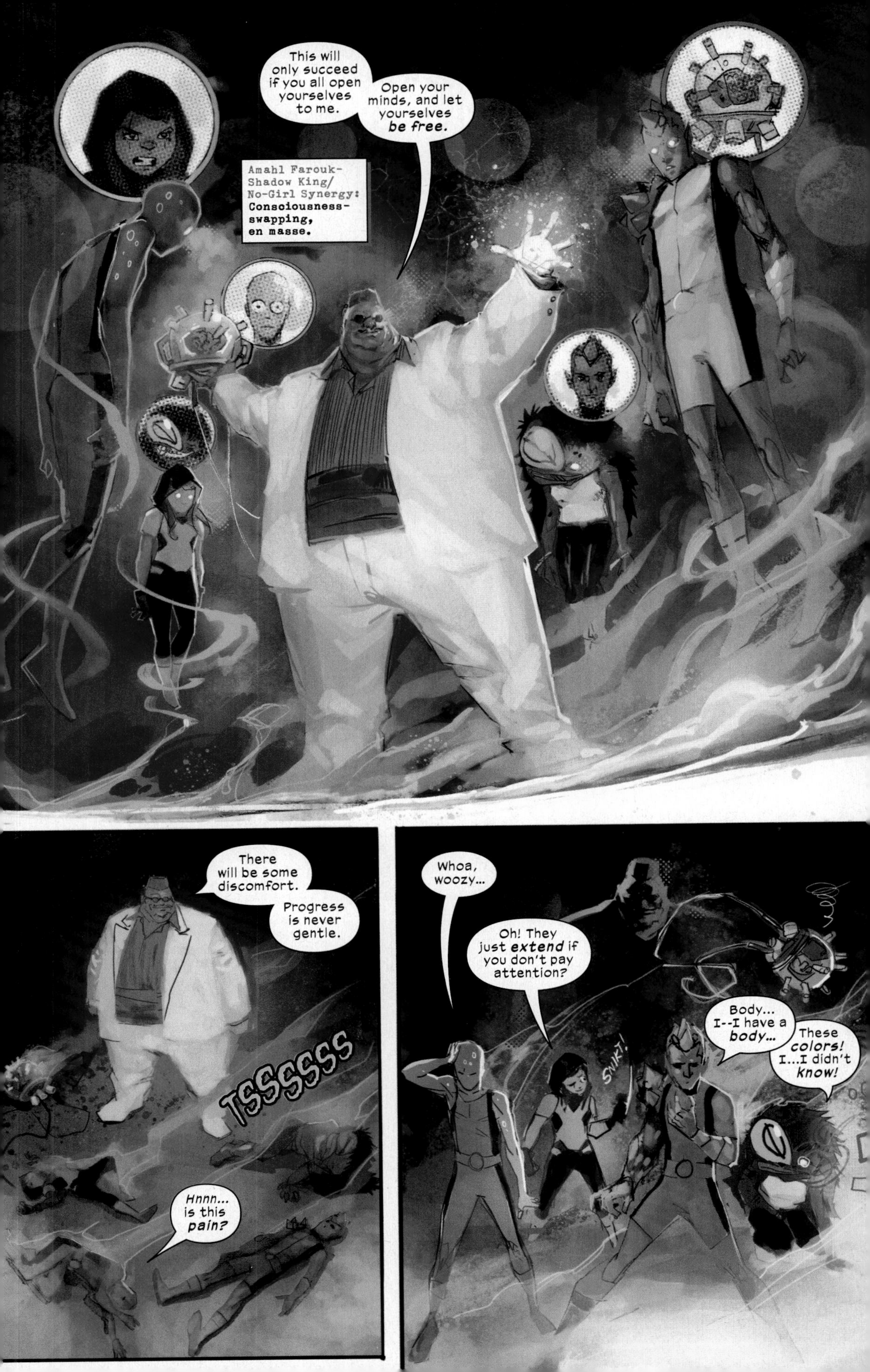
This will only succeed if you all open yourselves to me.
Open your minds, and let yourselves *be free.*
Amahl Farouk-Shadow King/ No-Girl Synergy: **Consciousness-swapping, en masse.**
There will be some discomfort.
Progress is never gentle.
TSSSSSS
Hnnn... is this *pain?*
Whoa, woozy...
Oh! They just *extend* if you don't pay attention?
SNIKT!
Body... I--I have a *body...*
These *colors!* I...I didn't *know!*

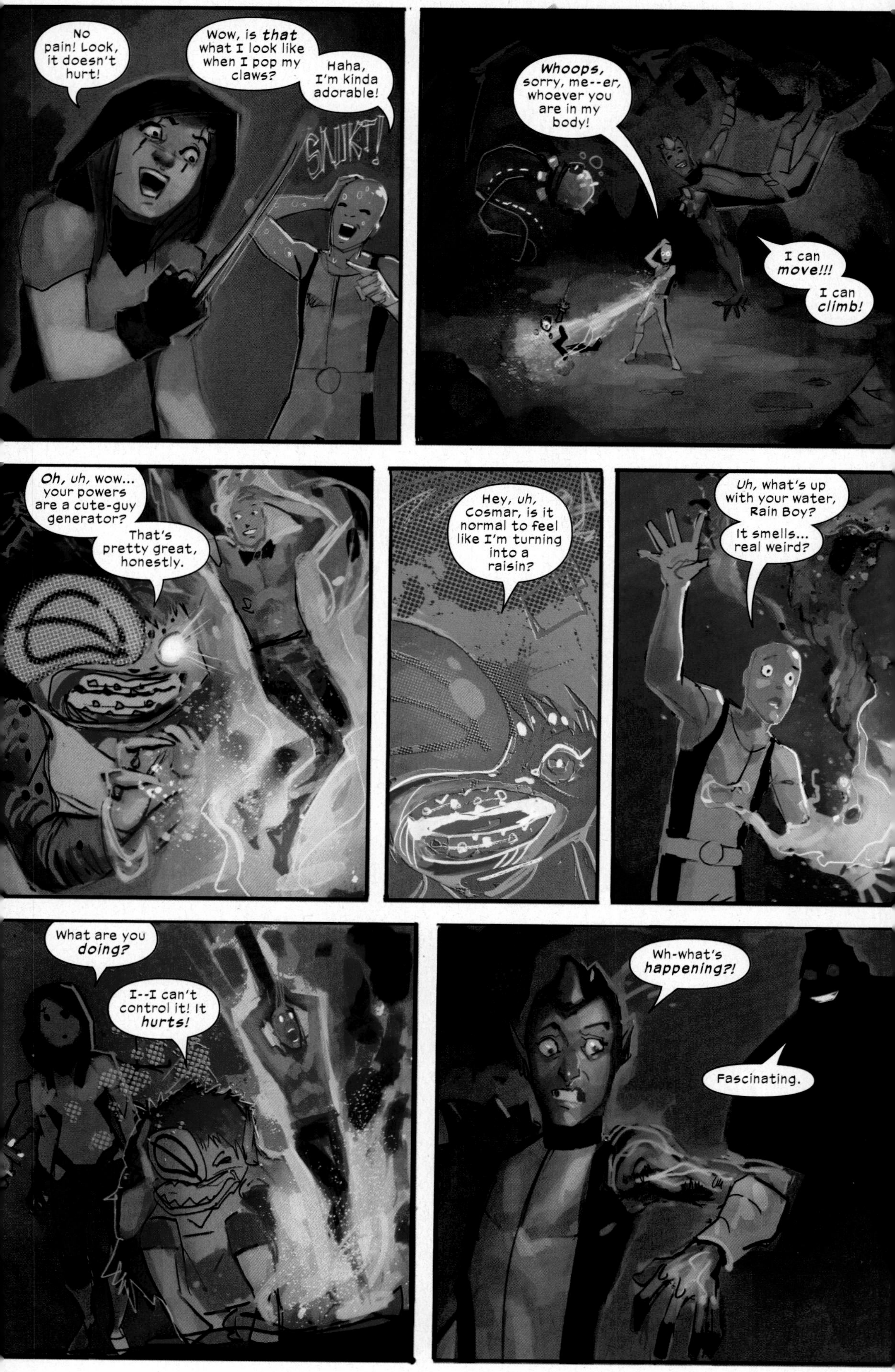

No pain! Look, it doesn't hurt!
Wow, is *that* what I look like when I pop my claws?
Haha, I'm kinda adorable!
SNIKT!
Whoops, sorry, me--er, whoever you are in my body!
I can *move!!!*
I can *climb!*
Oh, uh, wow... your powers are a cute-guy generator?
That's pretty great, honestly.
Hey, *uh,* Cosmar, is it normal to feel like I'm turning into a raisin?
Uh, what's up with your water, Rain Boy?
It smells... real weird?
What are you *doing?*
I--I can't control it! It *hurts!*
Wh-what's *happening?!*
Fascinating.

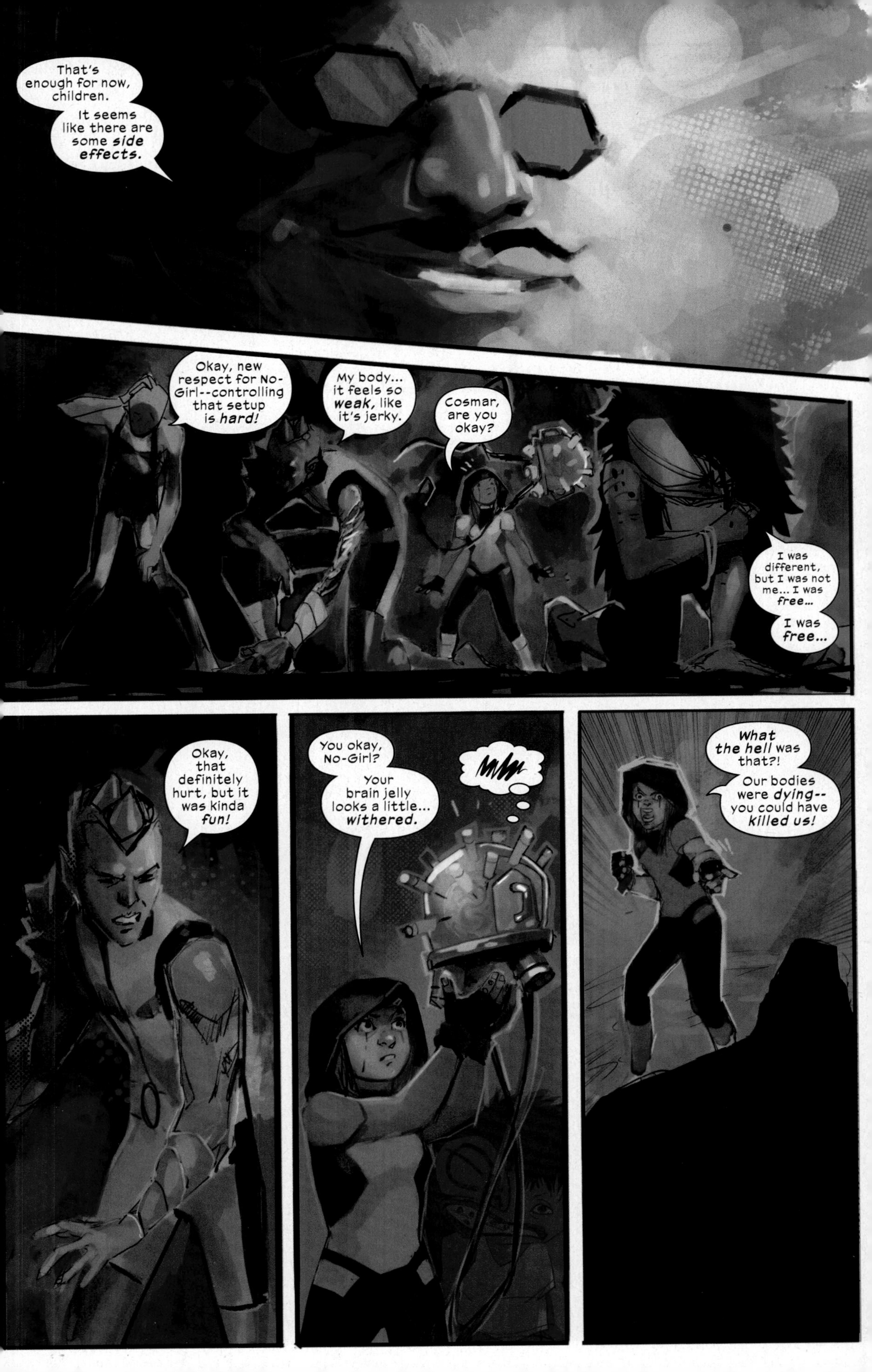
That's enough for now, children.
It seems like there are some *side effects.*
Okay, new respect for No-Girl--controlling that setup is *hard!*
My body... it feels so *weak*, like it's jerky.
Cosmar, are you okay?
I was different, but I was not me... I was *free...*
I was *free...*
Okay, that definitely hurt, but it was kinda *fun!*
You okay, No-Girl?
Your brain jelly looks a little... *withered.*
What the hell was that?!
Our bodies were *dying*-- you could have *killed us!*

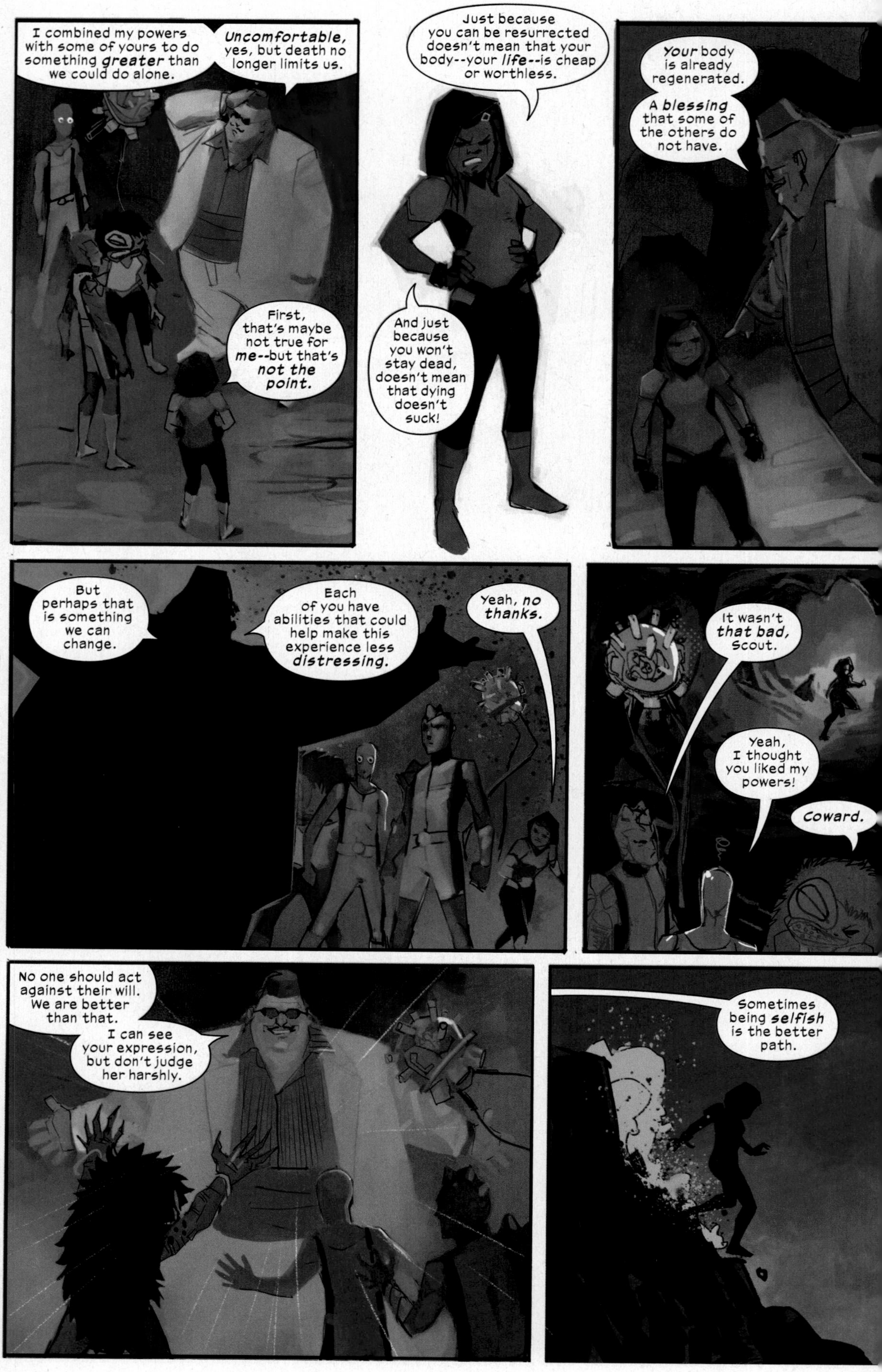
I combined my powers with some of yours to do something greater than we could do alone.
Uncomfortable, yes, but death no longer limits us.
First, that's maybe not true for me--but that's not the point.
Just because you can be resurrected doesn't mean that your body--your life--is cheap or worthless.
And just because you won't stay dead, doesn't mean that dying doesn't suck!
Your body is already regenerated.
A blessing that some of the others do not have.
But perhaps that is something we can change.
Each of you have abilities that could help make this experience less distressing.
Yeah, no thanks.
It wasn't that bad, Scout.
Yeah, I thought you liked my powers!
Coward.
No one should act against their will. We are better than that.
I can see your expression, but don't judge her harshly.
Sometimes being selfish is the better path.

We here at the Crooked Caller pride ourselves on keeping you up to date on the happenings in all the kingdoms of Otherworld.

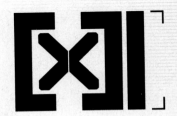

WHICH-BREED?

There've been reports of stragglers from Krakoa lingering about, sticking their noses in Otherworld business. And they're getting around.

The Caller's gotten word that a youngster has been seen in *Avalon*, *Sevalith*, the edges of *Blightspoke*, our own *Crooked Market* and all about the diplomatic ring.

As far as we can tell, there is no sinister agenda – mostly they've been reported to be interested in trade and asking nosy-but-benign questions--but seeing as they've had Actualization Essence and Candles of Revelation among their goods, we'll keep a close eye on them for future opportunities for our readers to get in on the action.

They also seem to have made a friend of the famously cantankerous Sheriff Whitechapel, which we wouldn't mention except that it could imply a new line to the riches of Blightspoke...

If any of you, discerning readers, have information on the movements of witchbreed* youth, let us know!

~ Quinn Crier, Staff Writer

*According to reports, the kid's anywhere between two and three meters tall, blue-skinned and horned. And, according to Ella the Gray from down near the border, the witchbreed also has quite the charming smile.

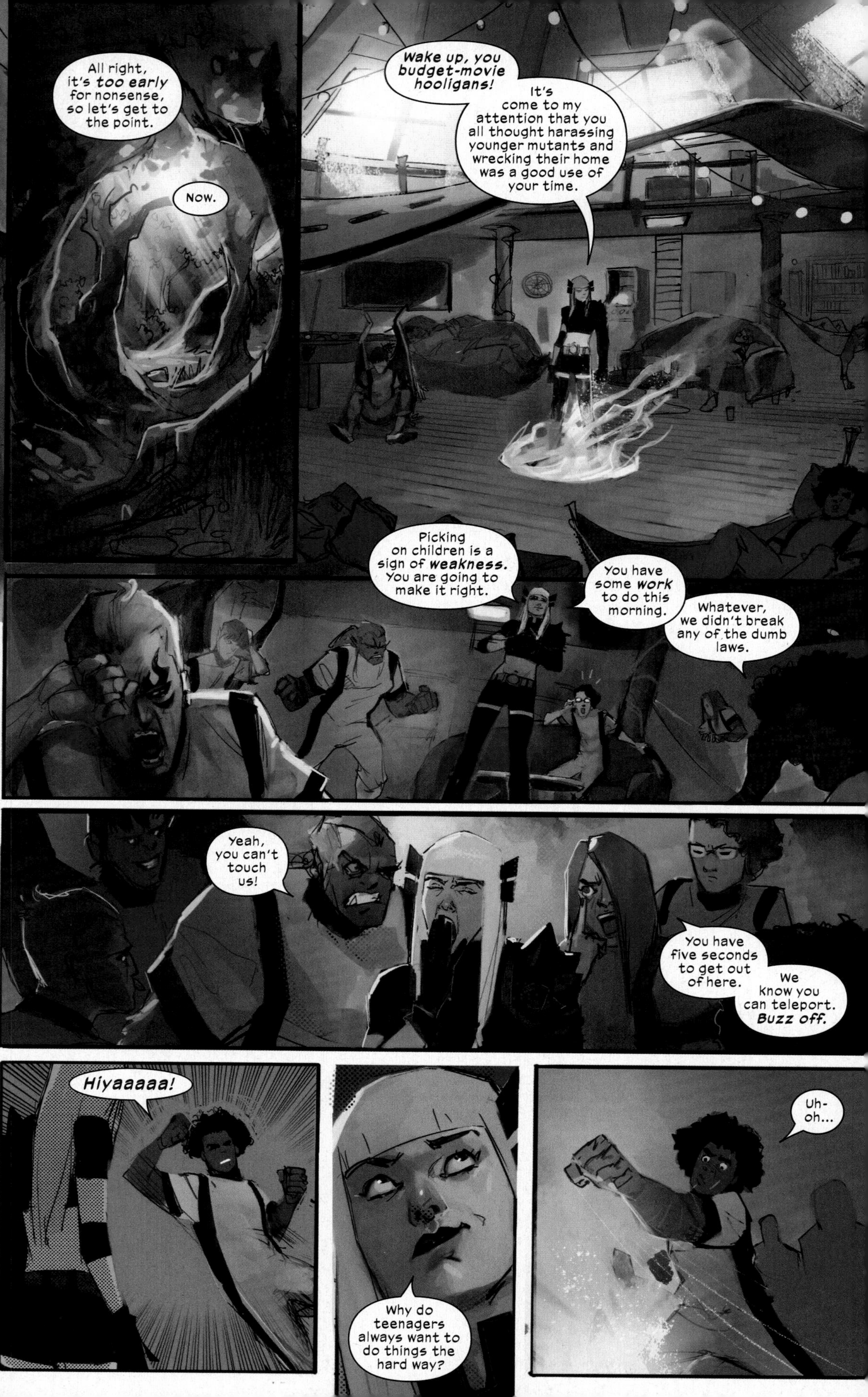

All right, it's *too early* for nonsense, so let's get to the point.
Now.
Wake up, you budget-movie hooligans!
It's come to my attention that you all thought harassing younger mutants and wrecking their home was a good use of your time.
Picking on children is a sign of *weakness.* You are going to make it right.
You have some *work* to do this morning.
Whatever, we didn't break any of the dumb laws.
Yeah, you can't touch us!
You have five seconds to get out of here.
We know you can teleport. *Buzz off.*
Hiyaaaaa!
Why do teenagers always want to do things the hard way?
Uh-oh...

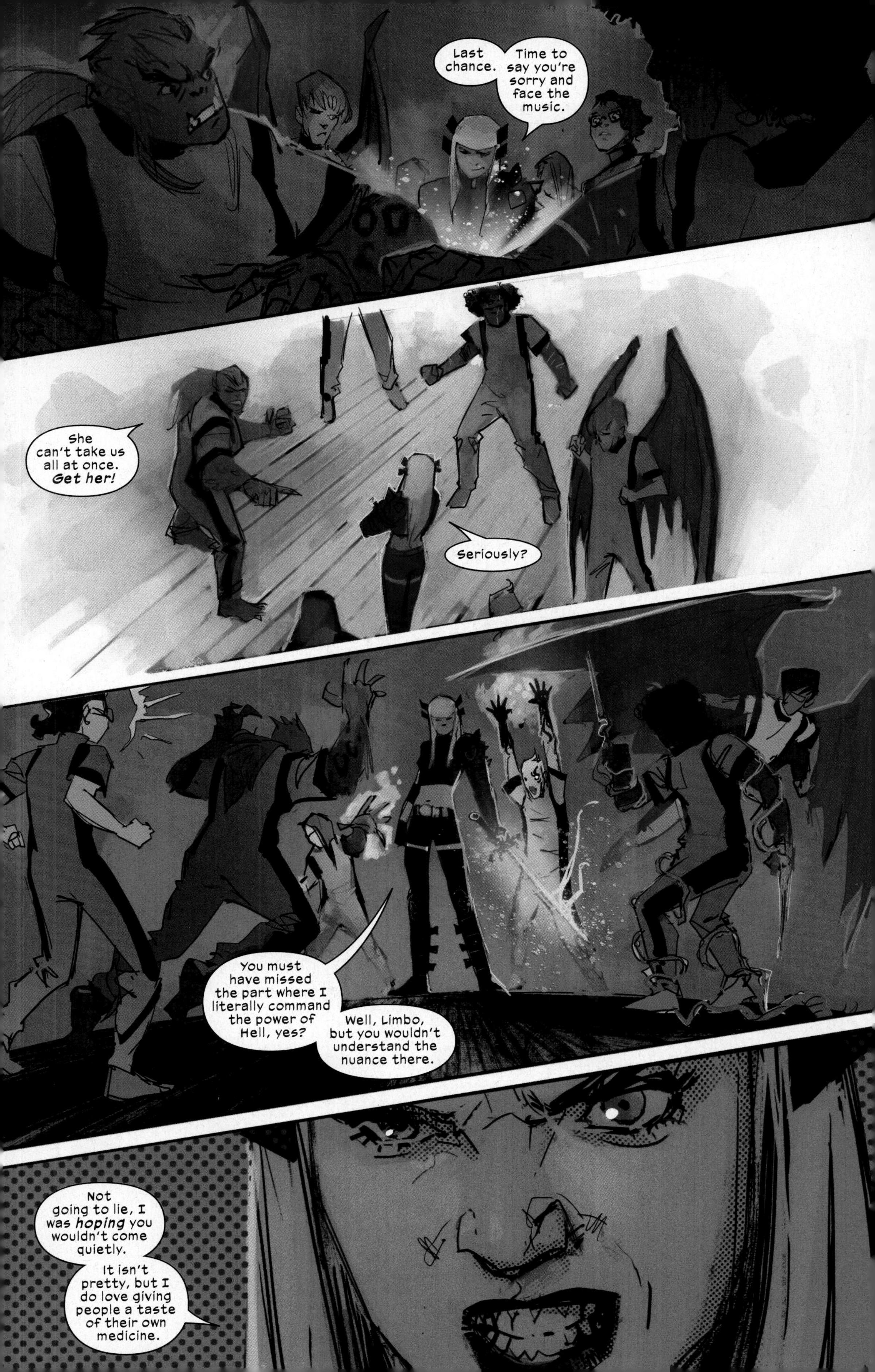

Last chance.
Time to say you're sorry and face the music.
She can't take us all at once. Get her!
Seriously?
You must have missed the part where I literally command the power of Hell, yes?
Well, Limbo, but you wouldn't understand the nuance there.
Not going to lie, I was hoping you wouldn't come quietly.
It isn't pretty, but I do love giving people a taste of their own medicine.

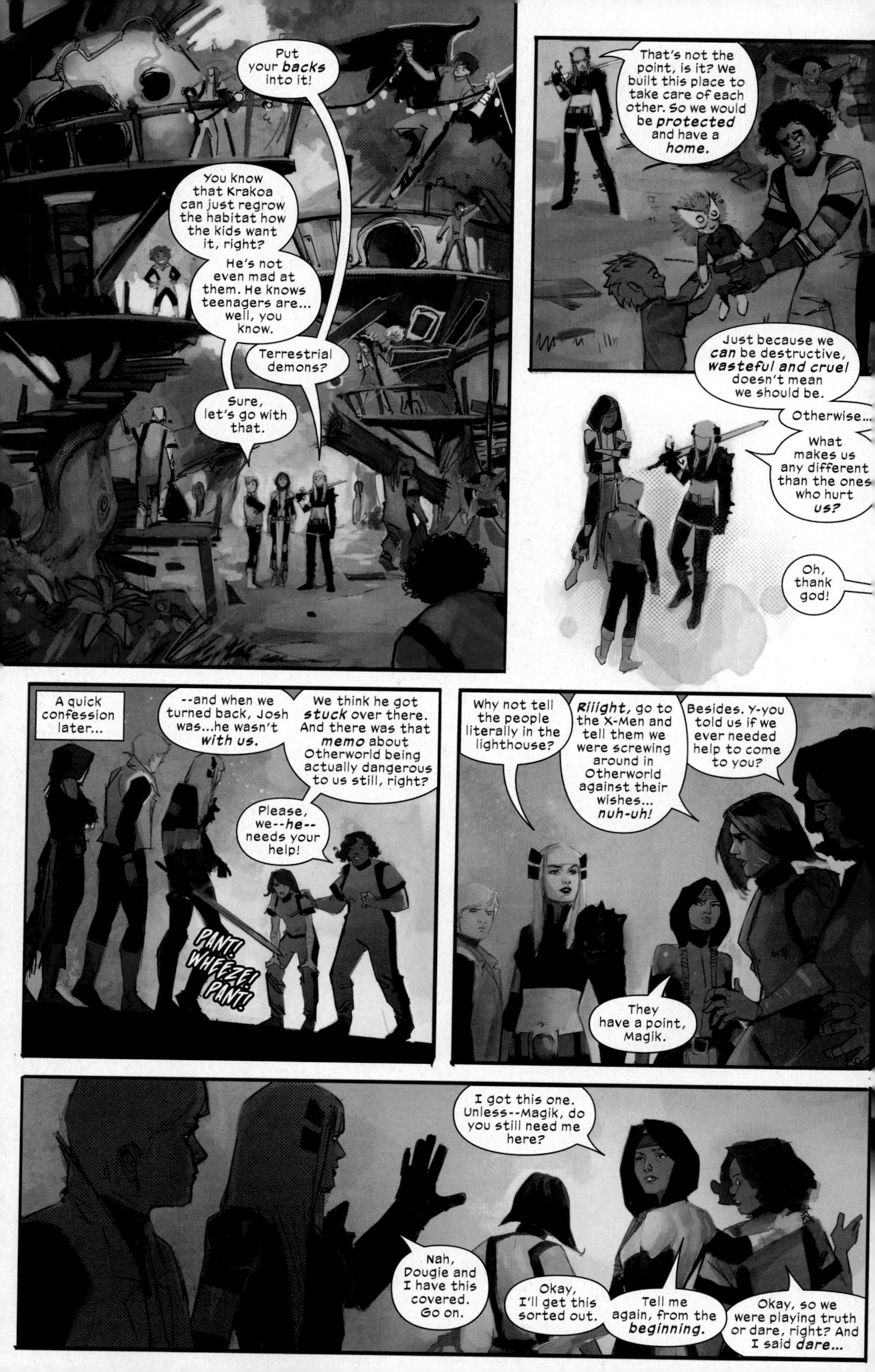

Put your backs into it!
You know that Krakoa can just regrow the habitat how the kids want it, right?
He's not even mad at them. He knows teenagers are... well, you know.
Terrestrial demons?
Sure, let's go with that.
That's not the point, is it? We built this place to take care of each other. So we would be protected and have a home.
Just because we can be destructive, wasteful and cruel doesn't mean we should be.
Otherwise...
What makes us any different than the ones who hurt us?
Oh, thank god!
A quick confession later...
--and when we turned back, Josh was...he wasn't with us.
We think he got stuck over there. And there was that memo about Otherworld being actually dangerous to us still, right?
Please, we--he--needs your help!
PANT! WHEEZE! PANT!
Why not tell the people literally in the lighthouse?
Riiight, go to the X-Men and tell them we were screwing around in Otherworld against their wishes... nuh-uh!
Besides. Y-you told us if we ever needed help to come to you?
They have a point, Magik.
I got this one. Unless--Magik, do you still need me here?
Nah, Dougie and I have this covered. Go on.
Okay, I'll get this sorted out.
Tell me again, from the beginning.
Okay, so we were playing truth or dare, right? And I said dare...

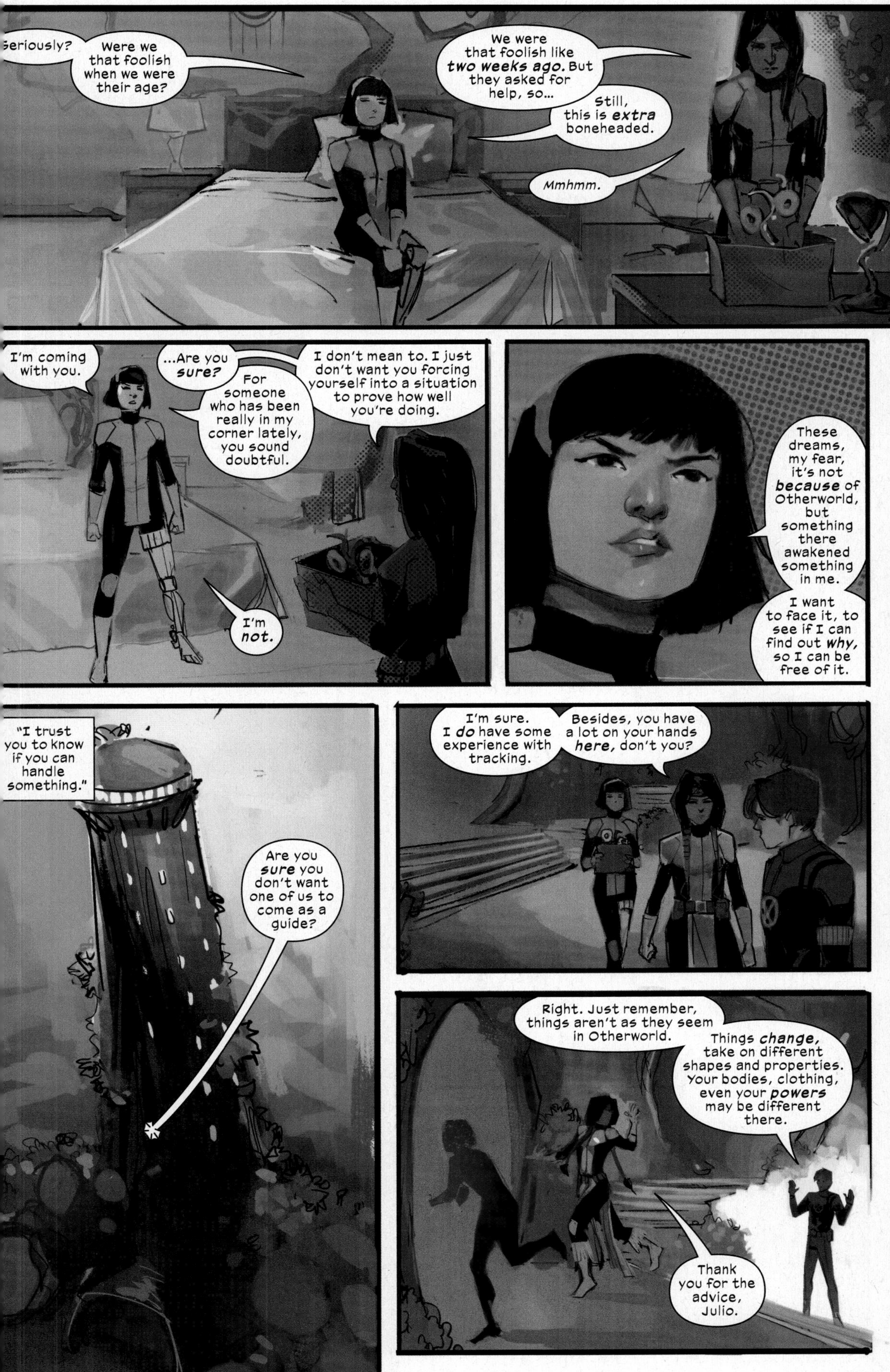
Seriously? Were we that foolish when we were their age?
We were that foolish like two weeks ago. But they asked for help, so...
Still, this is extra boneheaded.
Mmhmm.
I'm coming with you.
...Are you sure?
For someone who has been really in my corner lately, you sound doubtful.
I don't mean to. I just don't want you forcing yourself into a situation to prove how well you're doing.
I'm not.
These dreams, my fear, it's not because of Otherworld, but something there awakened something in me.
I want to face it, to see if I can find out why, so I can be free of it.
"I trust you to know if you can handle something."
Are you sure you don't want one of us to come as a guide?
I'm sure. I do have some experience with tracking.
Besides, you have a lot on your hands here, don't you?
Right. Just remember, things aren't as they seem in Otherworld.
Things change, take on different shapes and properties. Your bodies, clothing, even your powers may be different there.
Thank you for the advice, Julio.

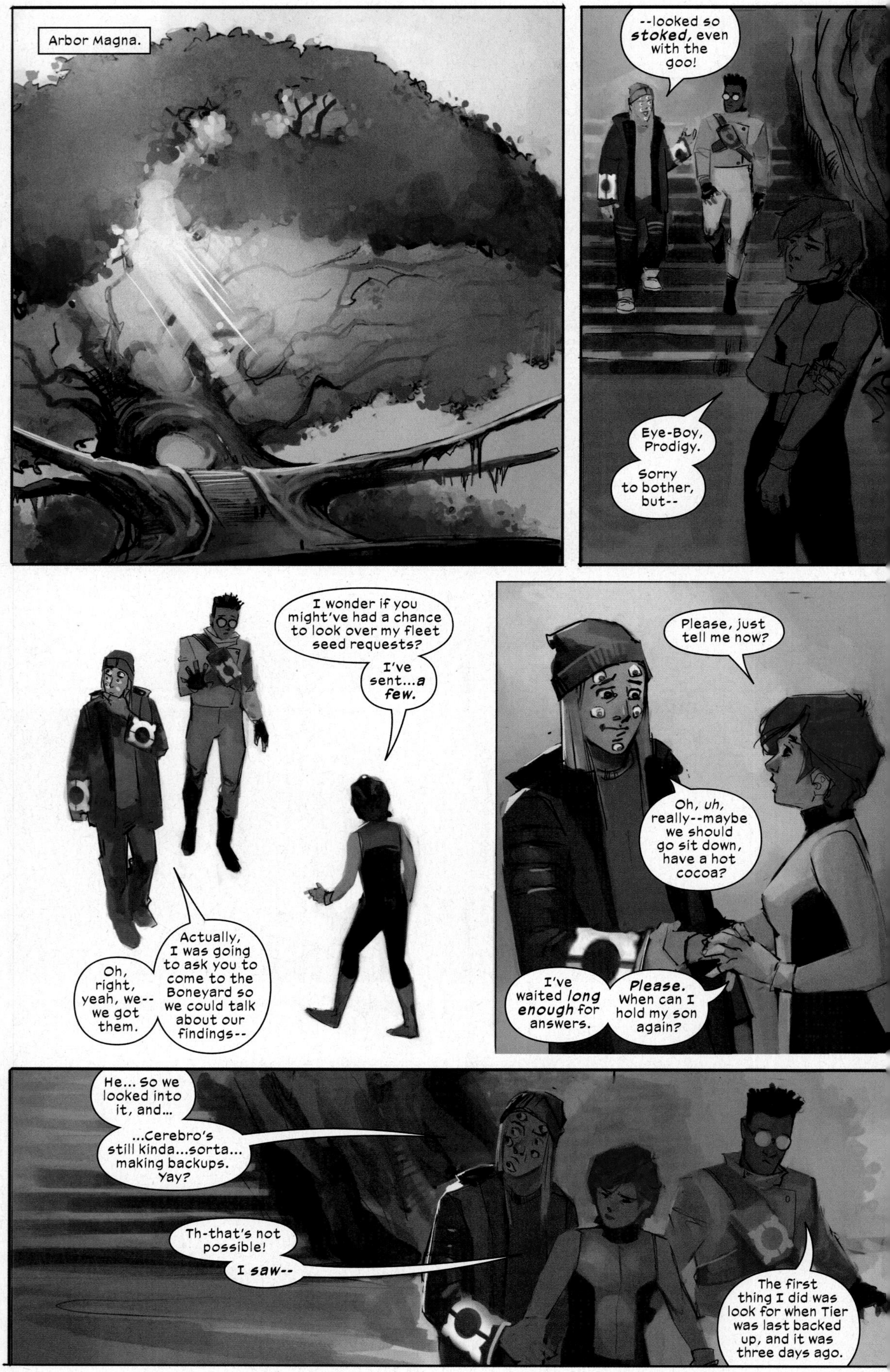

Arbor Magna.
--looked so *stoked,* even with the goo!
Eye-Boy, Prodigy.
Sorry to bother, but--
I wonder if you might've had a chance to look over my fleet seed requests?
I've sent...*a few.*
Actually, I was going to ask you to come to the Boneyard so we could talk about our findings--
Oh, right, yeah, we--we got them.
Please, just tell me now?
Oh, *uh,* really--maybe we should go sit down, have a hot cocoa?
I've waited *long enough* for answers.
Please. When can I hold my son again?
He... So we looked into it, and...
...Cerebro's still kinda...sorta... making backups. Yay?
Th-that's not possible!
I *saw--*
The first thing I did was look for when Tier was last backed up, and it was three days ago.

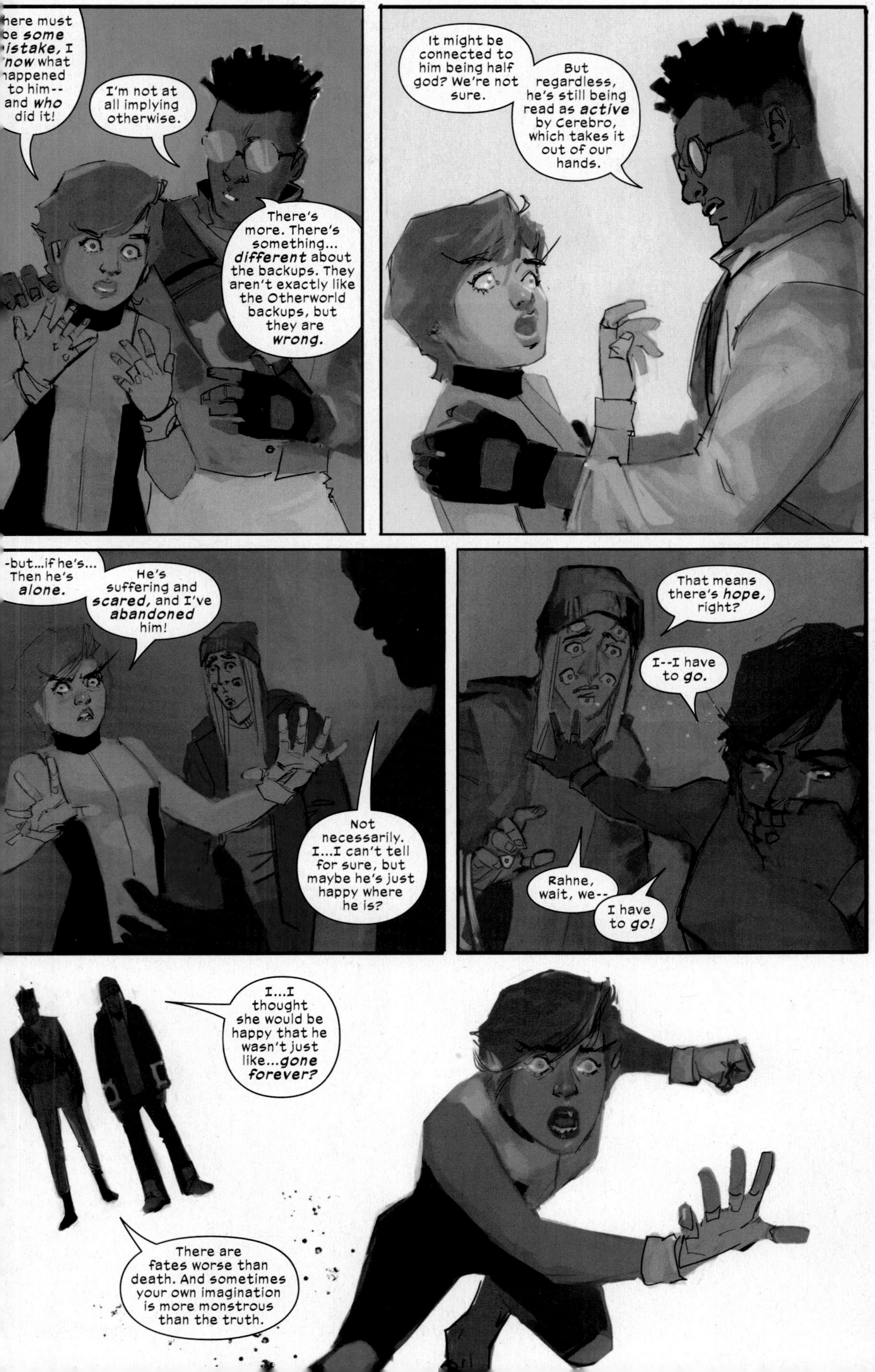
here must be some istake, I now what appened to him-- and who did it!
I'm not at all implying otherwise.
There's more. There's something... different about the backups. They aren't exactly like the Otherworld backups, but they are wrong.
It might be connected to him being half god? We're not sure.
But regardless, he's still being read as active by Cerebro, which takes it out of our hands.
-but...if he's... Then he's alone.
He's suffering and scared, and I've abandoned him!
Not necessarily. I...I can't tell for sure, but maybe he's just happy where he is?
That means there's hope, right?
I--I have to go.
Rahne, wait, we--
I have to go!
I...I thought she would be happy that he wasn't just like...gone forever?
There are fates worse than death. And sometimes your own imagination is more monstrous than the truth.

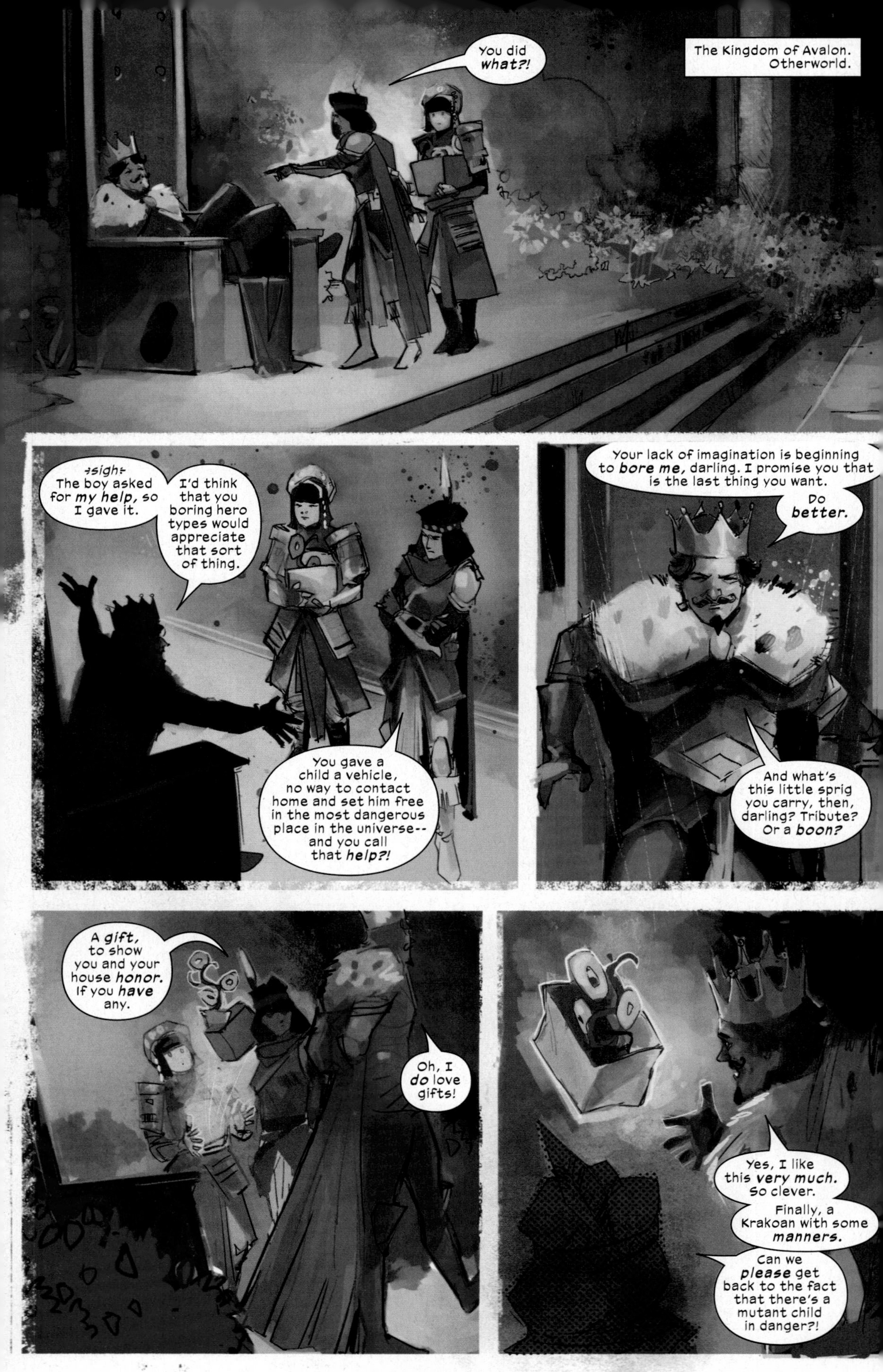

The Kingdom of Avalon. Otherworld.
You did *what?!*
sigh The boy asked for *my help,* so I gave it.
I'd think that you boring hero types would appreciate that sort of thing.
You gave a child a vehicle, no way to contact home and set him free in the most dangerous place in the universe-- and you call that *help?!*
Your lack of imagination is beginning to *bore me,* darling. I promise you that is the last thing you want.
Do *better.*
And what's this little sprig you carry, then, darling? Tribute? Or a *boon?*
A *gift,* to show you and your house *honor.* If you *have* any.
Oh, I *do* love gifts!
Yes, I like this *very much.* So clever.
Finally, a Krakoan with some *manners.*
Can we *please* get back to the fact that there's a mutant child in danger?!

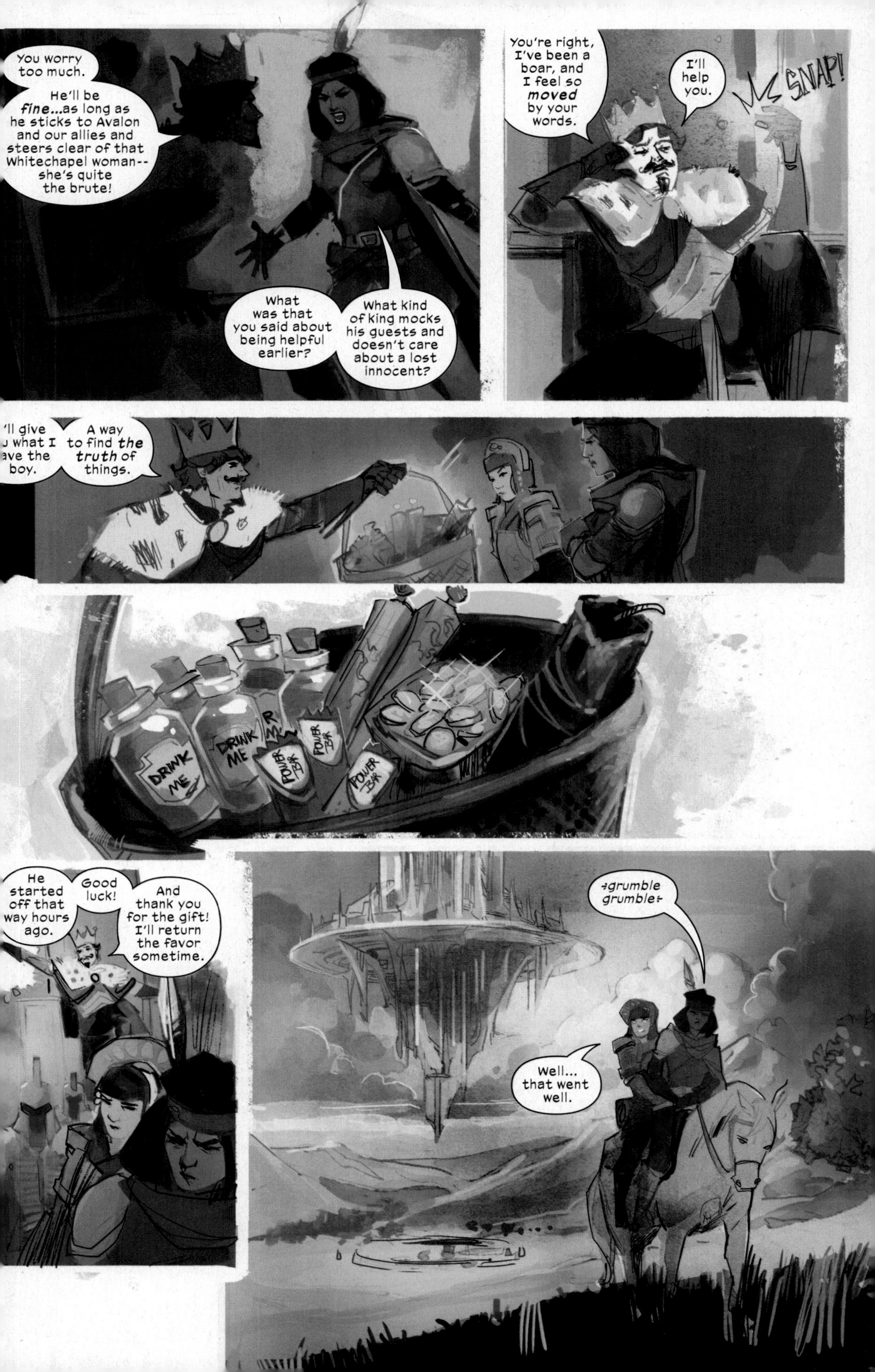

You worry too much.
He'll be *fine*...as long as he sticks to Avalon and our allies and steers clear of that Whitechapel woman--she's quite the brute!
What was that you said about being helpful earlier?
What kind of king mocks his guests and doesn't care about a lost innocent?
You're right, I've been a boar, and I feel so *moved* by your words.
I'll help you.
SNAP!
'll give u what I ave the boy.
A way to find *the truth* of things.
DRINK ME
DRINK ME
POWER BAR
POWER BAR
POWER BAR
He started off that way hours ago.
Good luck!
And thank you for the gift! I'll return the favor sometime.
grumble grumble
Well... that went well.

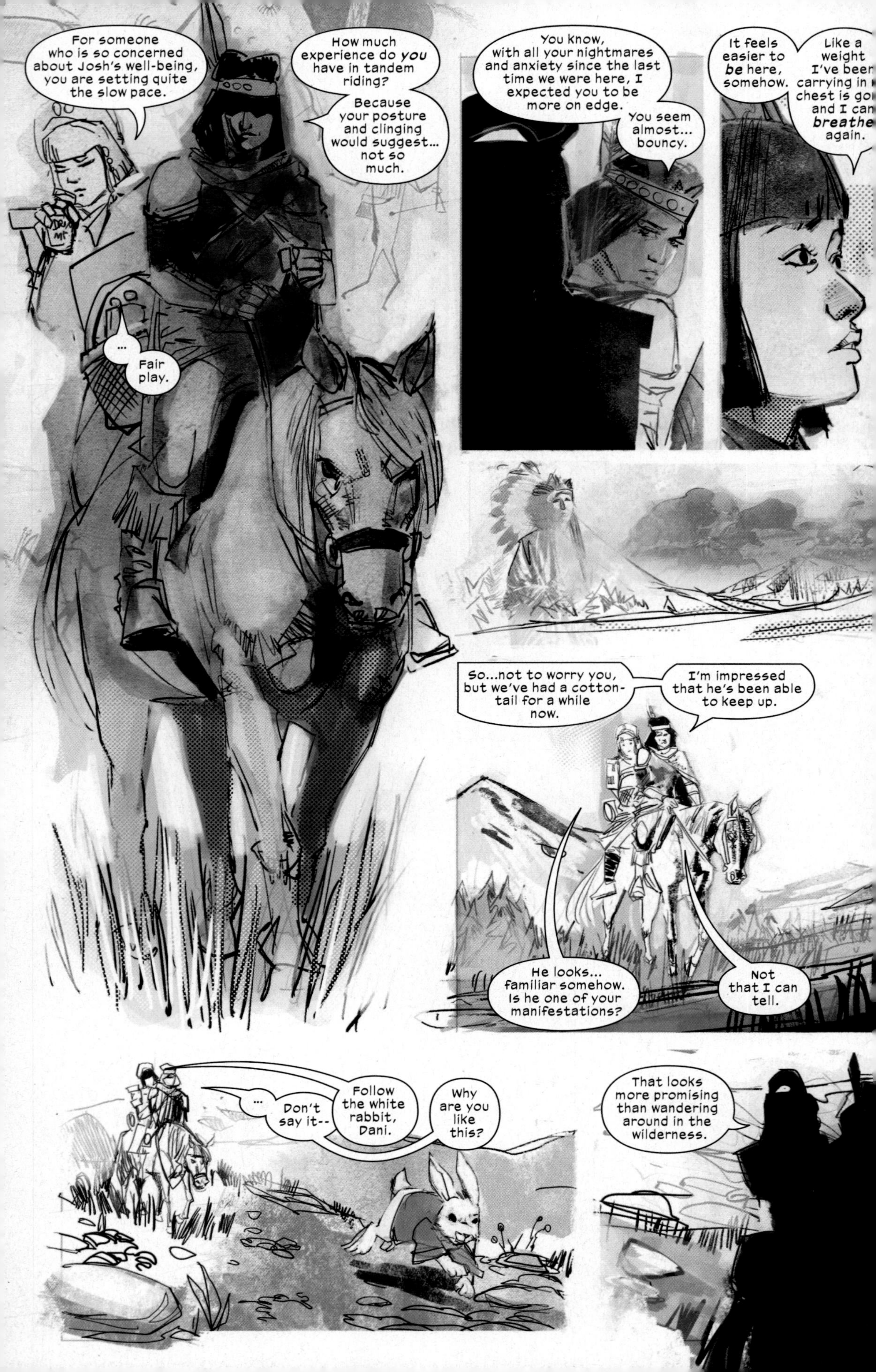

For someone who is so concerned about Josh's well-being, you are setting quite the slow pace.
How much experience do *you* have in tandem riding?
Because your posture and clinging would suggest... not so much.
...
Fair play.
You know, with all your nightmares and anxiety since the last time we were here, I expected you to be more on edge.
You seem almost... bouncy.
It feels easier to *be* here, somehow.
Like a weight I've been carrying in chest is go and I can *breathe* again.
So...not to worry you, but we've had a cottontail for a while now.
I'm impressed that he's been able to keep up.
He looks... familiar somehow. Is he one of your manifestations?
Not that I can tell.
Follow the white rabbit, Dani.
...
Don't say it--
Why are you like this?
That looks more promising than wandering around in the wilderness.

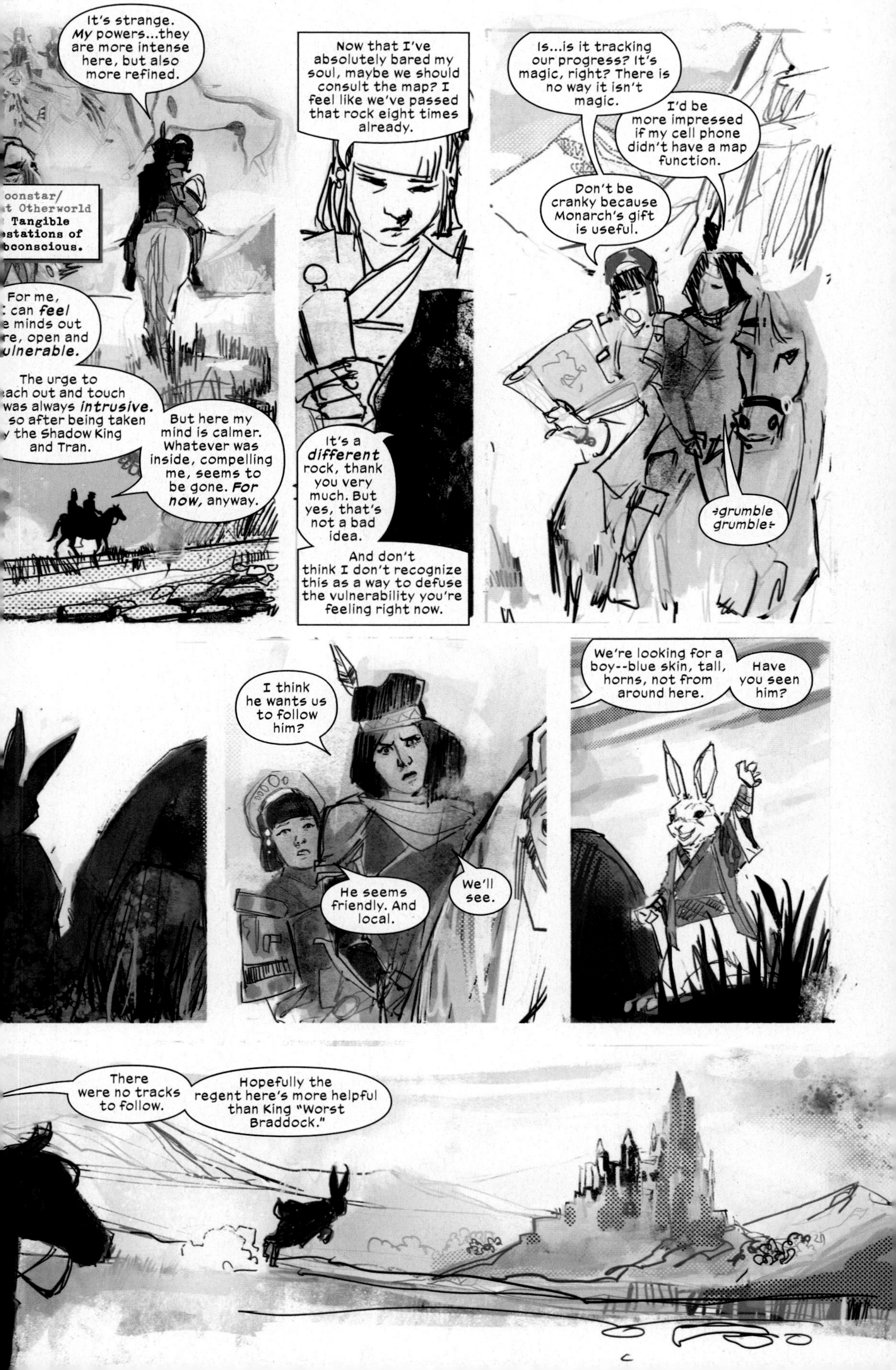

It's strange. My powers...they are more intense here, but also more refined.
oonstar/
t Otherworld
Tangible
estations of
bconscious.
For me,
can feel
e minds out
re, open and
ulnerable.
The urge to
each out and touch
was always intrusive.
so after being taken
the Shadow King
and Tran.
But here my mind is calmer. Whatever was inside, compelling me, seems to be gone. For now, anyway.
Now that I've absolutely bared my soul, maybe we should consult the map? I feel like we've passed that rock eight times already.
It's a different rock, thank you very much. But yes, that's not a bad idea.
And don't think I don't recognize this as a way to defuse the vulnerability you're feeling right now.
Is...is it tracking our progress? It's magic, right? There is no way it isn't magic.
I'd be more impressed if my cell phone didn't have a map function.
Don't be cranky because Monarch's gift is useful.
grumble grumble
I think he wants us to follow him?
He seems friendly. And local.
We'll see.
We're looking for a boy--blue skin, tall, horns, not from around here.
Have you seen him?
There were no tracks to follow.
Hopefully the regent here's more helpful than King "Worst Braddock."

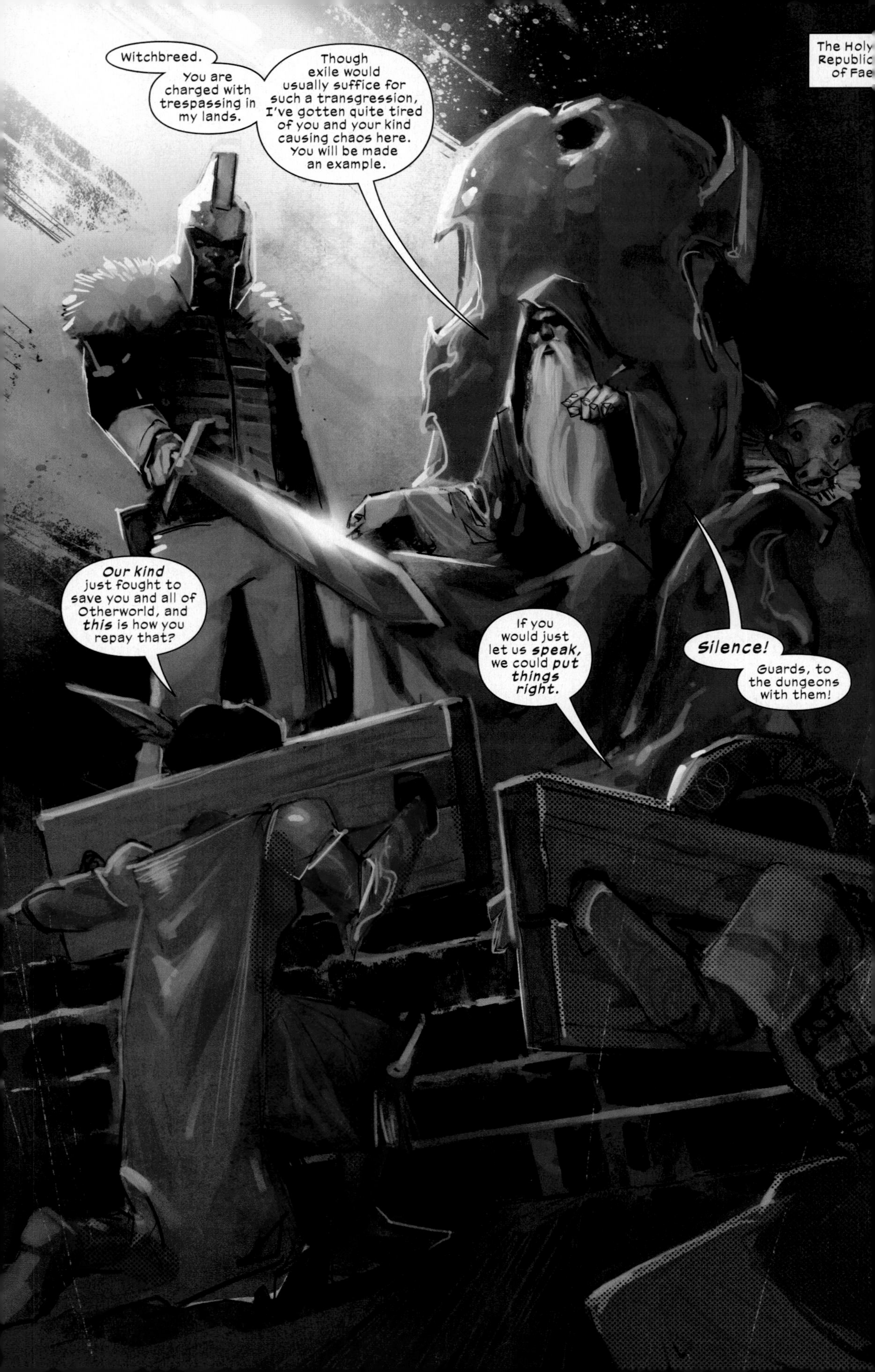
The Holy Republic of Fae
Witchbreed.
You are charged with trespassing in my lands.
Though exile would usually suffice for such a transgression, I've gotten quite tired of you and your kind causing chaos here. You will be made an example.
Our kind just fought to save you and all of Otherworld, and this is how you repay that?
If you would just let us speak, we could put things right.
Silence!
Guards, to the dungeons with them!

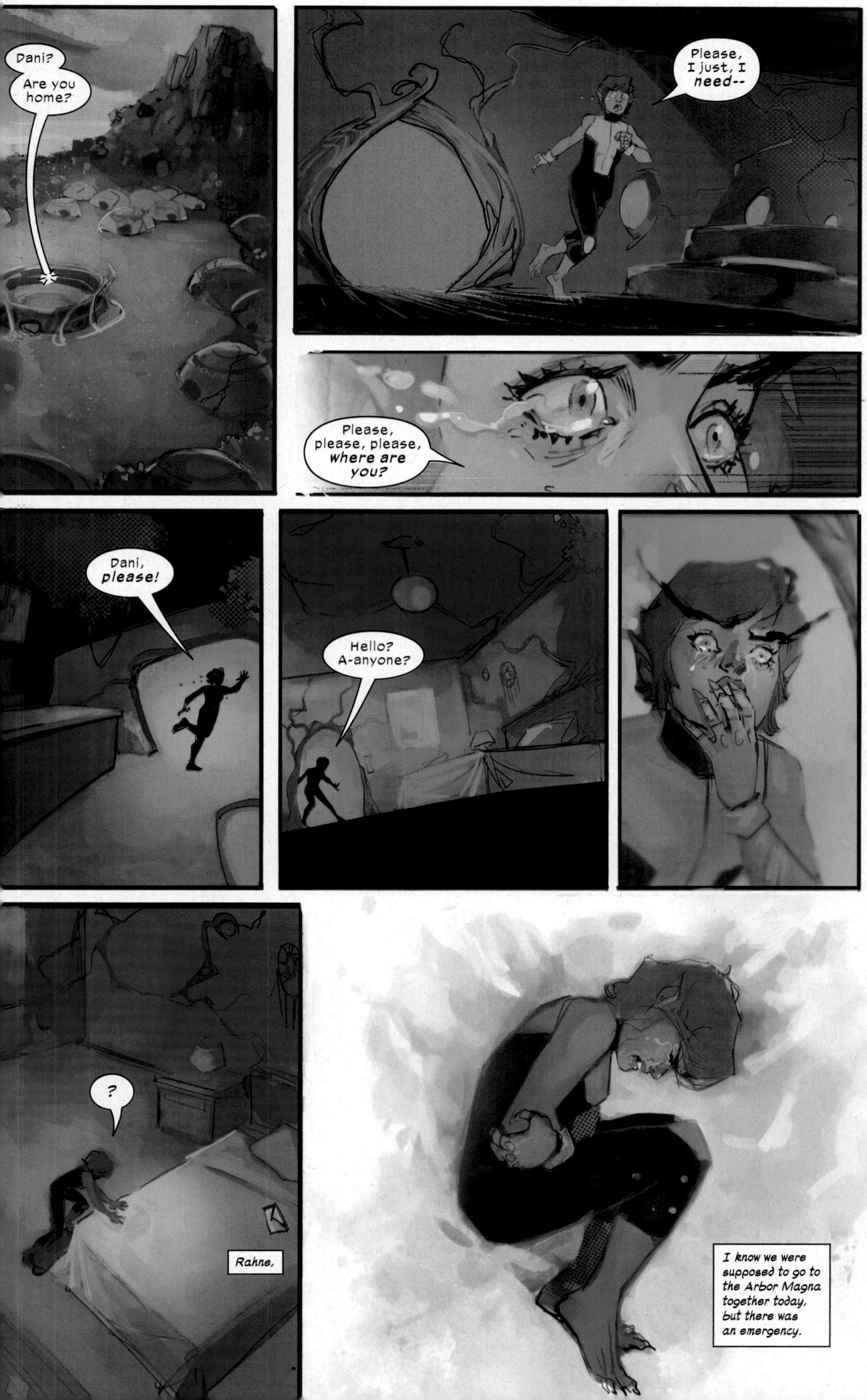

Dani?
Are you home?
Please, I just, I need--
Please, please, please, where are you?
Dani, please!
Hello? A-anyone?
?
Rahne,
I know we were supposed to go to the Arbor Magna together today, but there was an emergency.

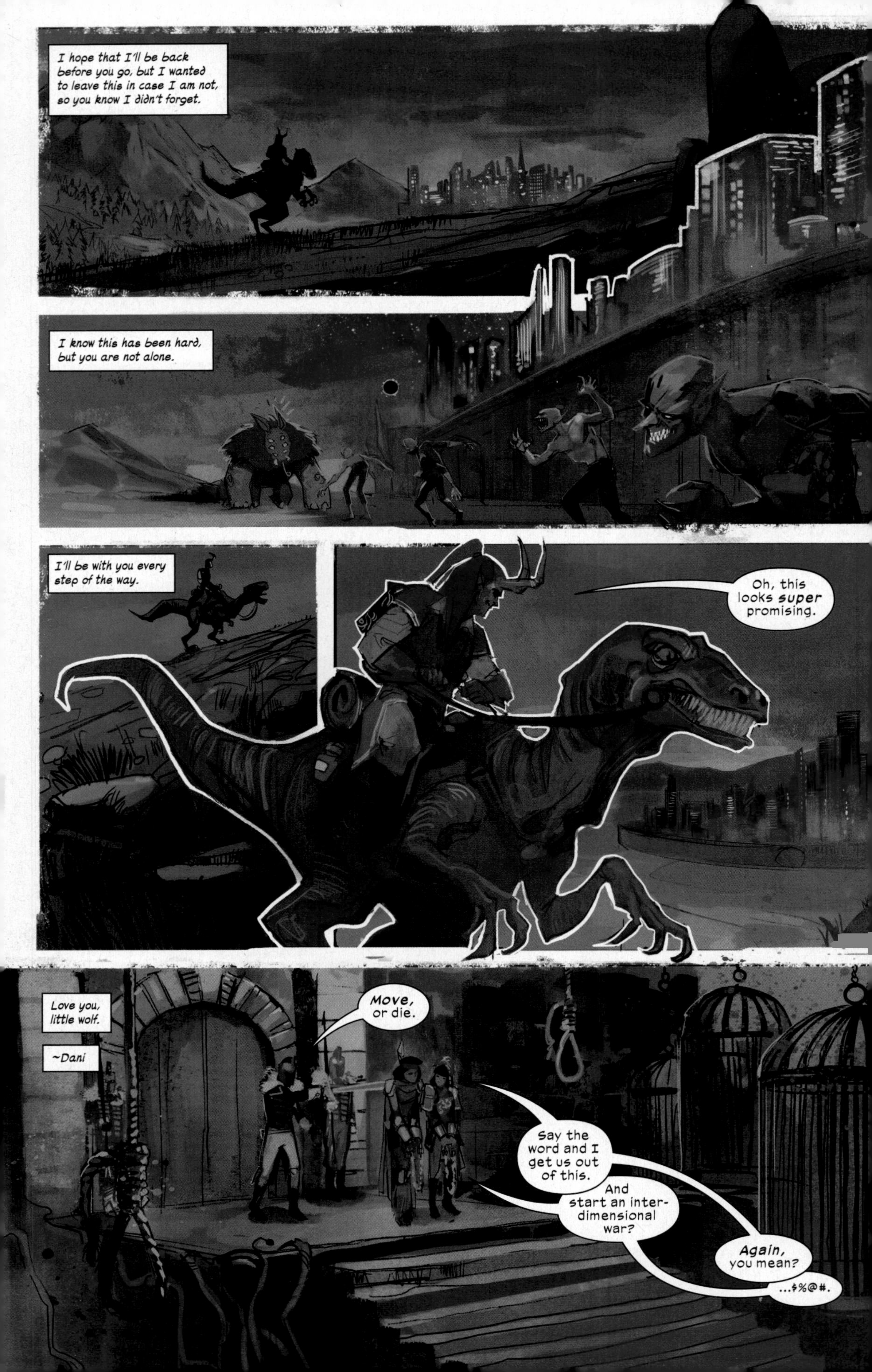
I hope that I'll be back before you go, but I wanted to leave this in case I am not, so you know I didn't forget.
I know this has been hard, but you are not alone.
I'll be with you every step of the way.
Oh, this looks **super** promising.
Love you, little wolf.
~Dani
Move, or die.
Say the word and I get us out of this.
And start an inter-dimensional war?
Again, you mean?
...$%@#.

[reign_of_x]

[kra_]
[koa_]

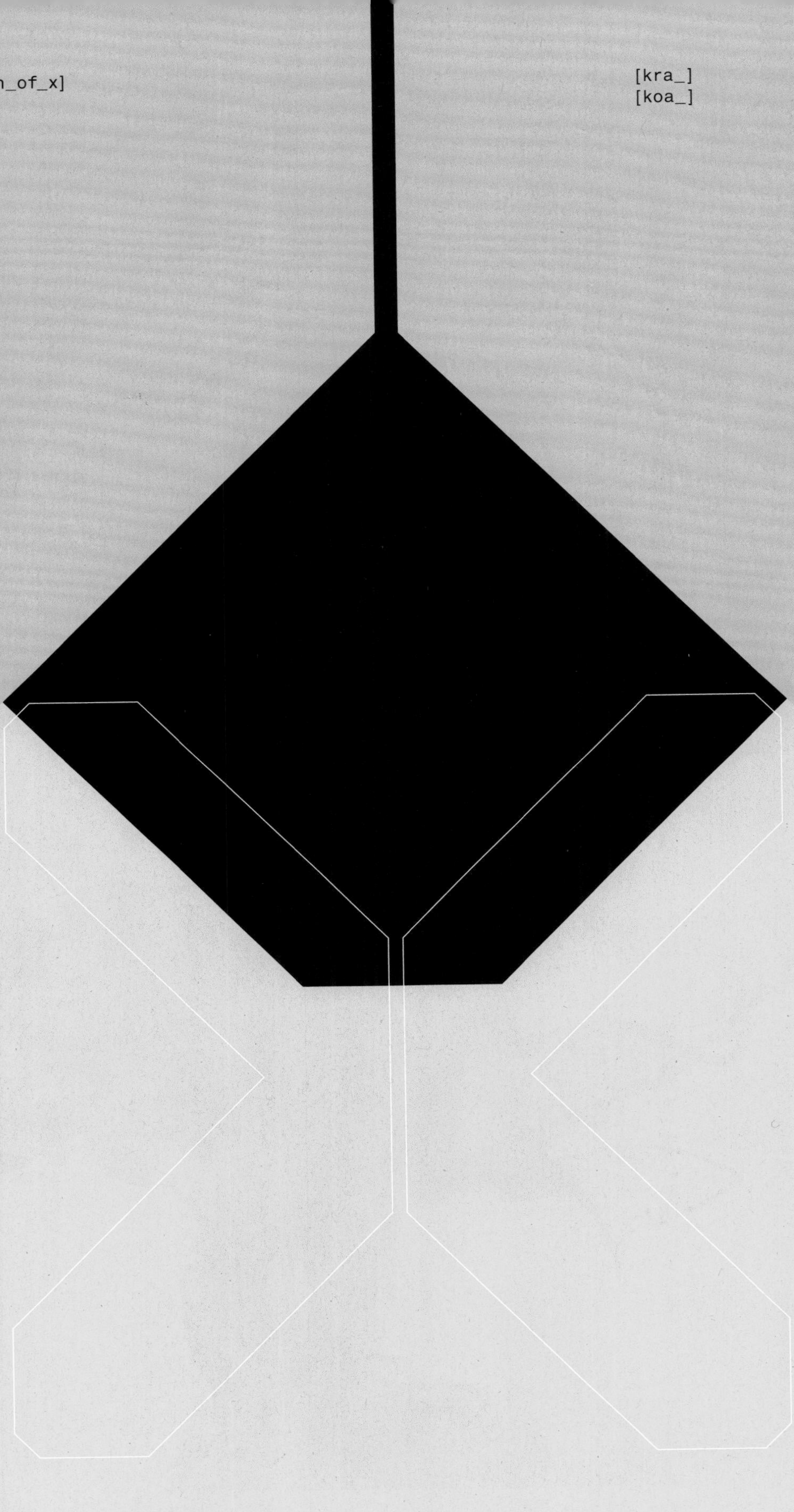

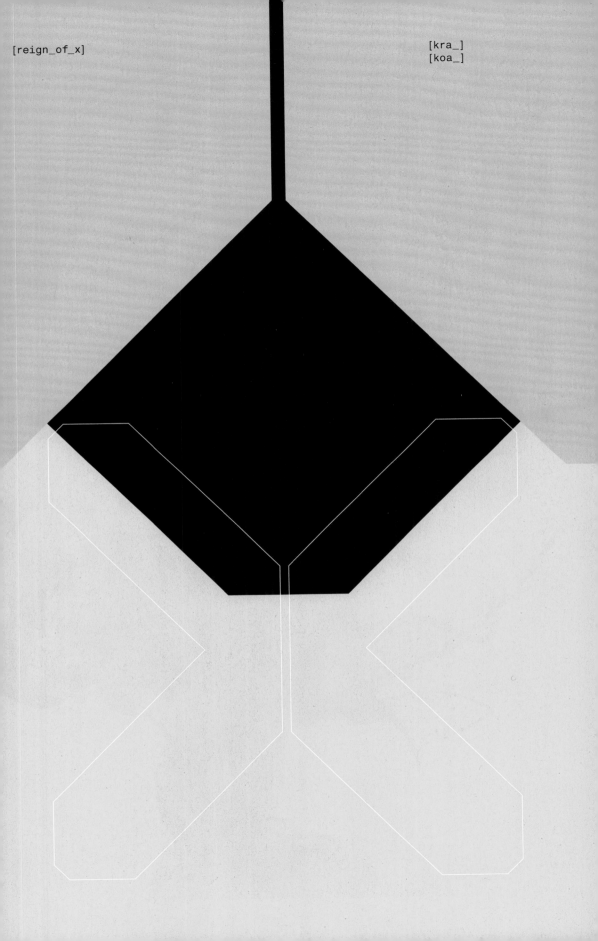

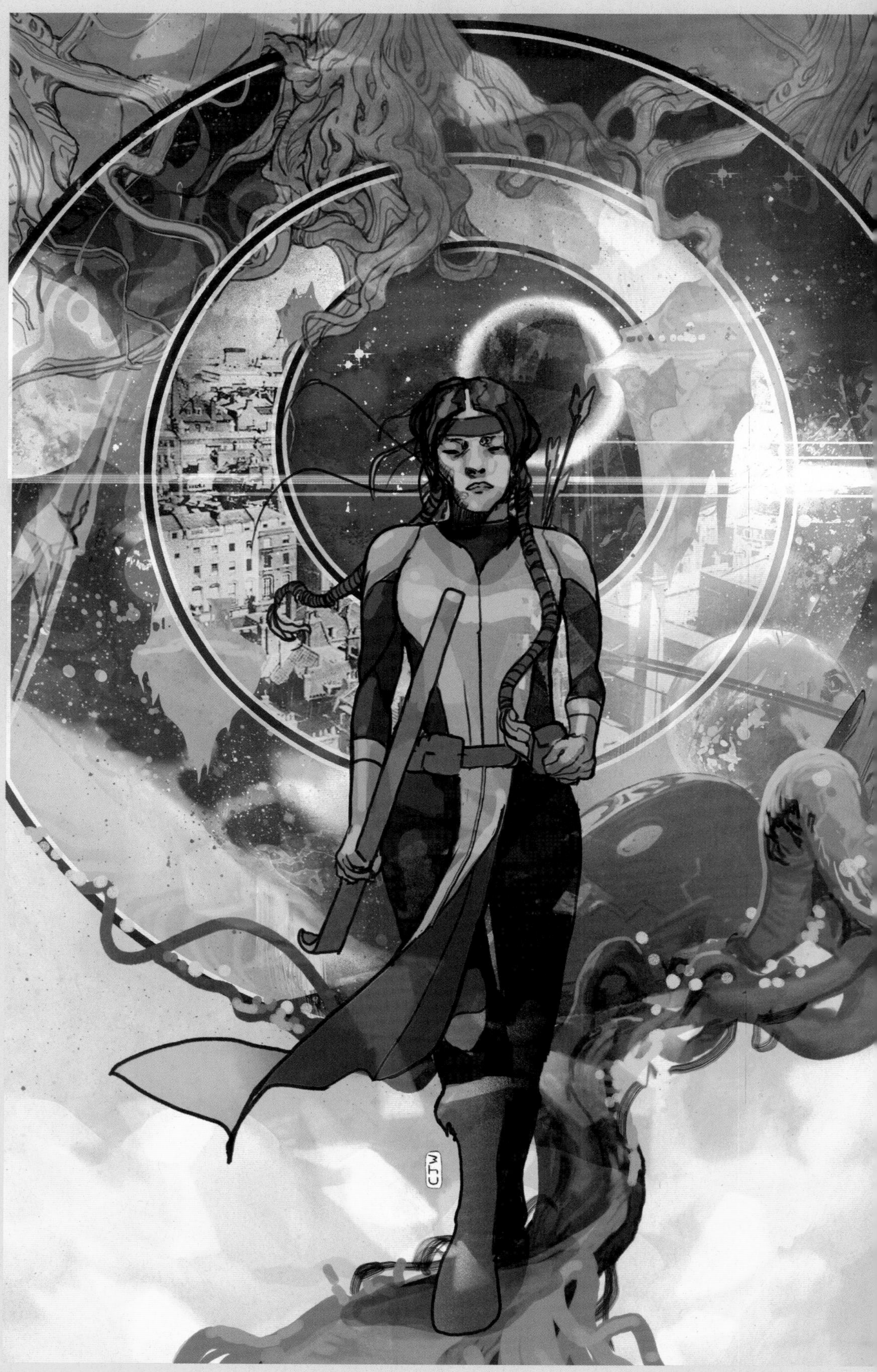
CTW

Follow the White Rabbit

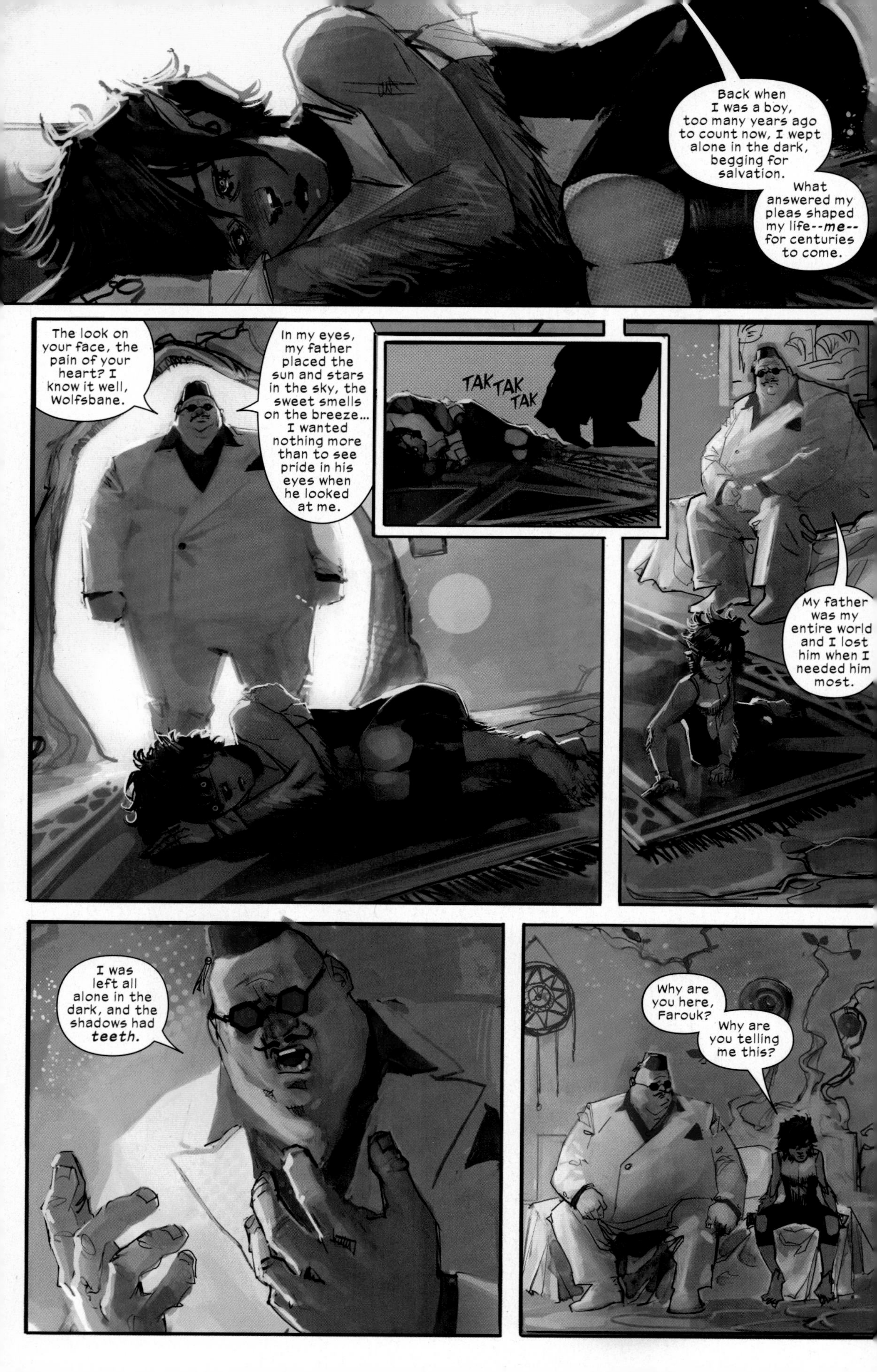

Back when I was a boy, too many years ago to count now, I wept alone in the dark, begging for salvation.
What answered my pleas shaped my life--me--for centuries to come.
The look on your face, the pain of your heart? I know it well, Wolfsbane.
In my eyes, my father placed the sun and stars in the sky, the sweet smells on the breeze... I wanted nothing more than to see pride in his eyes when he looked at me.
TAK TAK TAK
My father was my entire world and I lost him when I needed him most.
I was left all alone in the dark, and the shadows had teeth.
Why are you here, Farouk?
Why are you telling me this?

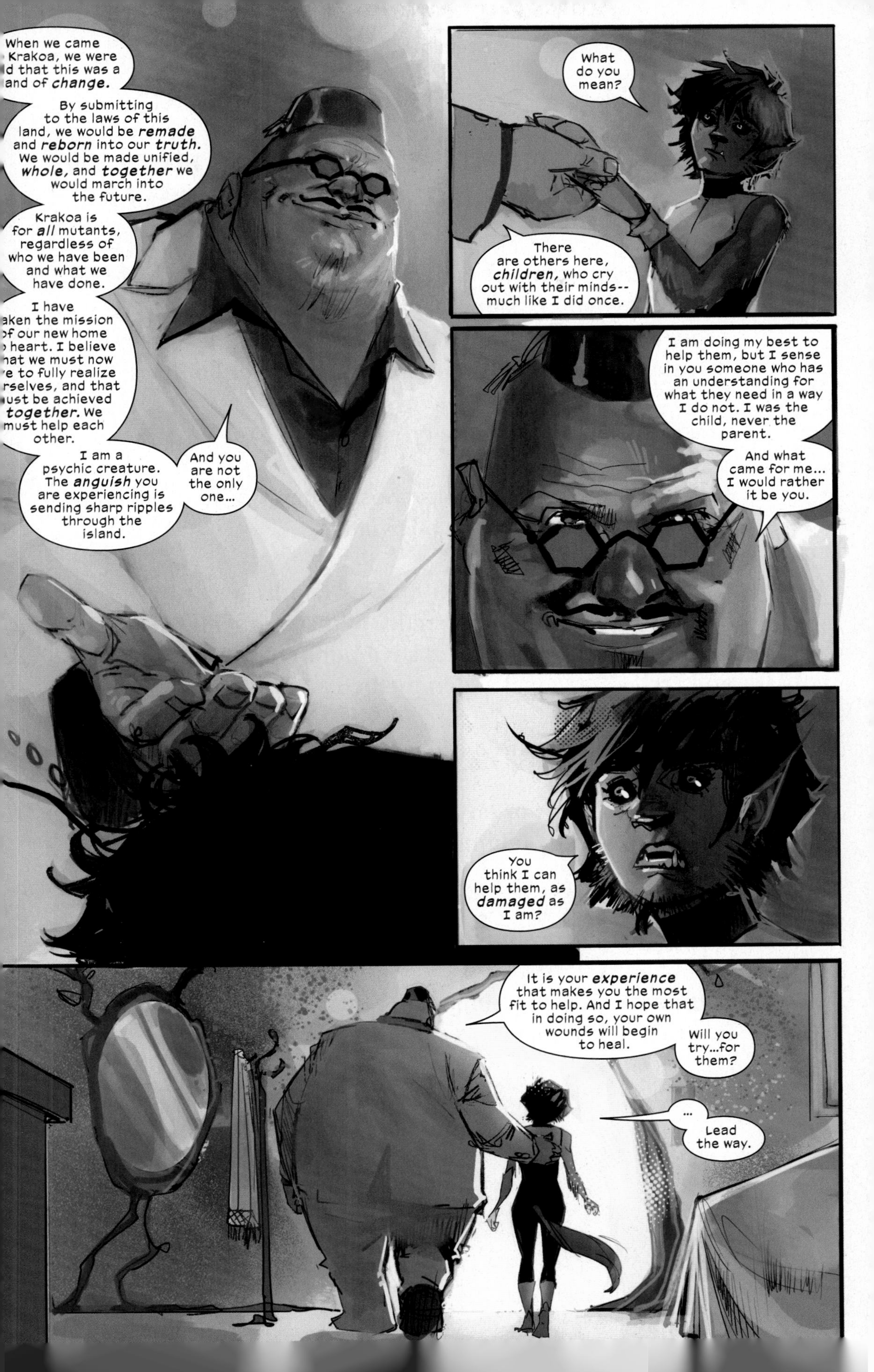
When we came
Krakoa, we were
d that this was a
and of *change.*
By submitting to the laws of this land, we would be ***remade*** and ***reborn*** into our ***truth.*** We would be made unified, ***whole,*** and ***together*** we would march into the future.
Krakoa is for ***all*** mutants, regardless of who we have been and what we have done.
I have
aken the mission
of our new home
heart. I believe
hat we must now
e to fully realize
rselves, and that
ust be achieved
together. We
must help each
other.
I am a psychic creature. The ***anguish*** you are experiencing is sending sharp ripples through the island.
And you are not the only one...
What do you mean?
There are others here, ***children,*** who cry out with their minds--much like I did once.
I am doing my best to help them, but I sense in you someone who has an understanding for what they need in a way I do not. I was the child, never the parent.
And what came for me... I would rather it be you.
You think I can help them, as ***damaged*** as I am?
It is your ***experience*** that makes you the most fit to help. And I hope that in doing so, your own wounds will begin to heal.
Will you try...for them?
...
Lead the way.

A PACT WITH HIS EXCELLENCY MERLYN, RULER OF THE HOLY REPUBLIC OF FAE

The witchbreed blasphemers, Danielle Moonstar and Xi'an Coy Manh, stand accused of crimes against The Holy Republic of Fae. Their crimes include trespassing, threatening the royal guard and speaking out of turn.

The punishment for these crimes: death.

His Excellency Merlyn has chosen mercy, and offered the witchbreed the following alternative:

Danielle Moonstar and Xi'an Coy Manh swear by blood and word, under penalty of instantaneous death, to infiltrate the blasphemous Kingdom of Roma Regina and reclaim a vessel stolen by the Lady Roma.

Success will result in a full pardon of all crimes.

Failure, desertion or any other breach of this pact will result in death by boiling blood.

Should they die during their mission, a posthumous pardon will be granted, as his Excellency is merciful.

This pact is sealed in blood and bound by his Excellency's power.

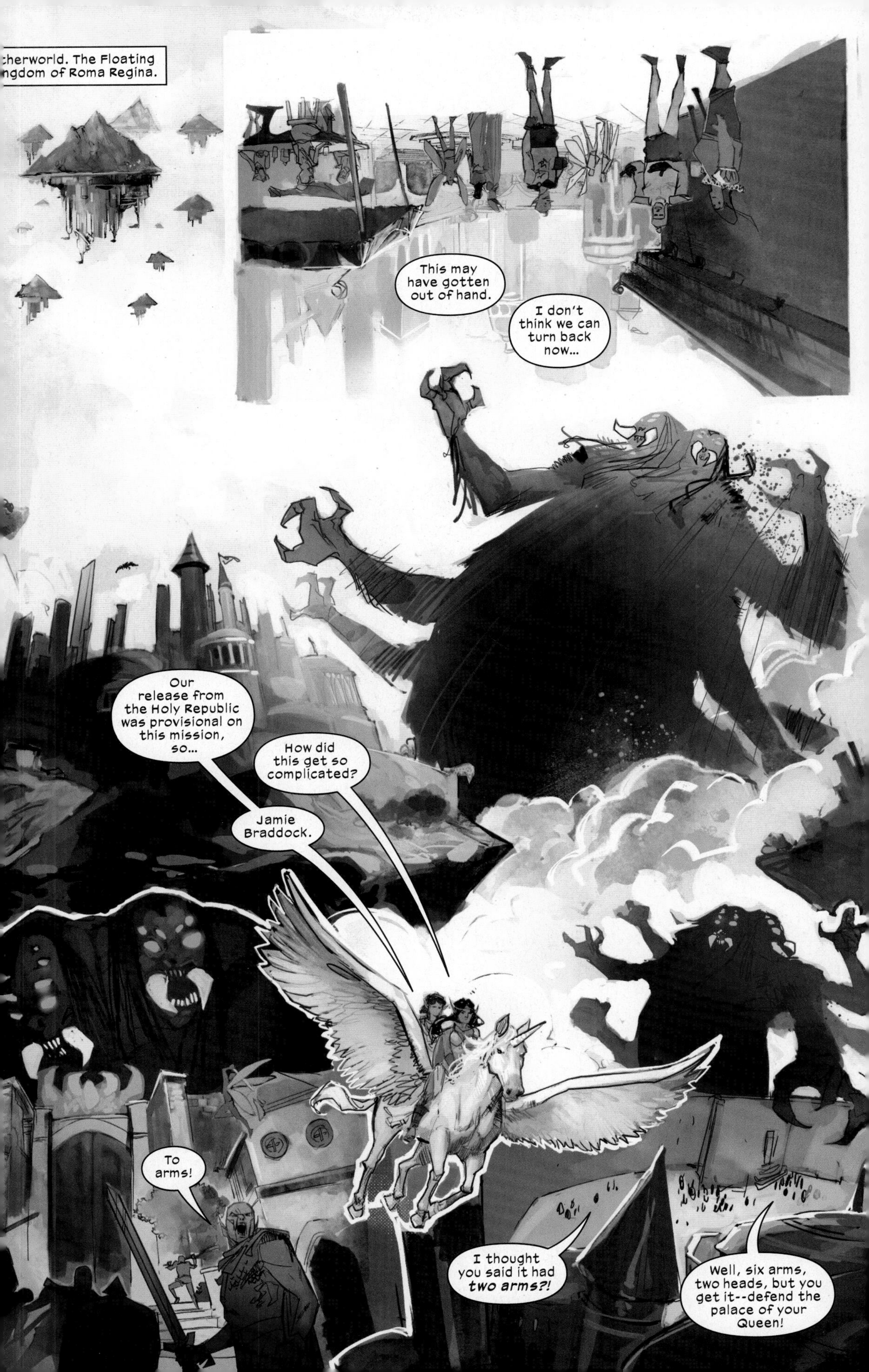
cherworld. The Floating
ngdom of Roma Regina.
This may have gotten out of hand.
I don't think we can turn back now...
Our release from the Holy Republic was provisional on this mission, so...
How did this get so complicated?
Jamie Braddock.
To arms!
I thought you said it had *two arms?!*
Well, six arms, two heads, but you get it--defend the palace of your Queen!

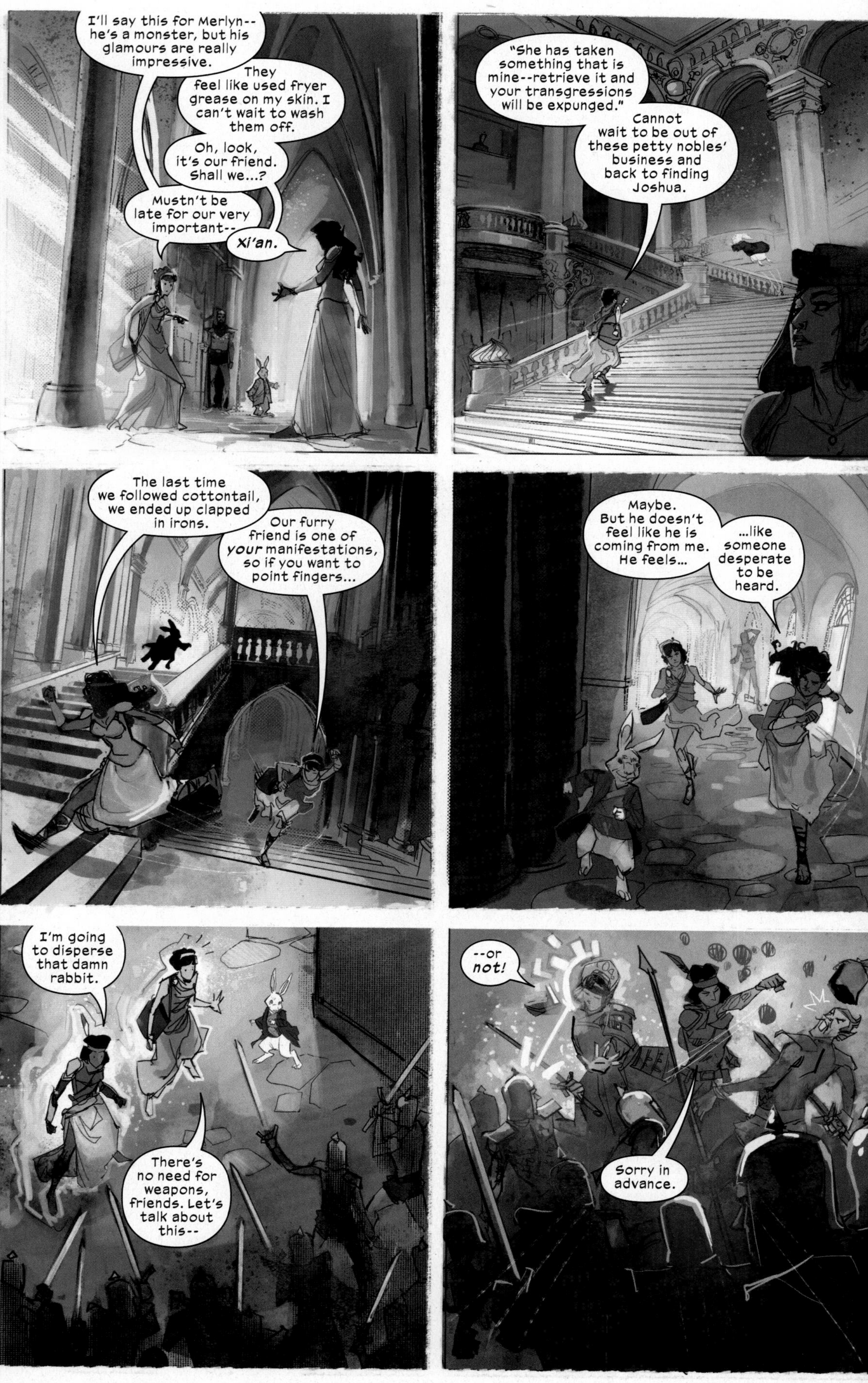

I'll say this for Merlyn--he's a monster, but his glamours are really impressive.
They feel like used fryer grease on my skin. I can't wait to wash them off.
Oh, look, it's our friend. Shall we...?
Mustn't be late for our very important--
Xi'an.
"She has taken something that is mine--retrieve it and your transgressions will be expunged."
Cannot wait to be out of these petty nobles' business and back to finding Joshua.
The last time we followed cottontail, we ended up clapped in irons.
Our furry friend is one of *your* manifestations, so if you want to point fingers...
Maybe. But he doesn't feel like he is coming from me. He feels...
...like someone desperate to be heard.
I'm going to disperse that damn rabbit.
There's no need for weapons, friends. Let's talk about this--
--or *not!*
Sorry in advance.

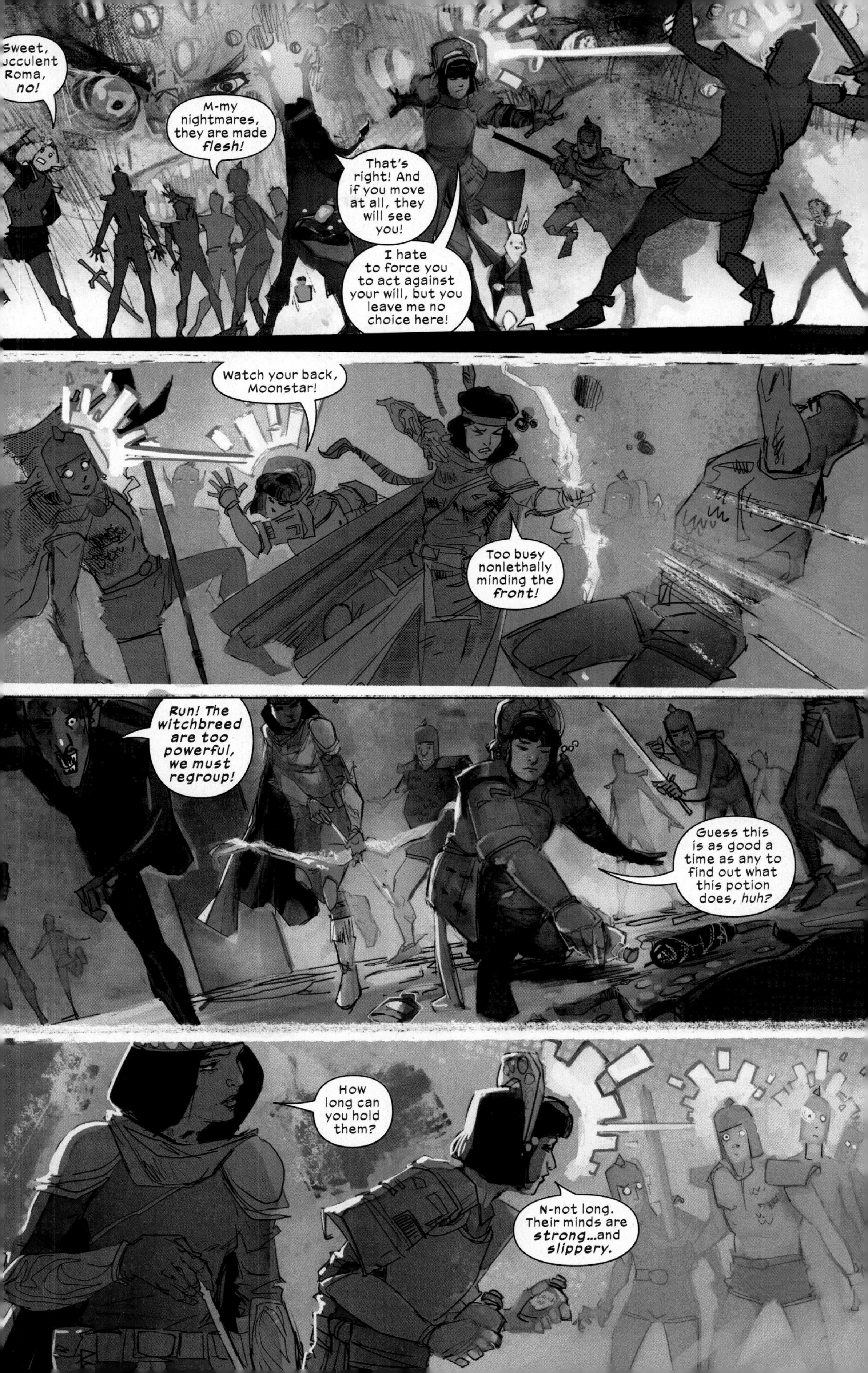
Sweet, ucculent Roma, no!
M-my nightmares, they are made flesh!
That's right! And if you move at all, they will see you!
I hate to force you to act against your will, but you leave me no choice here!
Watch your back, Moonstar!
Too busy nonlethally minding the front!
Run! The witchbreed are too powerful, we must regroup!
Guess this is as good a time as any to find out what this potion does, huh?
How long can you hold them?
N-not long. Their minds are strong...and slippery.

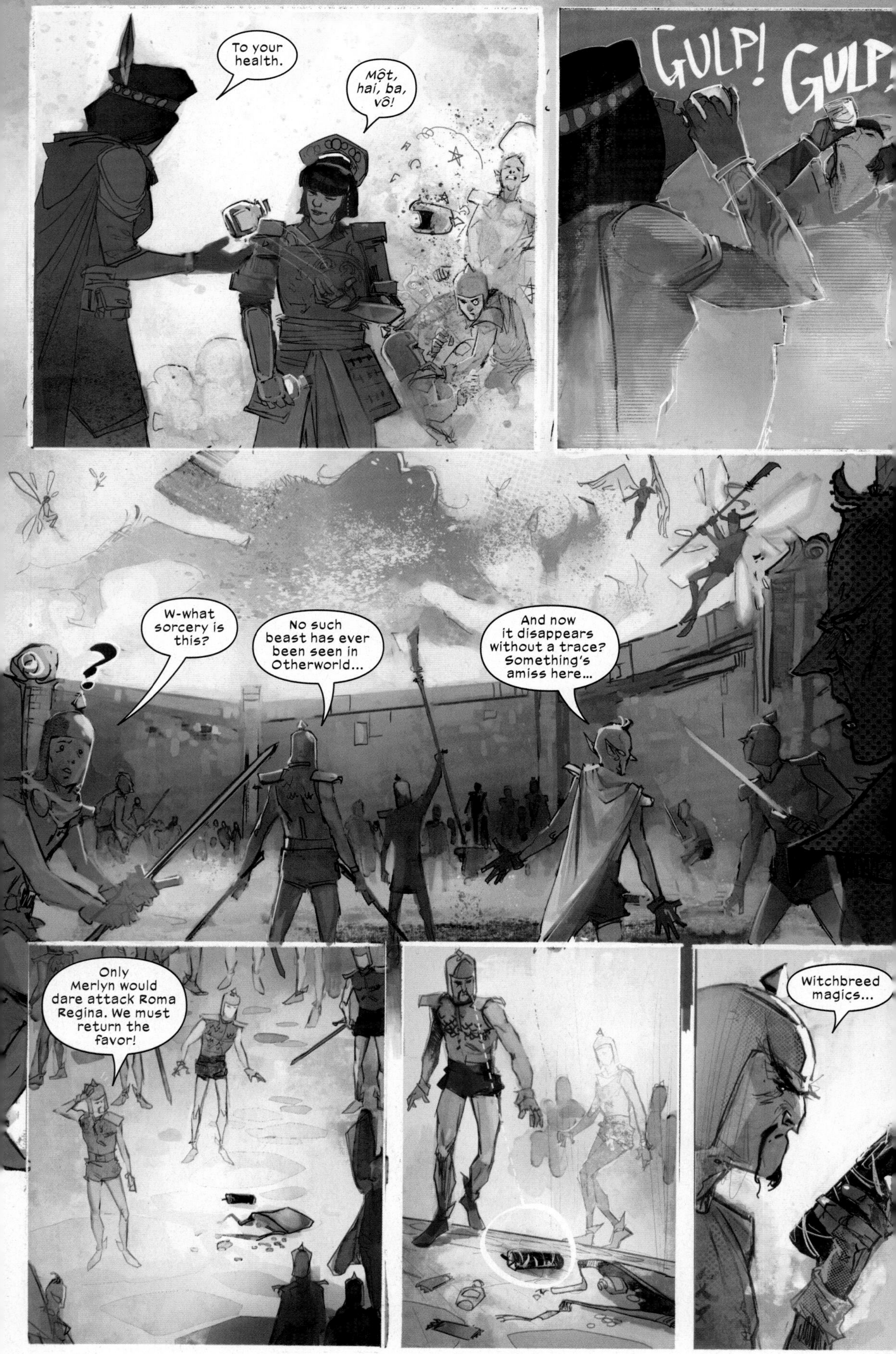

To your health.
Một, hai, ba, vô!
GULP! GULP!
W-what sorcery is this?
No such beast has ever been seen in Otherworld...
And now it disappears without a trace? Something's amiss here...
Only Merlyn would dare attack Roma Regina. We must return the favor!
Witchbreed magics...

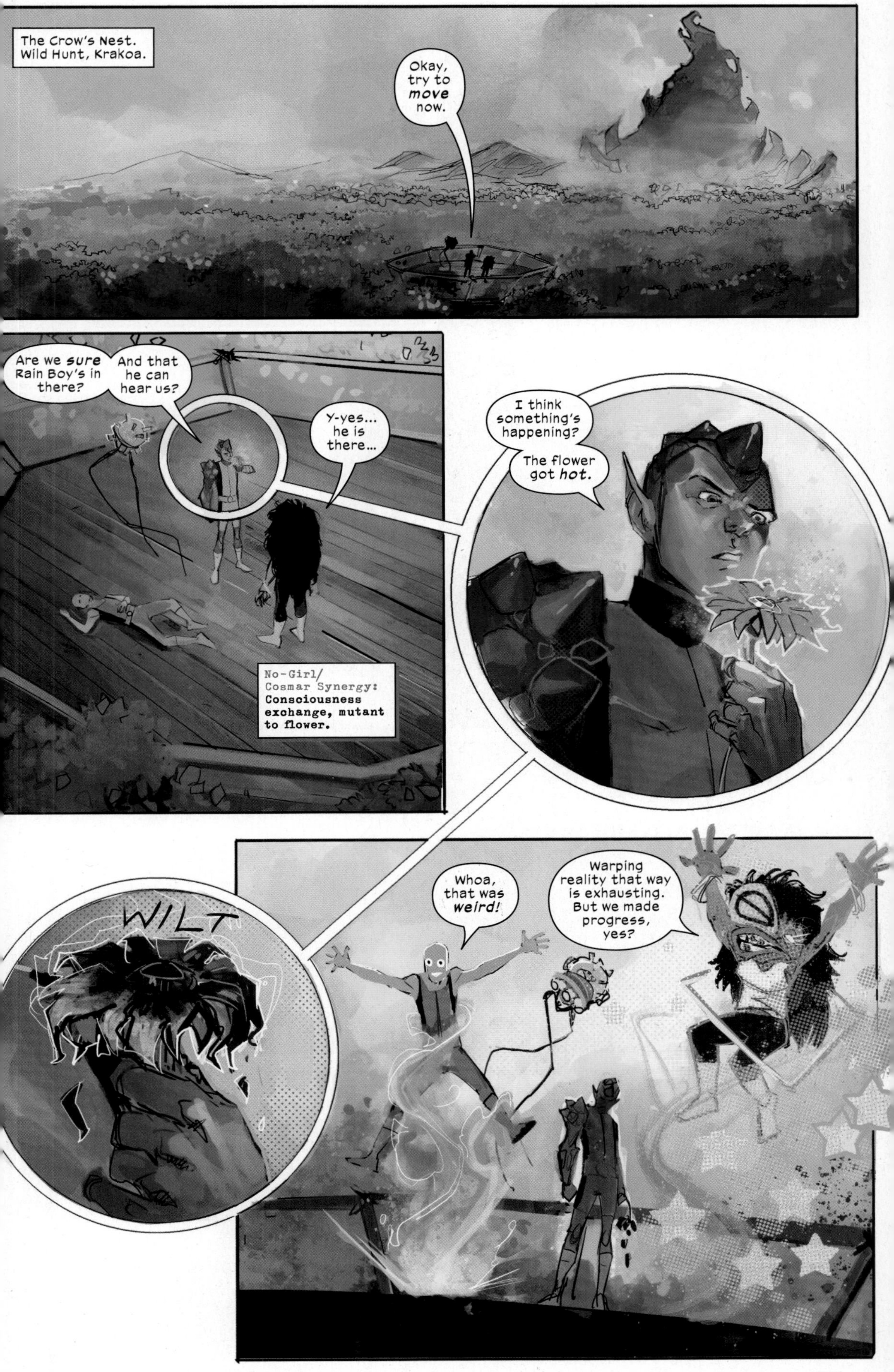

The Crow's Nest.
Wild Hunt, Krakoa.
Okay, try to *move* now.
Are we *sure* Rain Boy's in there?
And that he can hear us?
Y-yes... he is there...
No-Girl/ Cosmar Synergy: **Consciousness exchange, mutant to flower.**
I think something's happening?
The flower got *hot.*
WILT
Whoa, that was *weird!*
Warping reality that way is exhausting. But we made progress, yes?

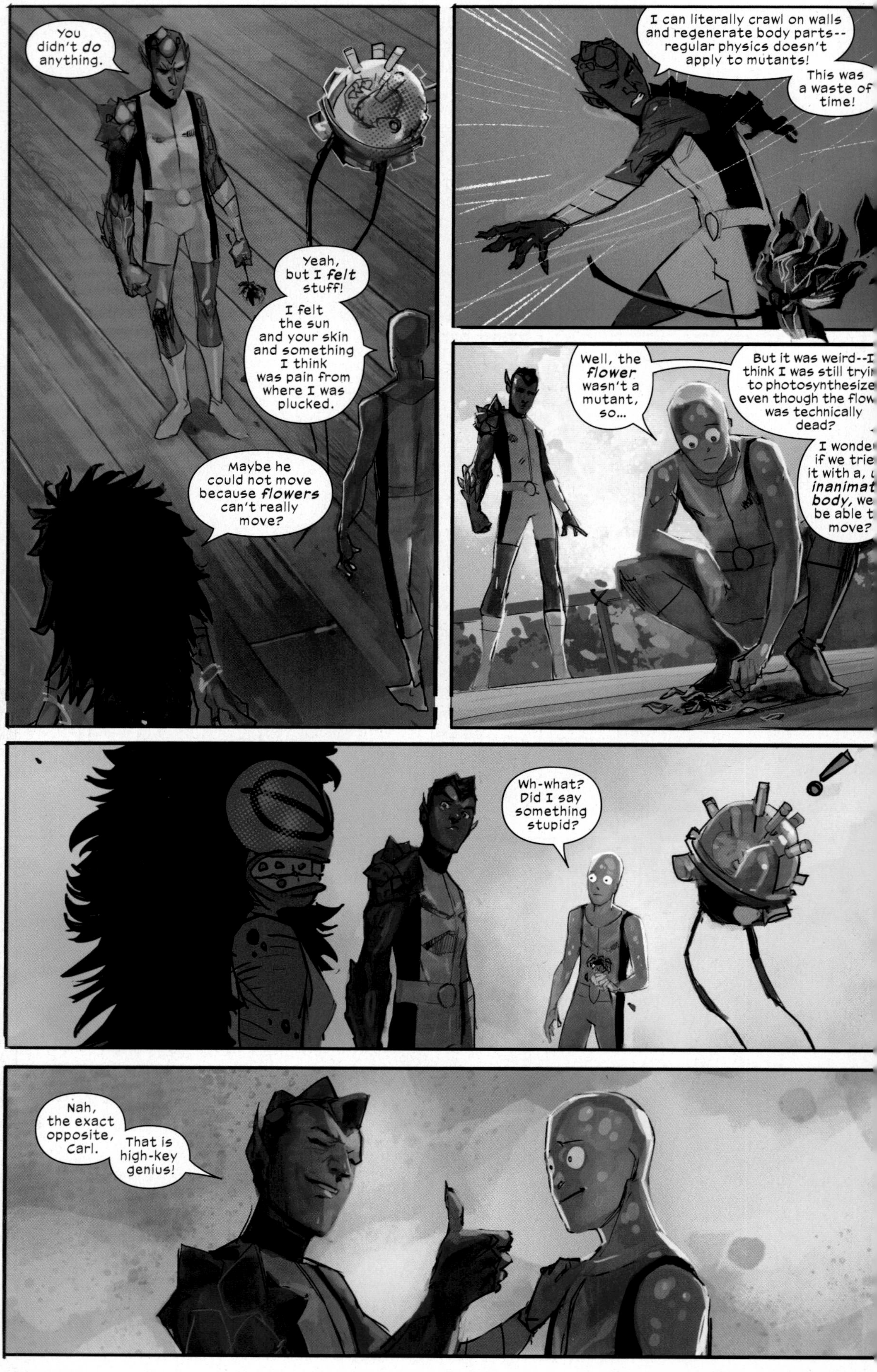
You didn't *do* anything.
I can literally crawl on walls and regenerate body parts--regular physics doesn't apply to mutants!
This was a waste of time!
Yeah, but I *felt* stuff!
I felt the sun and your skin and something I think was pain from where I was plucked.
Maybe he could not move because *flowers* can't really move?
Well, the *flower* wasn't a mutant, so...
But it was weird--I think I was still tryi to photosynthesize even though the flow was technically dead?
I wonde if we trie it with a, *inanimat body,* we be able t move?
Wh-what? Did I say something stupid?
!
Nah, the exact opposite, Carl.
That is high-key genius!

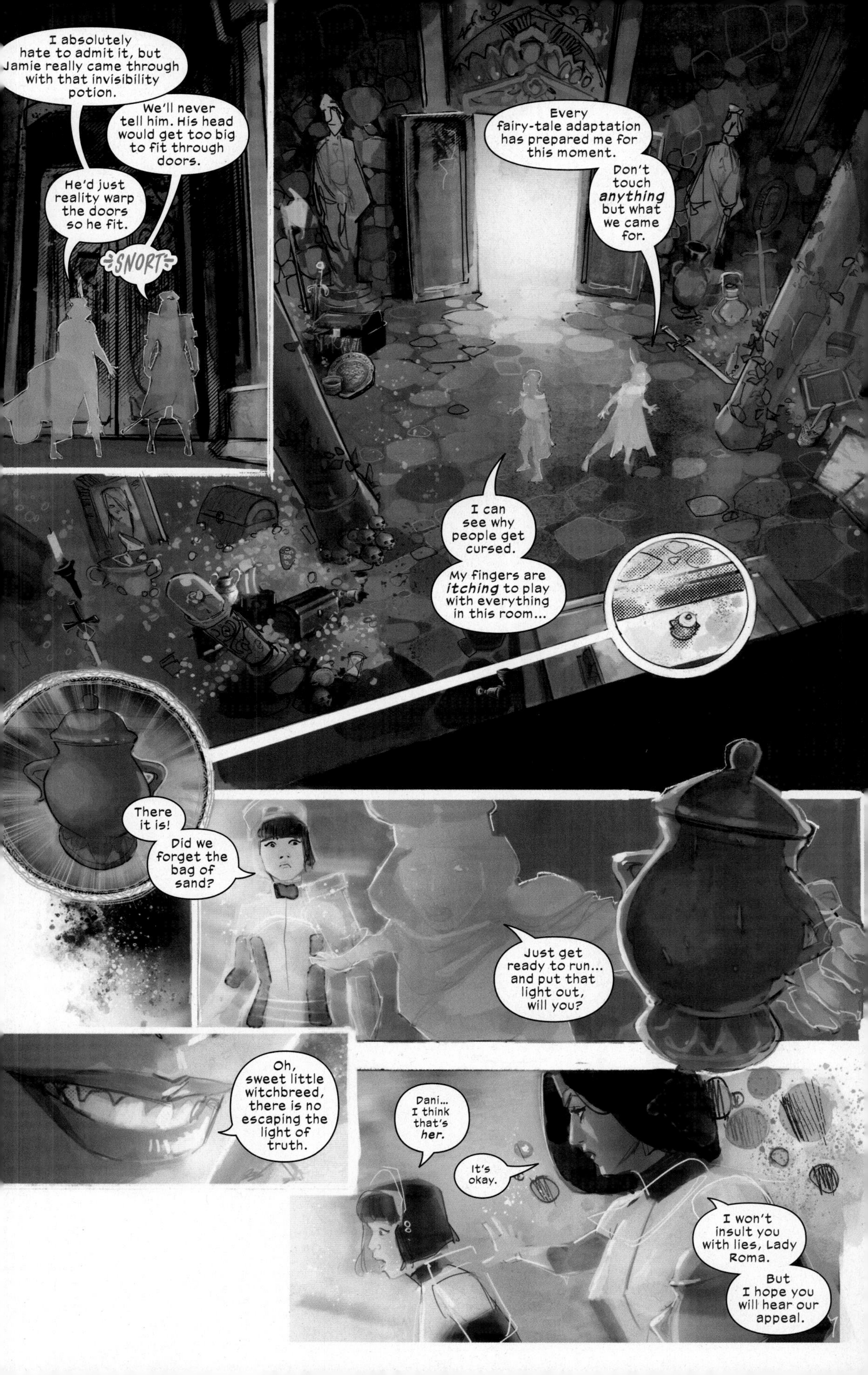
I absolutely hate to admit it, but Jamie really came through with that invisibility potion.
We'll never tell him. His head would get too big to fit through doors.
He'd just reality warp the doors so he fit.
SNORT
Every fairy-tale adaptation has prepared me for this moment.
Don't touch *anything* but what we came for.
I can see why people get cursed.
My fingers are *itching* to play with everything in this room...
There it is!
Did we forget the bag of sand?
Just get ready to run... and put that light out, will you?
Oh, sweet little witchbreed, there is no escaping the light of truth.
Dani... I think that's *her.*
It's okay.
I won't insult you with lies, Lady Roma.
But I hope you will hear our appeal.

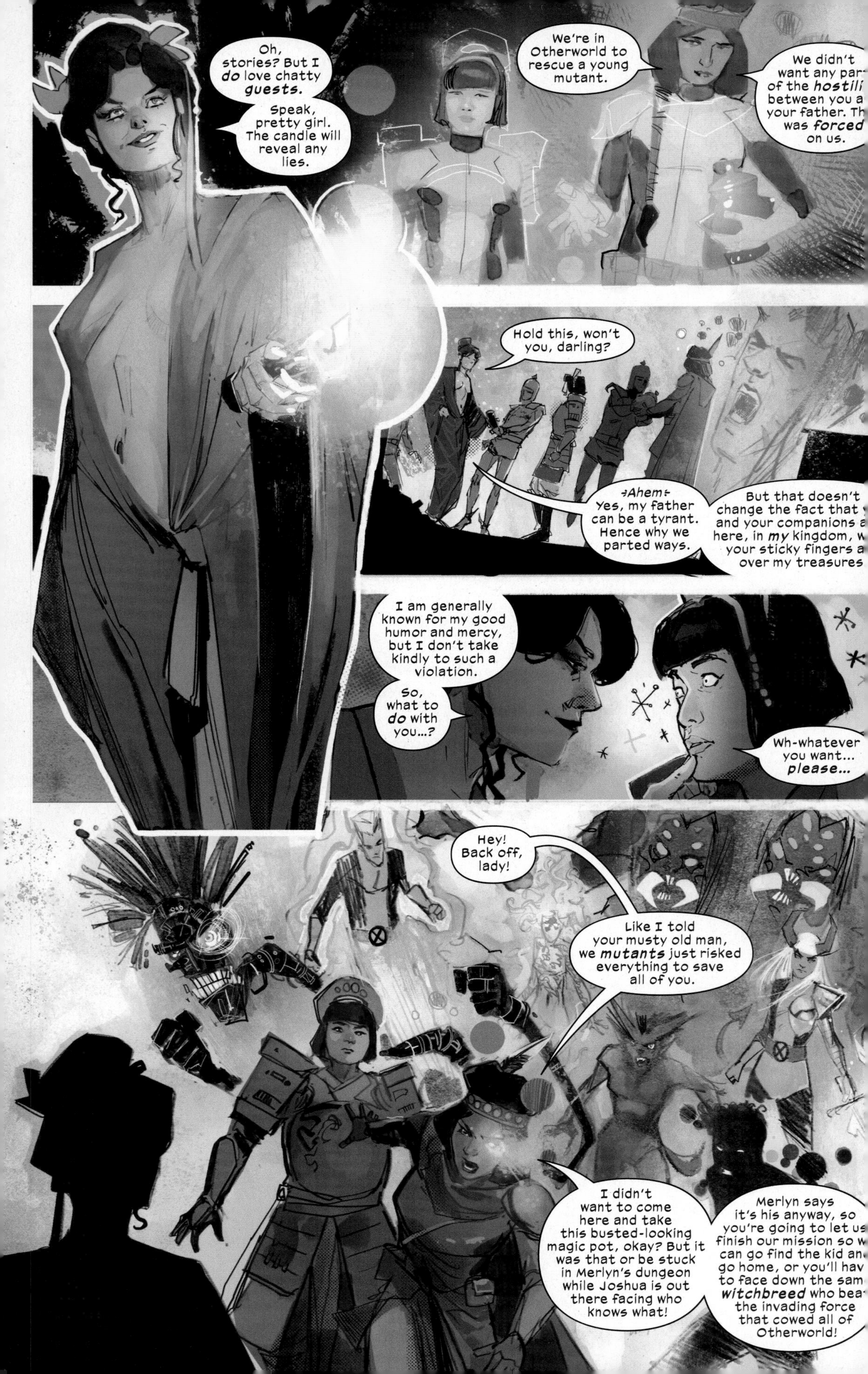
Oh, stories? But I *do* love chatty ***guests.***
Speak, pretty girl. The candle will reveal any lies.
We're in Otherworld to rescue a young mutant.
We didn't want any par of the ***hostili*** between you a your father. Th was ***forced*** on us.
Hold this, won't you, darling?
-Ahem- Yes, my father can be a tyrant. Hence why we parted ways.
But that doesn't change the fact that and your companions a here, in ***my*** kingdom, w your sticky fingers a over my treasures
I am generally known for my good humor and mercy, but I don't take kindly to such a violation.
So, what to ***do*** with you...?
Wh-whatever you want... ***please...***
Hey! Back off, lady!
Like I told your musty old man, we ***mutants*** just risked everything to save all of you.
I didn't want to come here and take this busted-looking magic pot, okay? But it was that or be stuck in Merlyn's dungeon while Joshua is out there facing who knows what!
Merlyn says it's his anyway, so you're going to let us finish our mission so w can go find the kid an go home, or you'll hav to face down the sam ***witchbreed*** who bea the invading force that cowed all of Otherworld!

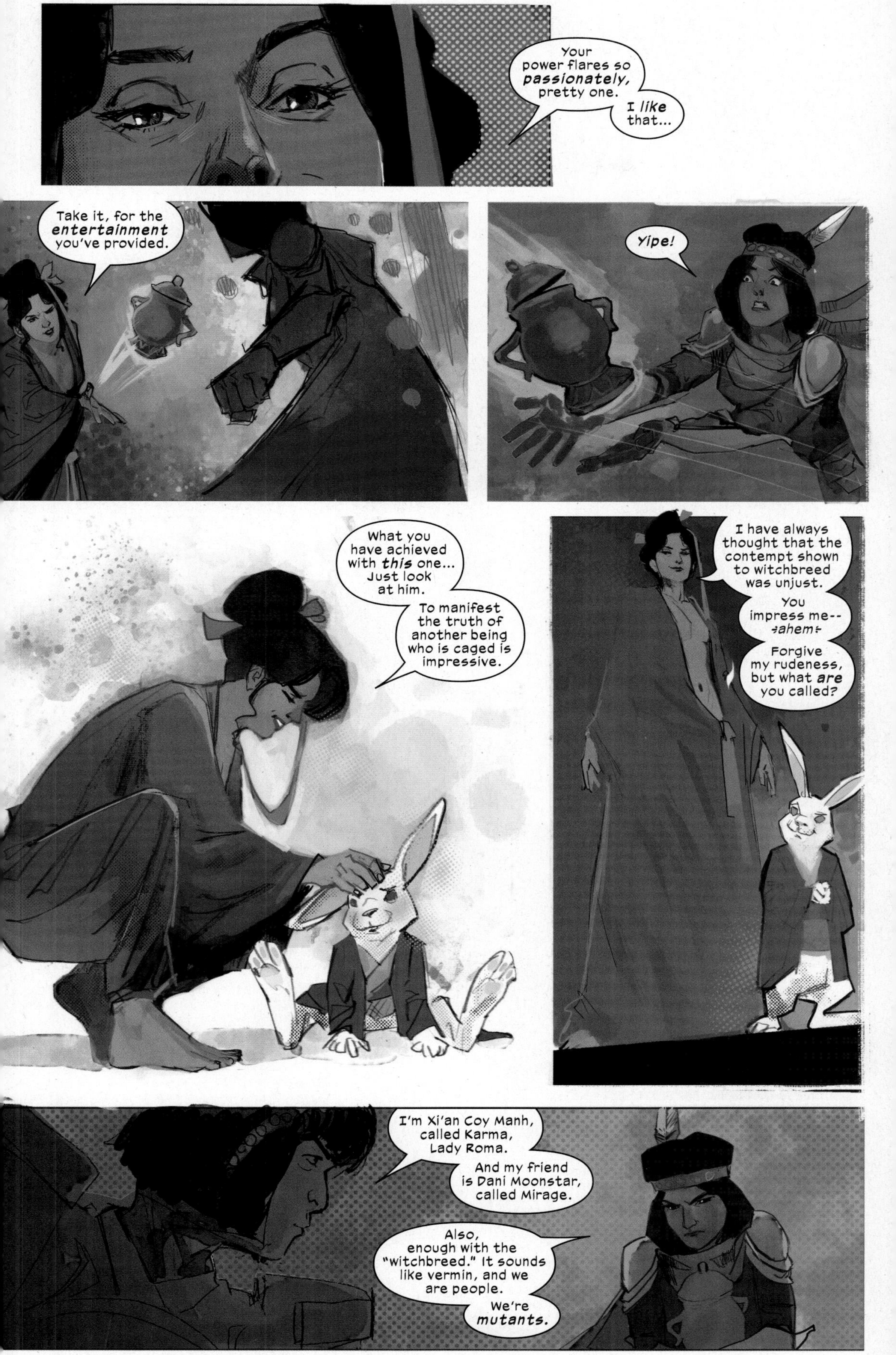

Your power flares so passionately, pretty one.
I like that...
Take it, for the entertainment you've provided.
Yipe!
What you have achieved with this one... Just look at him.
To manifest the truth of another being who is caged is impressive.
I have always thought that the contempt shown to witchbreed was unjust.
You impress me--
-ahem-
Forgive my rudeness, but what are you called?
I'm Xi'an Coy Manh, called Karma, Lady Roma.
And my friend is Dani Moonstar, called Mirage.
Also, enough with the "witchbreed." It sounds like vermin, and we are people.
We're mutants.

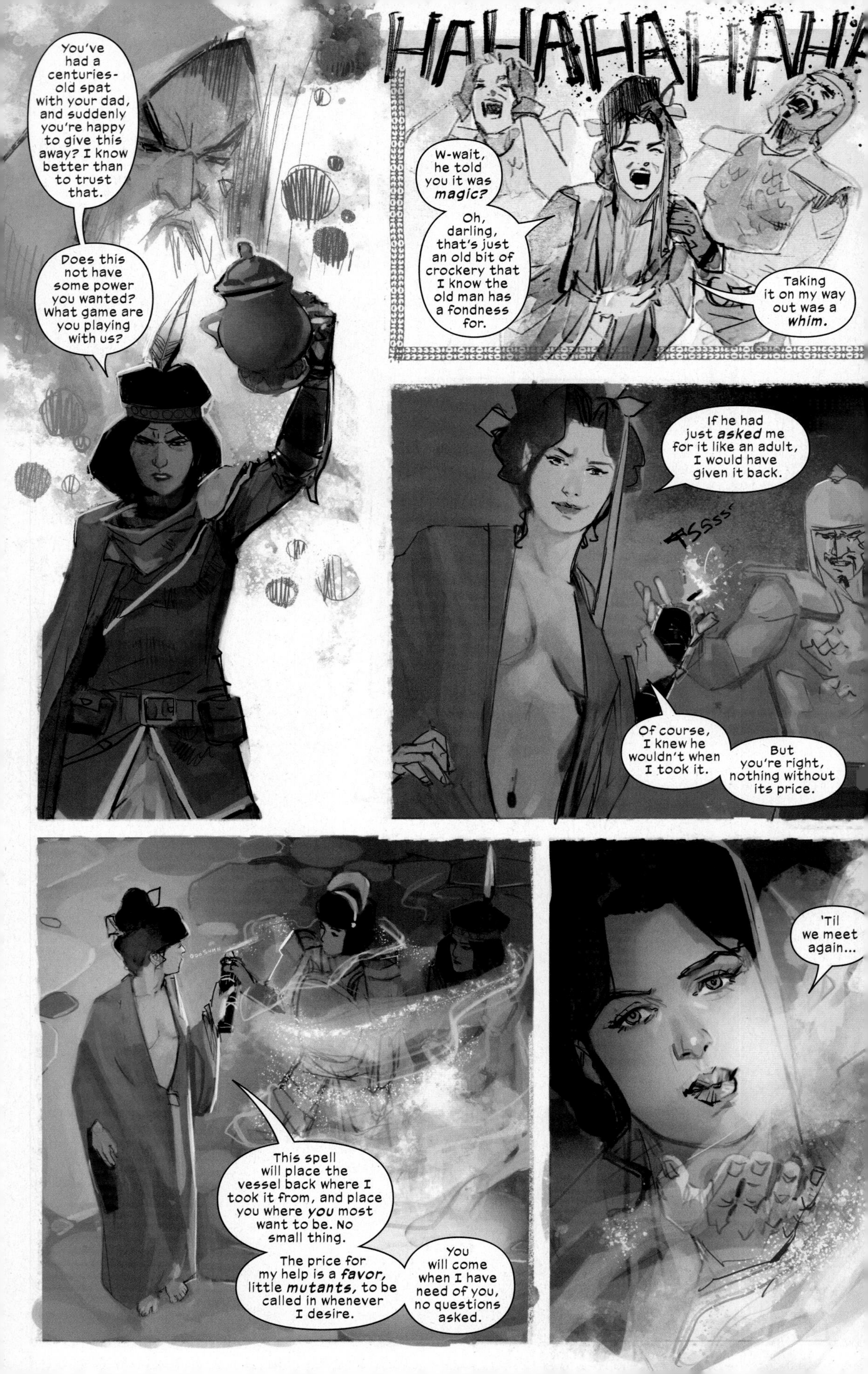

You've had a centuries-old spat with your dad, and suddenly you're happy to give this away? I know better than to trust that.
Does this not have some power you wanted? What game are you playing with us?
HAHAHAHAHA
W-wait, he told you it was *magic?*
Oh, darling, that's just an old bit of crockery that I know the old man has a fondness for.
Taking it on my way out was a *whim.*
If he had just *asked* me for it like an adult, I would have given it back.
FSSSS
Of course, I knew he wouldn't when I took it.
But you're right, nothing without its price.
This spell will place the vessel back where I took it from, and place you where *you* most want to be. No small thing.
The price for my help is a *favor,* little *mutants,* to be called in whenever I desire.
You will come when I have need of you, no questions asked.
'Til we meet again...

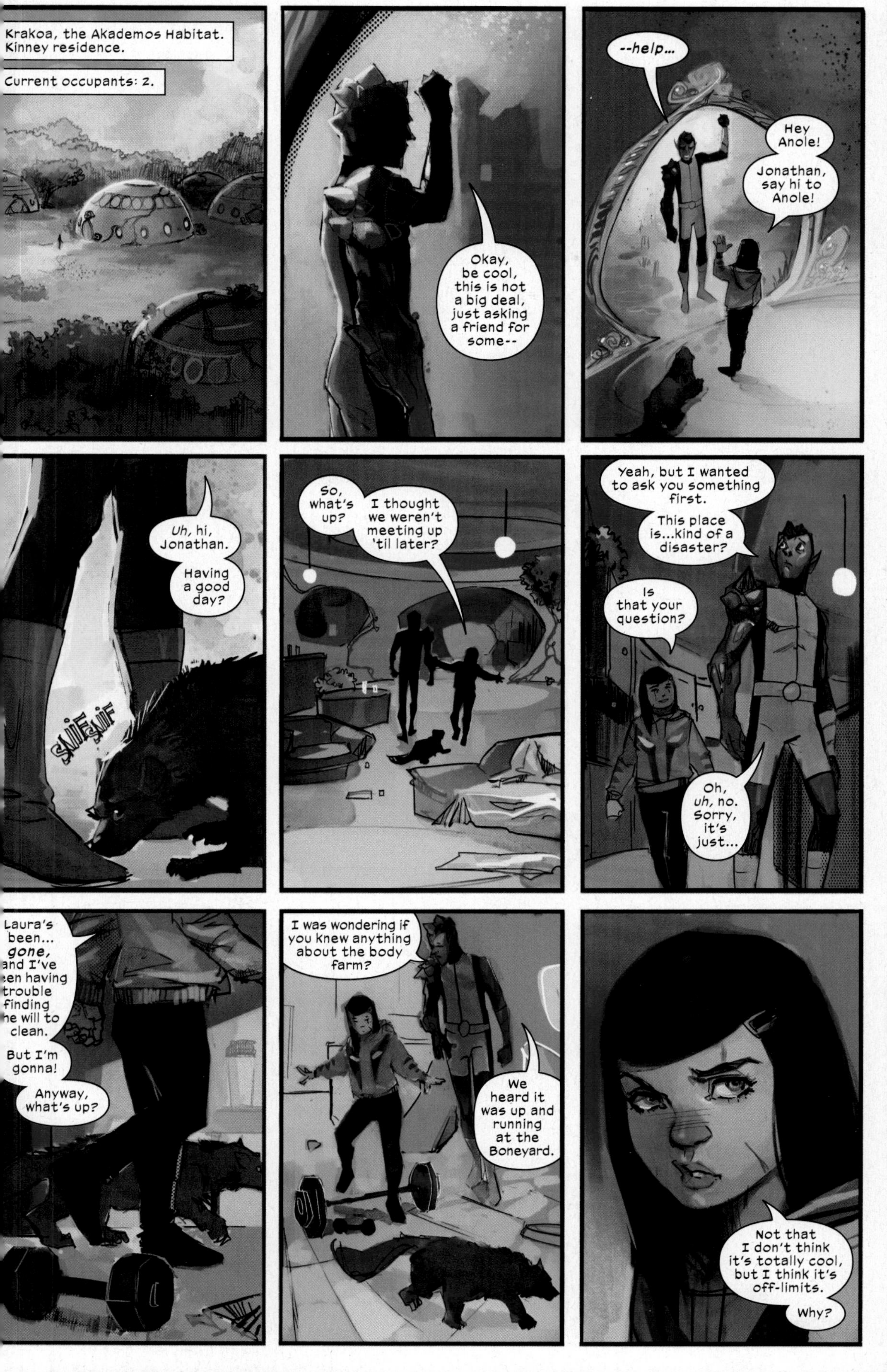

Krakoa, the Akademos Habitat. Kinney residence.
Current occupants: 2.
Okay, be cool, this is not a big deal, just asking a friend for some--
--help...
Hey Anole!
Jonathan, say hi to Anole!
Uh, hi, Jonathan.
Having a good day?
SNIFF SNIFF
So, what's up?
I thought we weren't meeting up 'til later?
Yeah, but I wanted to ask you something first.
This place is...kind of a disaster?
Is that your question?
Oh, uh, no. Sorry, it's just...
Laura's been... gone, and I've been having trouble finding the will to clean.
But I'm gonna!
Anyway, what's up?
I was wondering if you knew anything about the body farm?
We heard it was up and running at the Boneyard.
Not that I don't think it's totally cool, but I think it's off-limits.
Why?

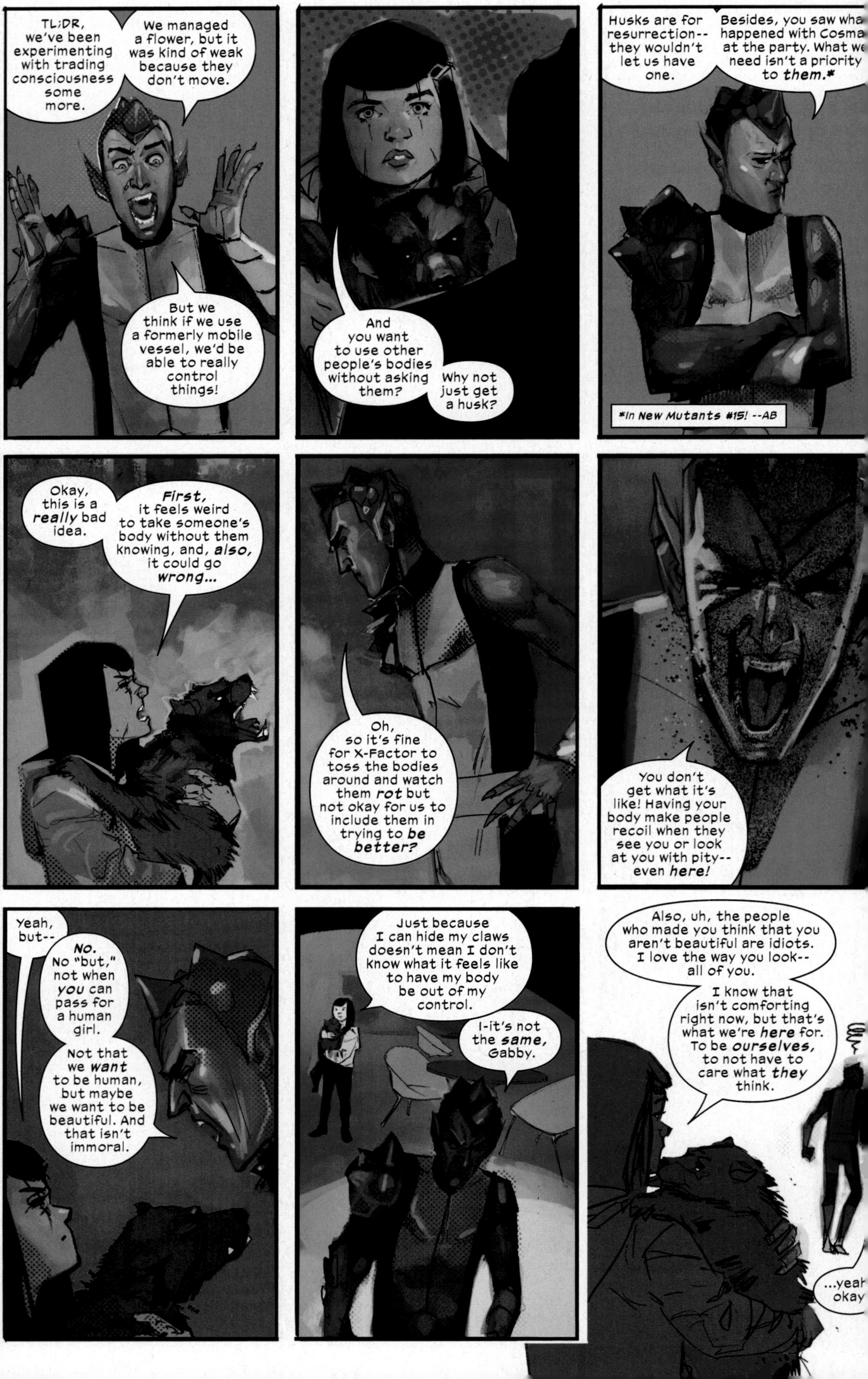

TL;DR, we've been experimenting with trading consciousness some more.
We managed a flower, but it was kind of weak because they don't move.
But we think if we use a formerly mobile vessel, we'd be able to really control things!
And you want to use other people's bodies without asking them?
Why not just get a husk?
Husks are for resurrection--they wouldn't let us have one.
Besides, you saw wha happened with Cosma at the party. What we need isn't a priority to *them.**
*In New Mutants #15! --AB
Okay, this is a *really* bad idea.
First, it feels weird to take someone's body without them knowing, and, *also,* it could go *wrong...*
Oh, so it's fine for X-Factor to toss the bodies around and watch them *rot* but not okay for us to include them in trying to *be better?*
You don't get what it's like! Having your body make people recoil when they see you or look at you with pity--even *here!*
Yeah, but--
No. No "but," not when *you* can pass for a human girl.
Not that we *want* to be human, but maybe we want to be beautiful. And that isn't immoral.
Just because I can hide my claws doesn't mean I don't know what it feels like to have my body be out of my control.
I-it's not the *same,* Gabby.
Also, uh, the people who made you think that you aren't beautiful are idiots. I love the way you look--all of you.
I know that isn't comforting right now, but that's what we're *here* for. To be *ourselves,* to not have to care what *they* think.
...yeah okay

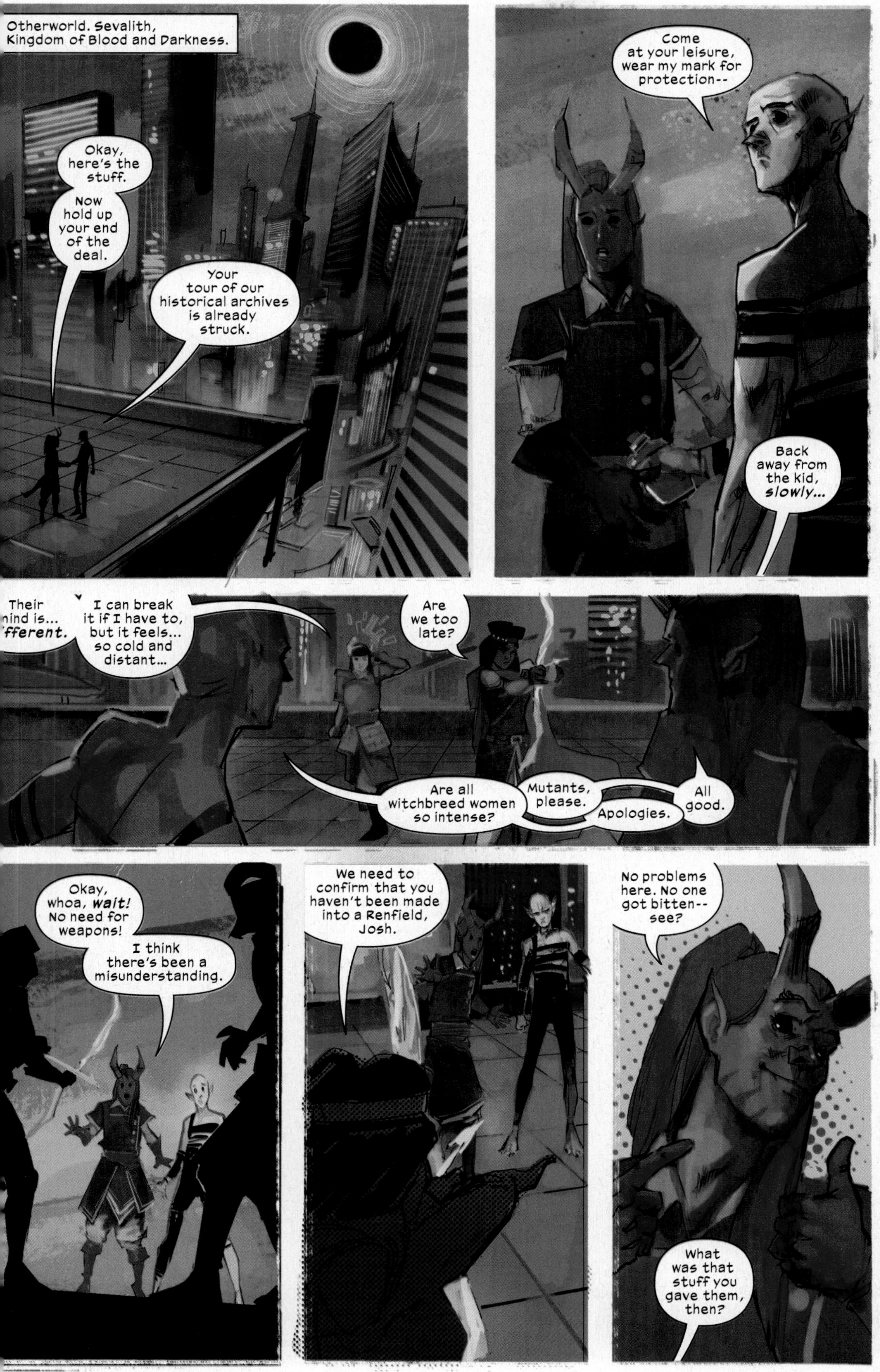
Otherworld. Sevalith, Kingdom of Blood and Darkness.
Okay, here's the stuff.
Now hold up your end of the deal.
Your tour of our historical archives is already struck.
Come at your leisure, wear my mark for protection--
Back away from the kid, *slowly...*
Their mind is... *fferent.*
I can break it if I have to, but it feels... so cold and distant...
Are we too late?
Are all witchbreed women so intense?
Mutants, please.
Apologies.
All good.
Okay, whoa, *wait!* No need for weapons!
I think there's been a misunderstanding.
We need to confirm that you haven't been made into a Renfield, Josh.
No problems here. No one got bitten--see?
What was that stuff you gave them, then?

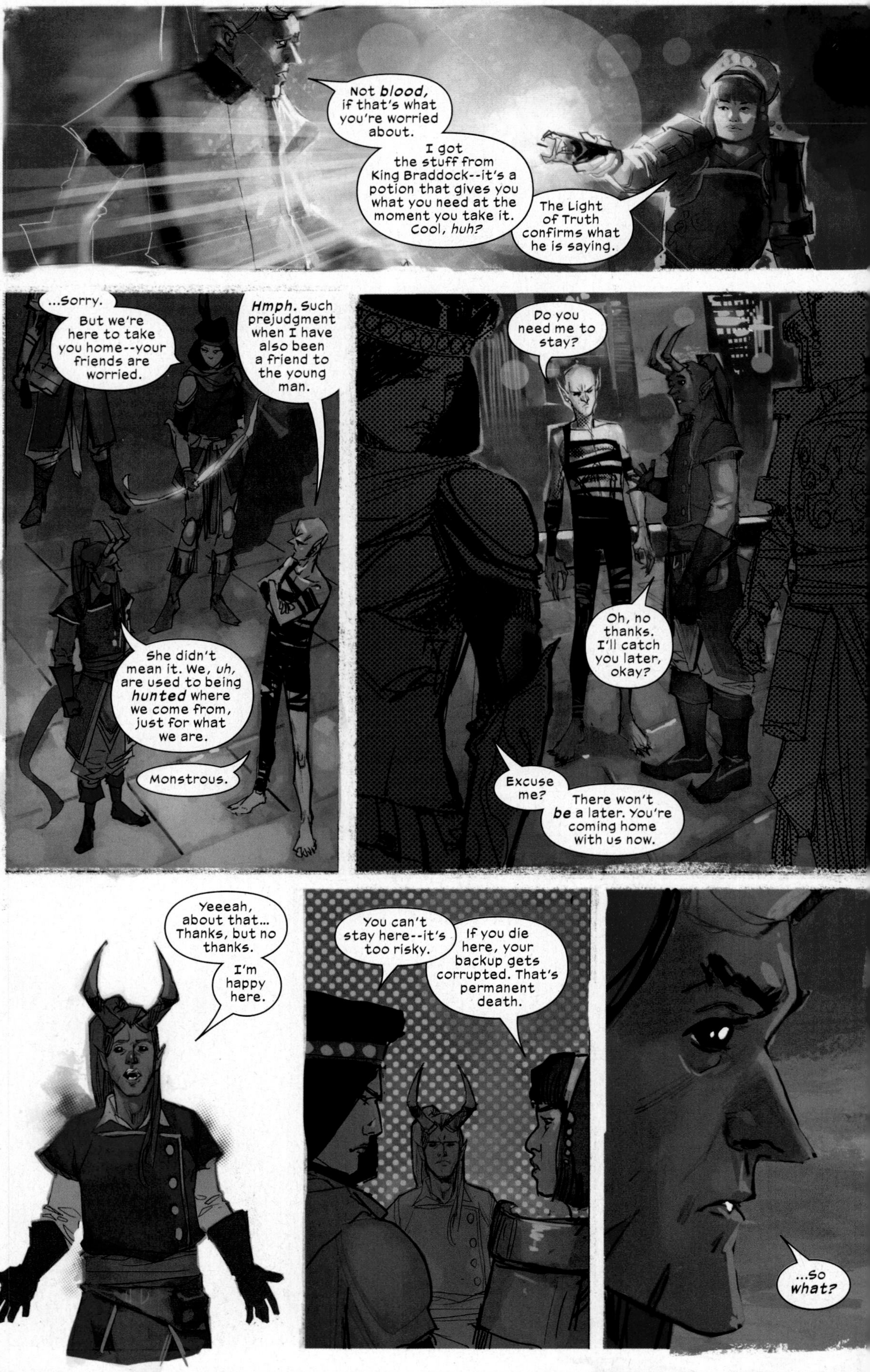

Not *blood,* if that's what you're worried about.
I got the stuff from King Braddock--it's a potion that gives you what you need at the moment you take it. Cool, *huh?*
The Light of Truth confirms what he is saying.
...Sorry.
But we're here to take you home--your friends are worried.
Hmph. Such prejudgment when I have also been a friend to the young man.
She didn't mean it. We, *uh,* are used to being *hunted* where we come from, just for what we are.
Monstrous.
Do you need me to stay?
Oh, no thanks. I'll catch you later, okay?
Excuse me?
There won't *be* a later. You're coming home with us now.
Yeeeah, about that... Thanks, but no thanks.
I'm happy here.
You can't stay here--it's too risky.
If you die here, your backup gets corrupted. That's permanent death.
...So *what?*

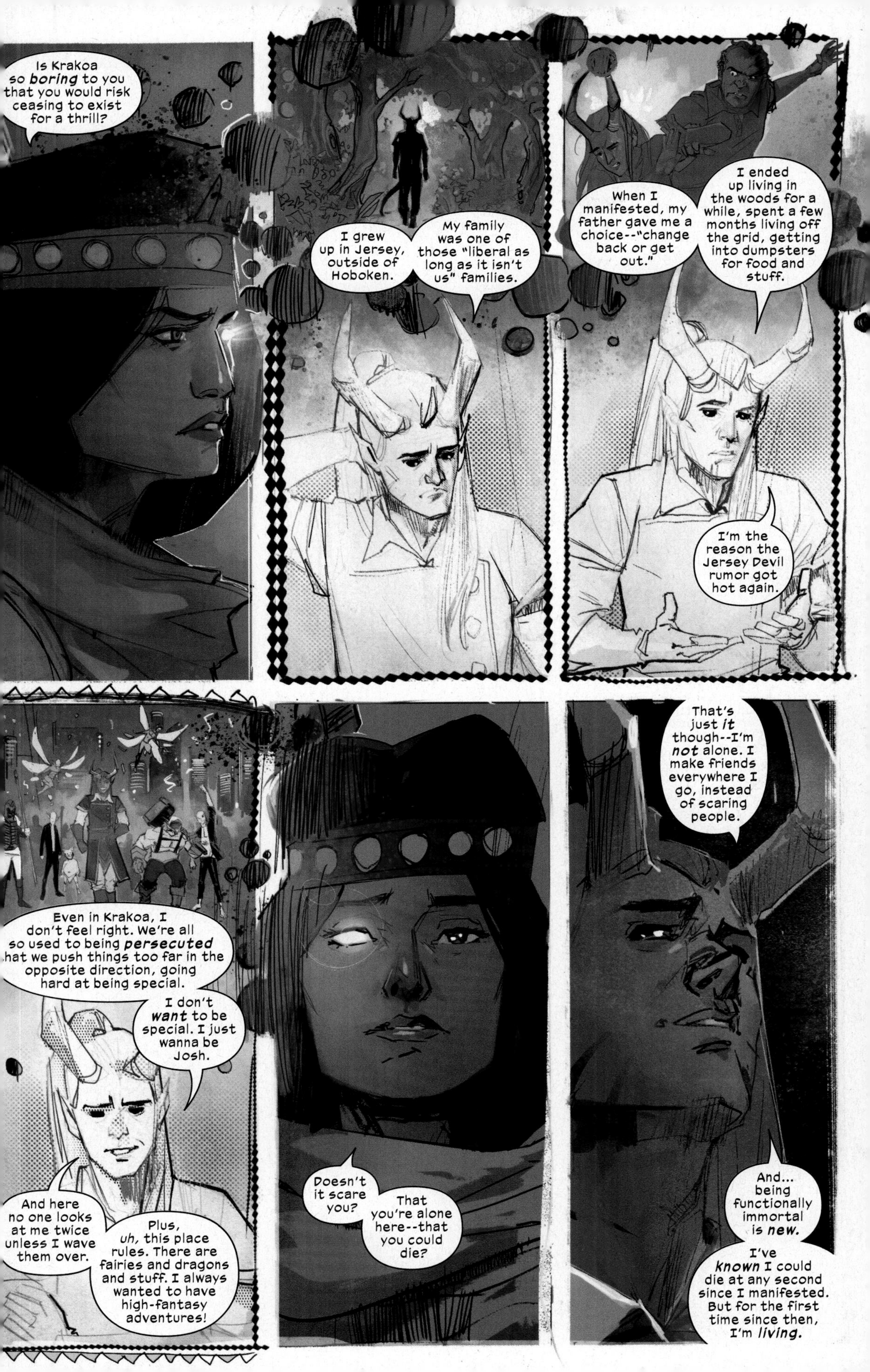
Is Krakoa so *boring* to you that you would risk ceasing to exist for a thrill?
I grew up in Jersey, outside of Hoboken.
My family was one of those "liberal as long as it isn't us" families.
When I manifested, my father gave me a choice--"change back or get out."
I ended up living in the woods for a while, spent a few months living off the grid, getting into dumpsters for food and stuff.
I'm the reason the Jersey Devil rumor got hot again.
Even in Krakoa, I don't feel right. We're all so used to being *persecuted* hat we push things too far in the opposite direction, going hard at being special.
I don't *want* to be special. I just wanna be Josh.
And here no one looks at me twice unless I wave them over.
Plus, *uh,* this place rules. There are fairies and dragons and stuff. I always wanted to have high-fantasy adventures!
Doesn't it scare you?
That you're alone here--that you could die?
That's just *it* though--I'm *not* alone. I make friends everywhere I go, instead of scaring people.
And... being functionally immortal is *new.*
I've *known* I could die at any second since I manifested. But for the first time since then, I'm *living.*

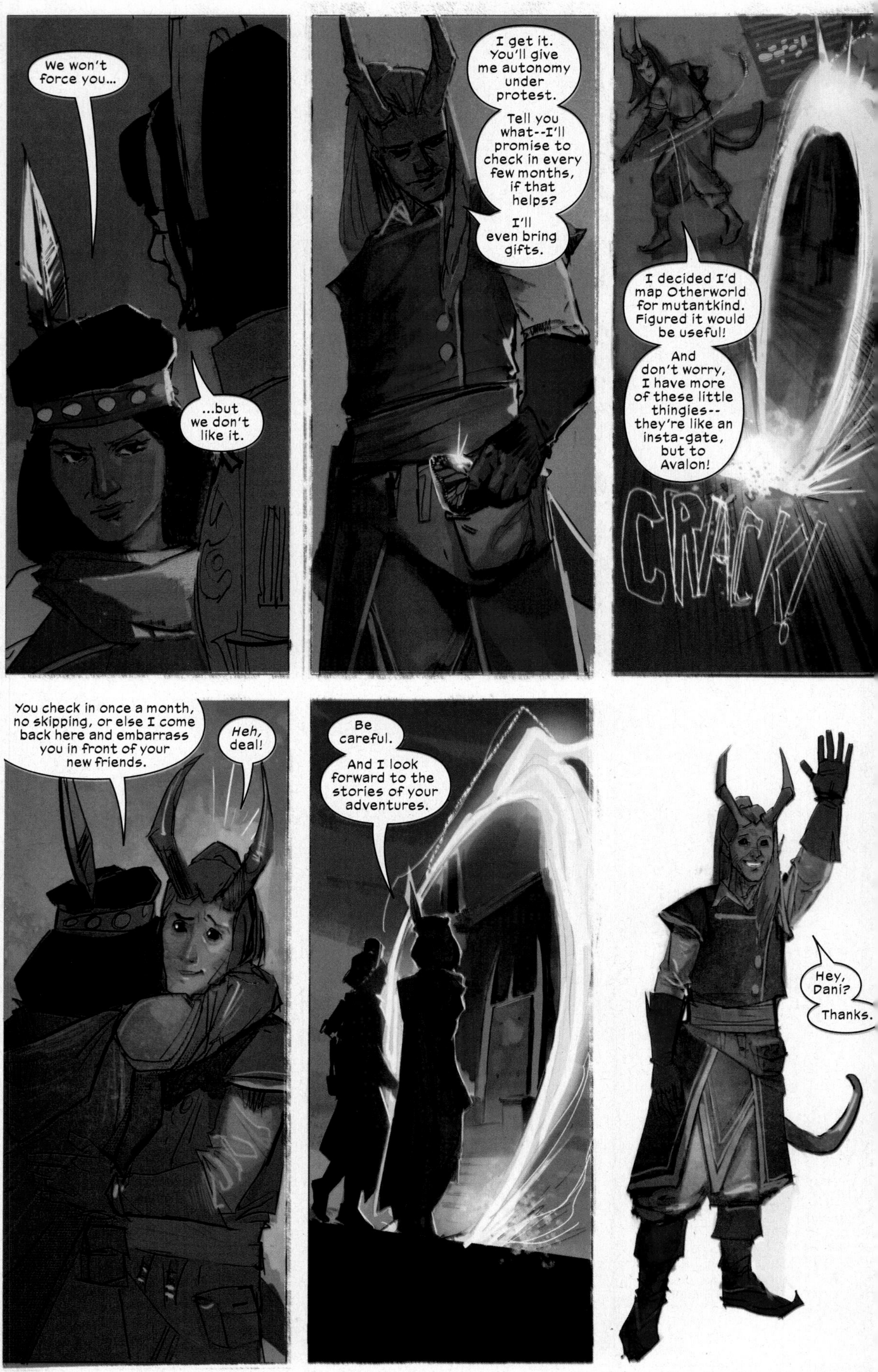
We won't force you...
...but we don't like it.
I get it. You'll give me autonomy under protest.
Tell you what--I'll promise to check in every few months, if that helps?
I'll even bring gifts.
I decided I'd map Otherworld for mutantkind. Figured it would be useful!
And don't worry, I have more of these little thingies--they're like an insta-gate, but to Avalon!
CRACK!
You check in once a month, no skipping, or else I come back here and embarrass you in front of your new friends.
Heh, deal!
Be careful.
And I look forward to the stories of your adventures.
Hey, Dani?
Thanks.

WARPATH JOURNAL, ENTRY 003

Write down all the compliments you can remember that you've received.

I have gotten many compliments over my life, so recounting them all isn't useful here. But some that I go back to in my mind are the following:

Domino tells me I fill out my uniform well. It's a vain joy, but I would be lying if I said it didn't make me feel good.

Wolverine once told me that of all the people who threw him in a Fastball Special, I was the most mindful of his body, and that I could "toss him any time."

Silver Samurai once told me he enjoys my knifework.

Write about something that is frustrating to you.

I don't like the idea of talking out of school, so to speak, but, this space may be useful as a tool to examine my reactions.

Lately, Warlock has taken to avoiding Cypher, and instead is following others around, imitating the way we move, look and sometimes speak.

I understand that he is not mocking us -- while he has a well-developed sense of humor, it is mostly at his own expense. He isn't the kind of being that finds fun in cruelty. It reminds me of a child trying to find their own identity through play, which isn't a bad thing, but something about his behavior irks me.

If I wasn't currently training groups of mutants (of various ages) without the bothersome feeling, I would say it is because I don't do well with certain stages of learning/self-exploration, but that isn't it.

I am a person of action -- I confront things that need confronting and deal with them head on -- but I haven't here, and that bothers me almost more than Warlock. His sincerity and confusion are too much to look at sometimes, and I don't know if confrontation is what he needs right now.

So I am not able to act, just observe. Which is...very frustrating.

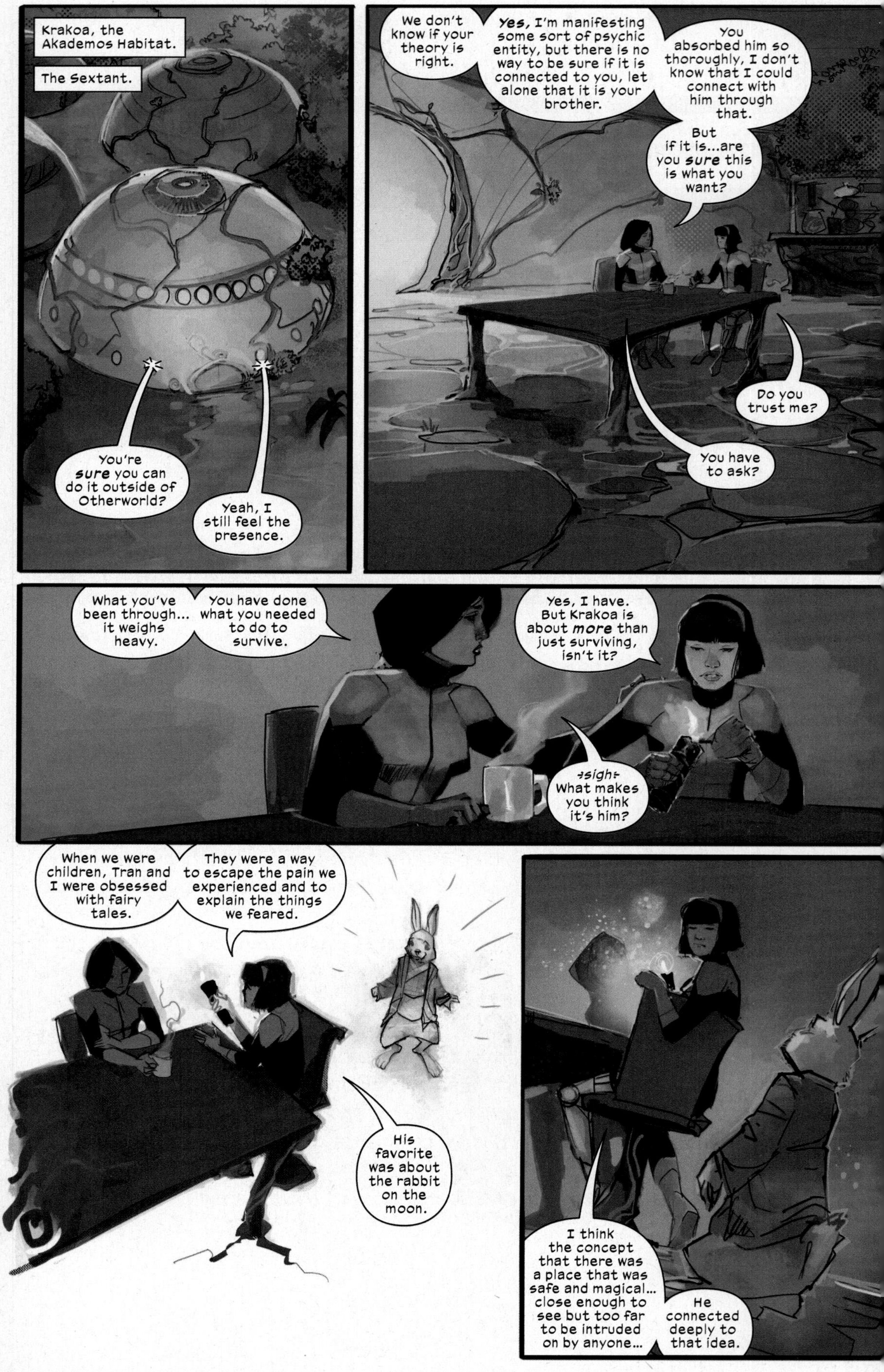

Krakoa, the Akademos Habitat.
The Sextant.
You're *sure* you can do it outside of Otherworld?
Yeah, I still feel the presence.
We don't know if your theory is right.
Yes, I'm manifesting some sort of psychic entity, but there is no way to be sure if it is connected to you, let alone that it is your brother.
You absorbed him so thoroughly, I don't know that I could connect with him through that.
But if it is...are you *sure* this is what you want?
Do you trust me?
You have to ask?
What you've been through... it weighs heavy.
You have done what you needed to do to survive.
Yes, I have. But Krakoa is about *more* than just surviving, isn't it?
sigh What makes you think it's him?
When we were children, Tran and I were obsessed with fairy tales.
They were a way to escape the pain we experienced and to explain the things we feared.
His favorite was about the rabbit on the moon.
I think the concept that there was a place that was safe and magical... close enough to see but too far to be intruded on by anyone...
He connected deeply to that idea.

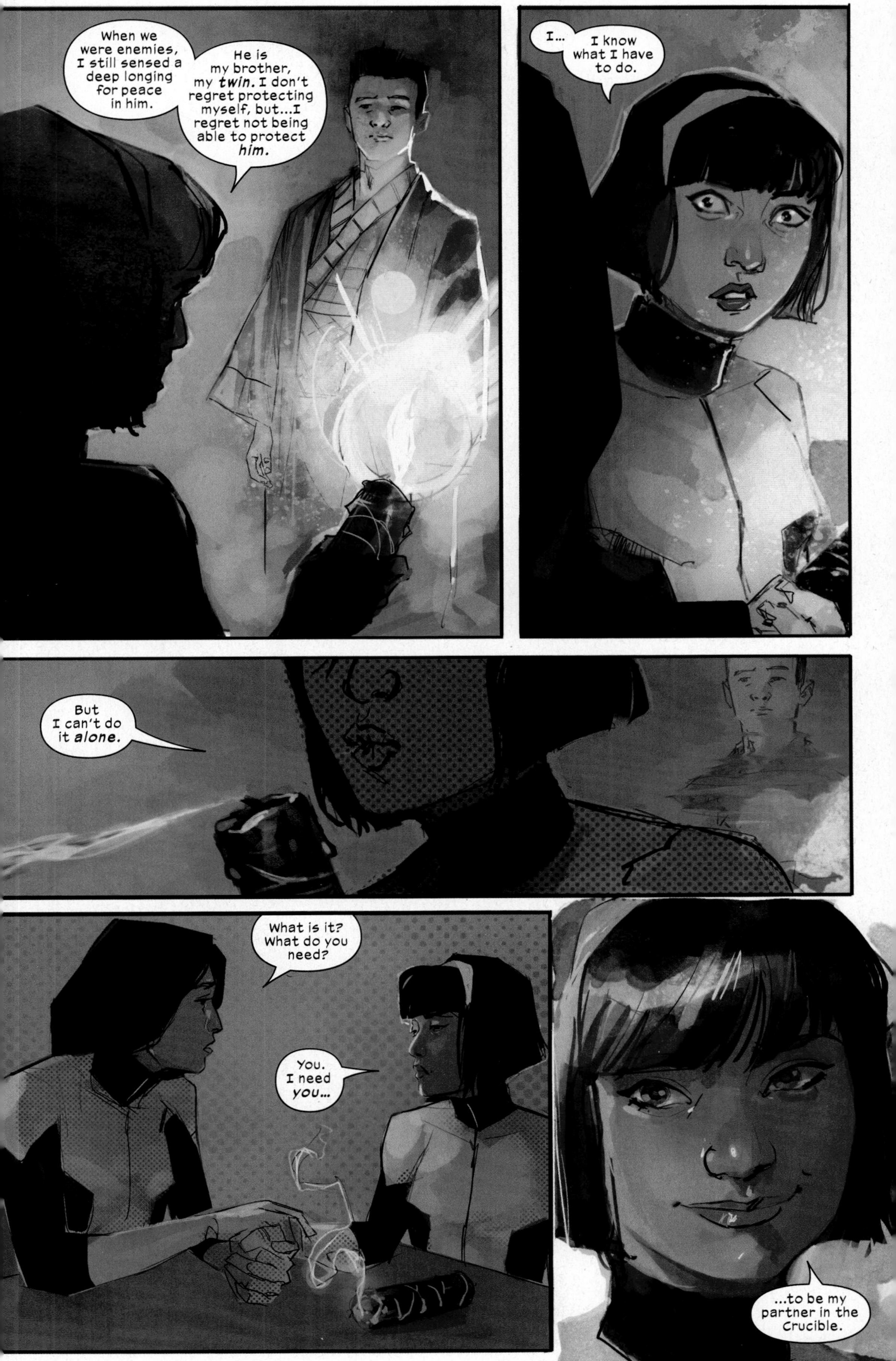
When we were enemies, I still sensed a deep longing for peace in him.
He is my brother, my *twin.* I don't regret protecting myself, but...I regret not being able to protect *him.*
I...
I know what I have to do.
But I can't do it *alone.*
What is it? What do you need?
You. I need *you*...
...to be my partner in the Crucible.

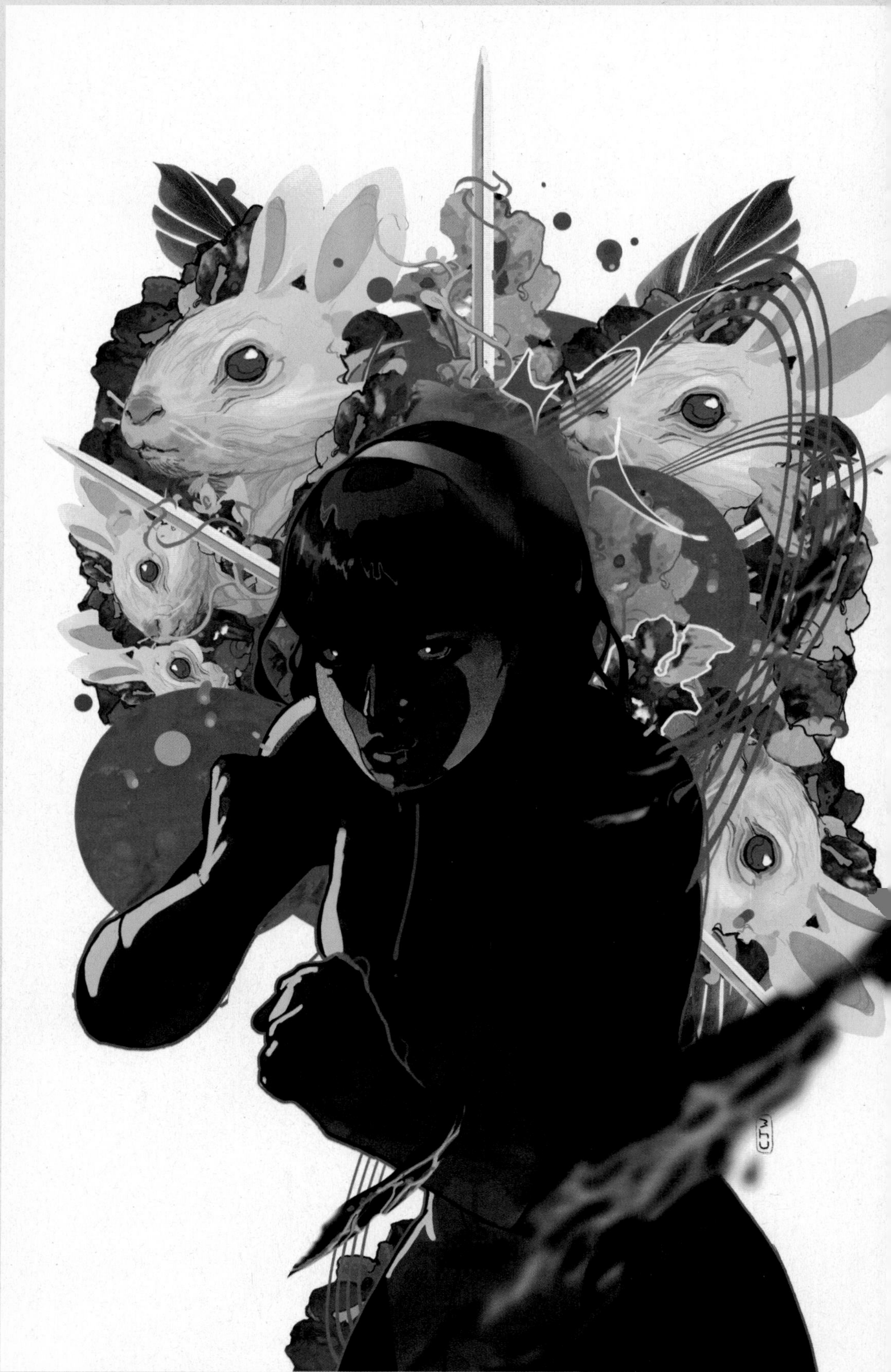

Homecoming

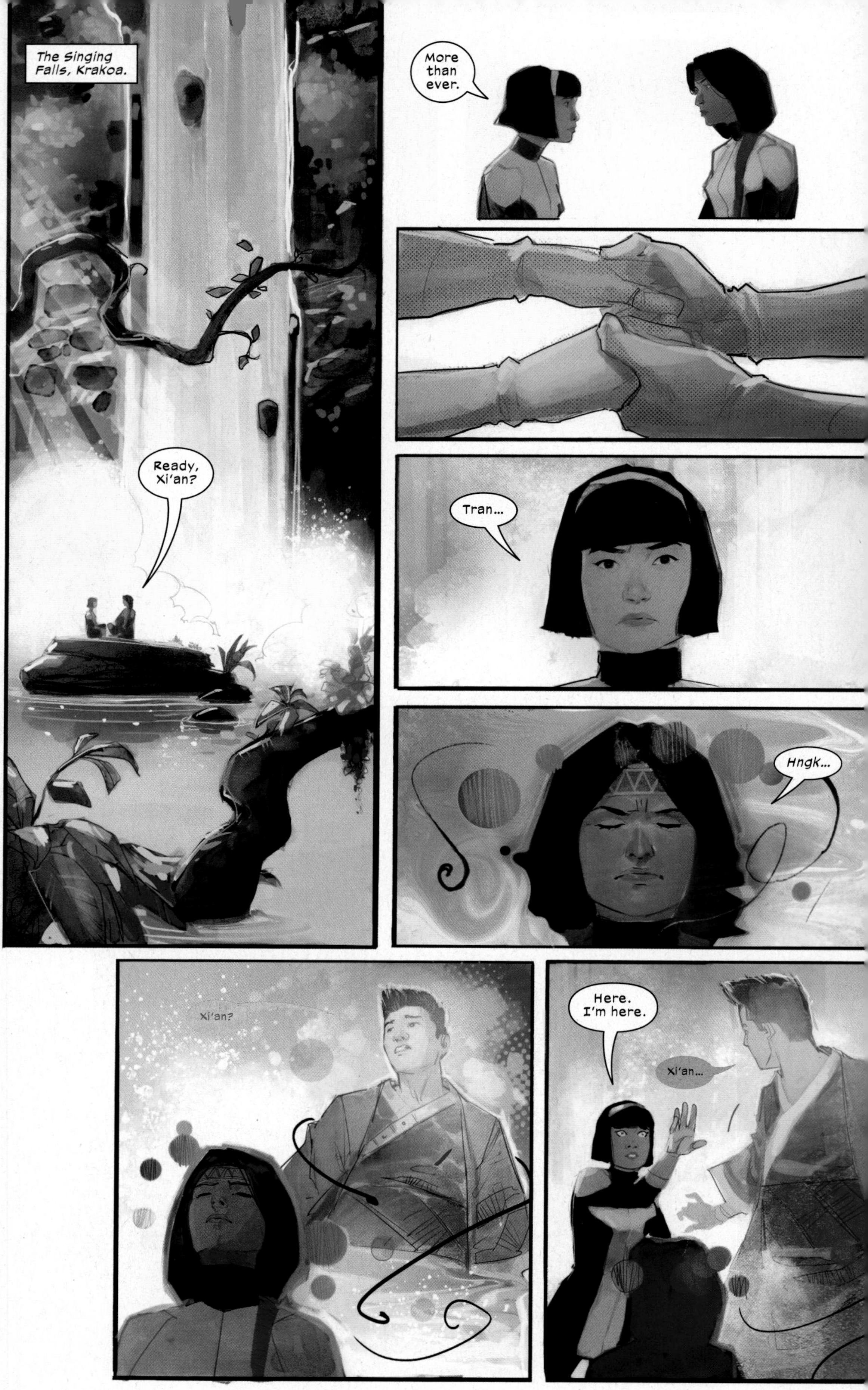
The Singing Falls, Krakoa.
Ready, Xi'an?
More than ever.
Tran...
Hngk...
Xi'an?
Here. I'm here.
Xi'an...

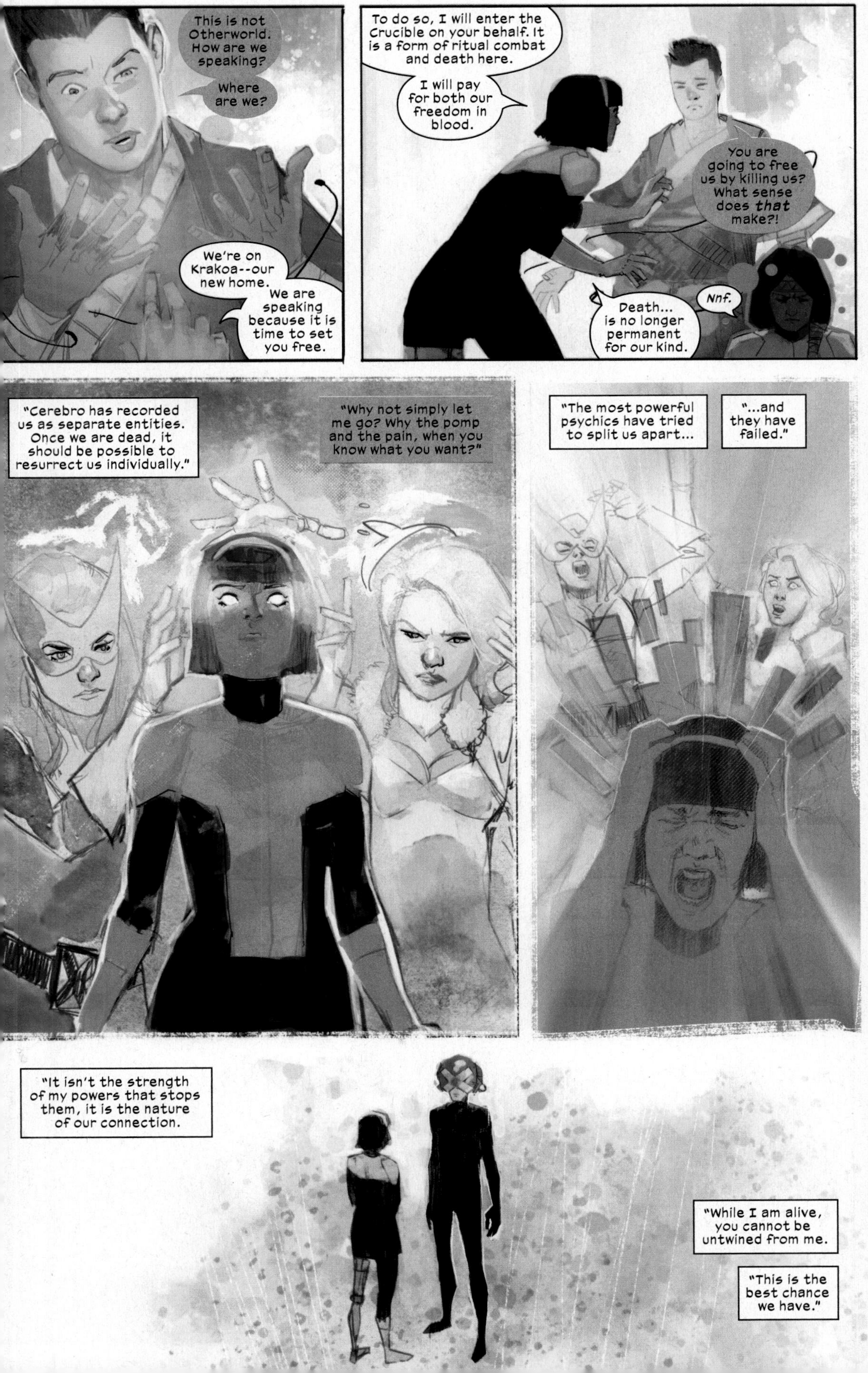
This is not Otherworld. How are we speaking?
Where are we?
We're on Krakoa--our new home.
We are speaking because it is time to set you free.
To do so, I will enter the Crucible on your behalf. It is a form of ritual combat and death here.
I will pay for both our freedom in blood.
You are going to free us by killing us? What sense does *that* make?!
Death... is no longer permanent for our kind.
Nnf.
"Cerebro has recorded us as separate entities. Once we are dead, it should be possible to resurrect us individually."
"Why not simply let me go? Why the pomp and the pain, when you know what you want?"
"The most powerful psychics have tried to split us apart...
"...and they have failed."
"It isn't the strength of my powers that stops them, it is the nature of our connection.
"While I am alive, you cannot be untwined from me.
"This is the best chance we have."

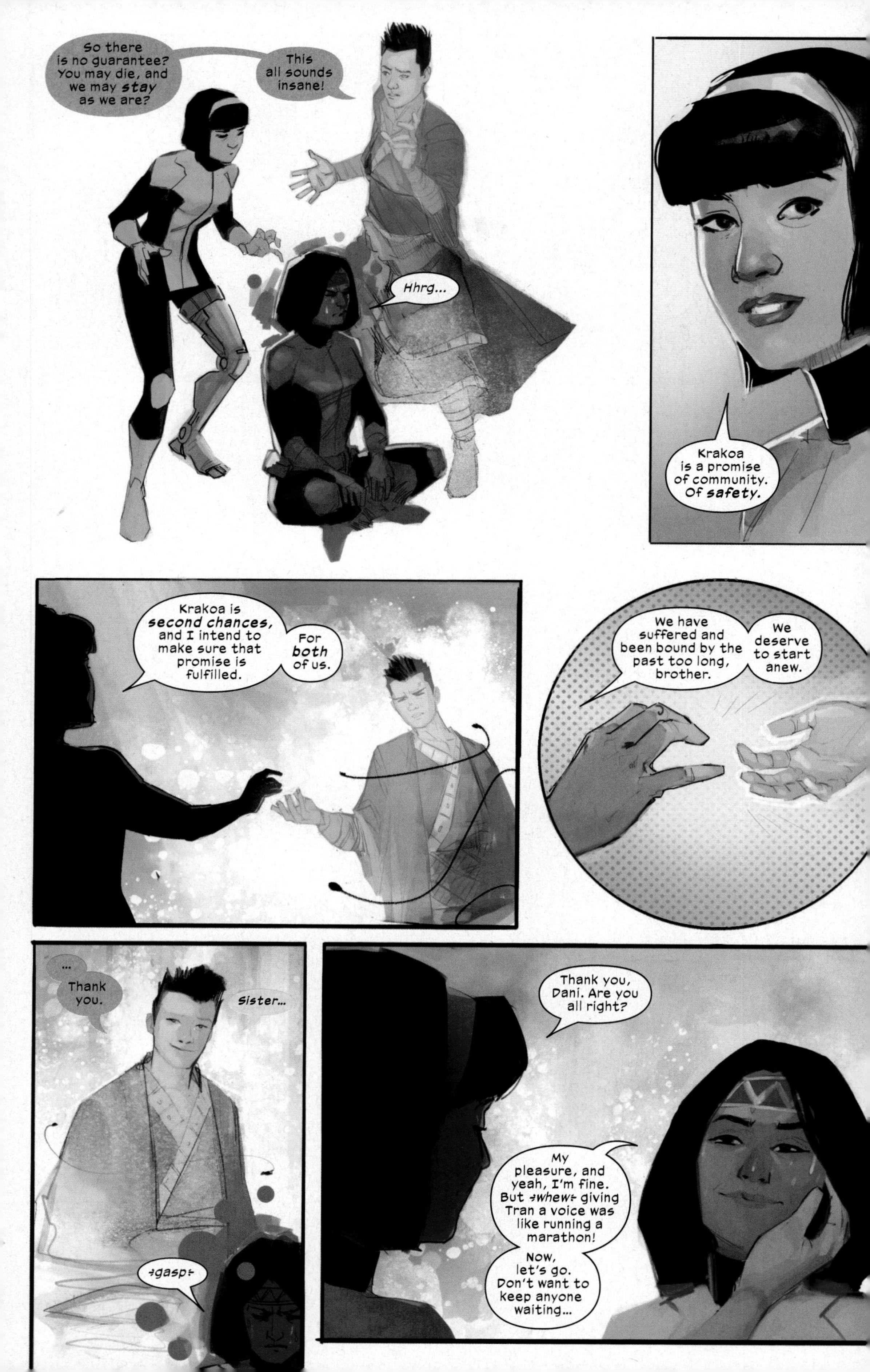
So there is no guarantee? You may die, and we may stay as we are?
This all sounds insane!
Hhrg...
Krakoa is a promise of community. Of safety.
Krakoa is second chances, and I intend to make sure that promise is fulfilled.
For both of us.
We have suffered and been bound by the past too long, brother.
We deserve to start anew.
... Thank you.
Sister...
-gasp-
Thank you, Dani. Are you all right?
My pleasure, and yeah, I'm fine. But -whew- giving Tran a voice was like running a marathon!
Now, let's go. Don't want to keep anyone waiting...

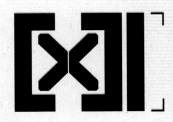

PSYCHIC RESCUE REPORT (FAILURE)

SUBJECTS: Karma (Xi'an Coy Manh), Tran Coy Manh

RELEVANT CONTEXT:

- Subjects are twin siblings who share a similar power set.

- Initial psychic bonding occurred during a conflict, in which Karma absorbed Tran's "life essence" in total.

- Tran gained influence over Karma for a time and succeeded in releasing his "soul" from her through magical interference.

- A secondary bonding incident occurred, through magical intervention involving Magik's soulsword.

- This bonding suppressed Tran's ability to influence Karma.

PROCEDURE(S): Psychic extraction

PARTICIPANTS: Karma [& Tran], Psylocke (Kwannon), Prestige (Rachel Summers), Marvel Girl (Jean Grey) & White Queen (Emma Frost) [in tandem], Professor X

ATTEMPTS: 4

PROCEDURE(S): Magical/soulsword extraction

PARTICIPANTS: Karma [& Tran], Magik (Illyana Rasputina)

ATTEMPTS: 1

NOTES: The connection forged through the power of the soulsword seems to have activated a reciprocal consciousness latch between the subjects, which cannot be undone while they are both alive. All attempts have resulted in failure. Pushing beyond would likely result in permanent psychic damage to all involved (and possibly anyone within a "blast" radius of a few miles).

Further, it appears that even though Magik's sword was involved in re-binding Tran to Karma, it cannot undo it.

That Cerebro reads the twins as separate entities is hopeful, however. Theoretically, with the proper attention and intention during the Resurrection process, separation **should** be possible, though there is a real possibility that the two will be changed permanently even if they are. Karma has been informed of this risk and has chosen to move forward with her plans for the Crucible.

May her faith in us be rewarded.

-- Professor X

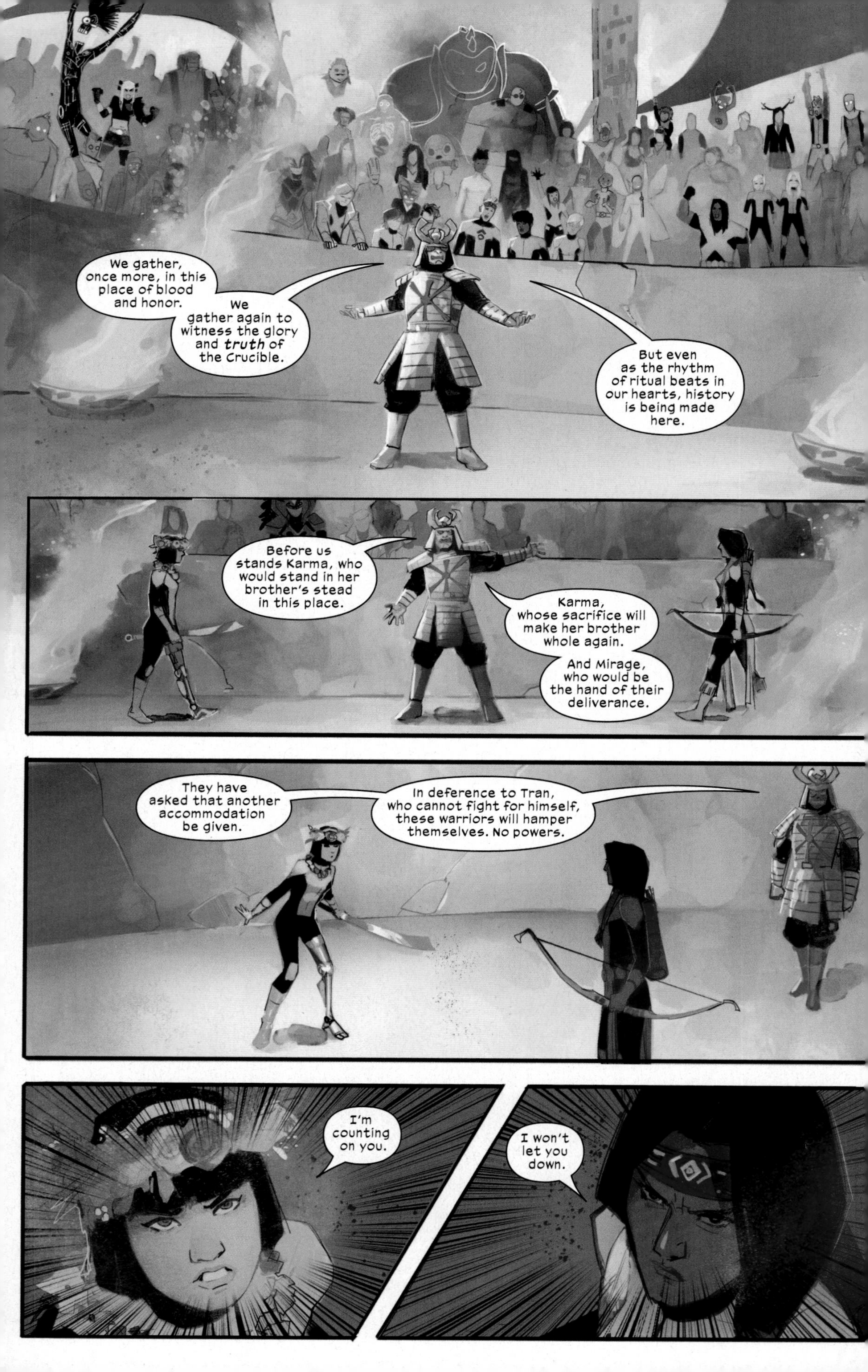
We gather, once more, in this place of blood and honor.
We gather again to witness the glory and *truth* of the Crucible.
But even as the rhythm of ritual beats in our hearts, history is being made here.
Before us stands Karma, who would stand in her brother's stead in this place.
Karma, whose sacrifice will make her brother whole again.
And Mirage, who would be the hand of their deliverance.
They have asked that another accommodation be given.
In deference to Tran, who cannot fight for himself, these warriors will hamper themselves. No powers.
I'm counting on you.
I won't let you down.

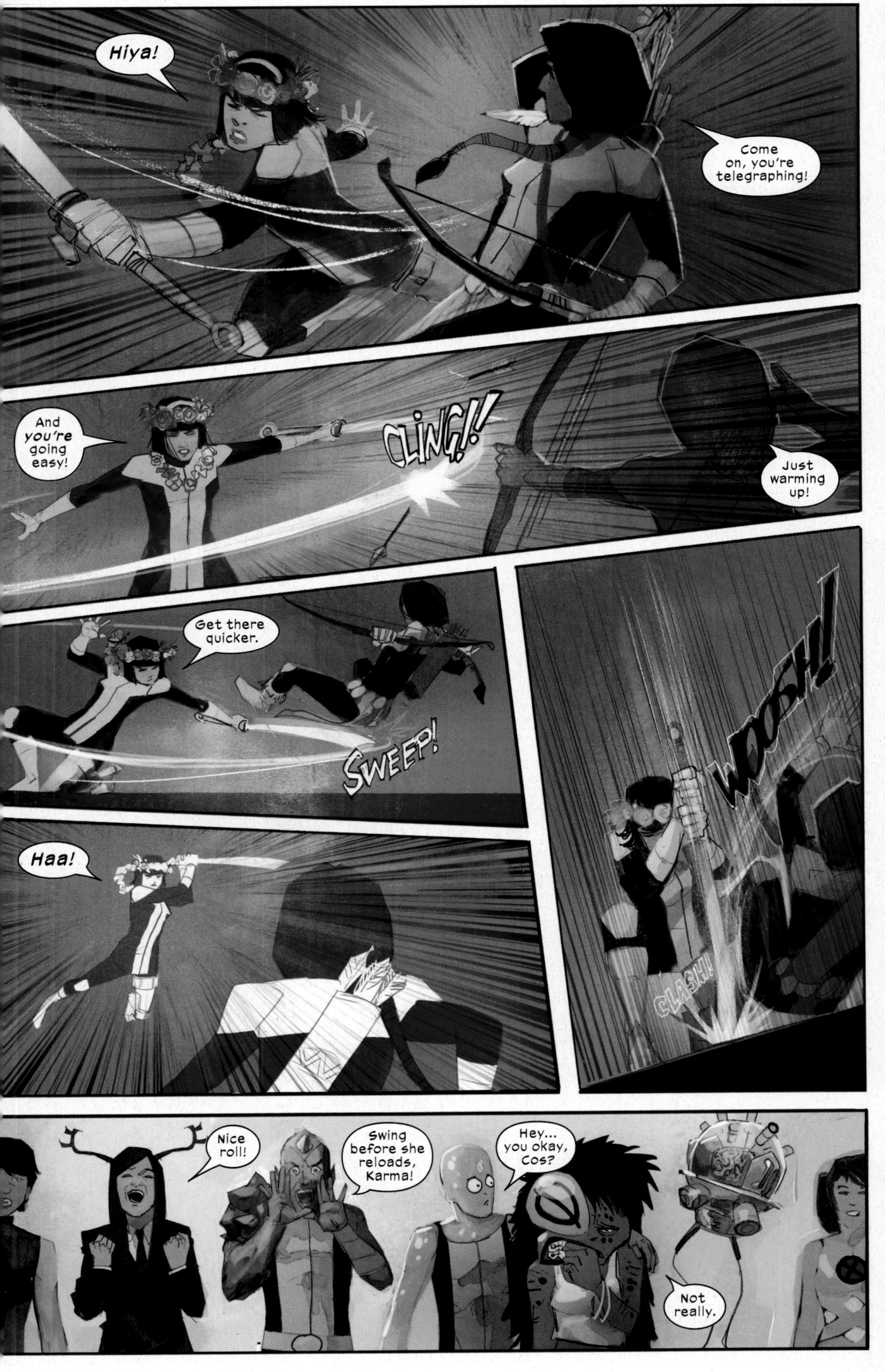
Hiya!
Come on, you're telegraphing!
And you're going easy!
CLING!!
Just warming up!
Get there quicker.
SWEEP!
WOOSH!
Haa!
CLASH!
Nice roll!
Swing before she reloads, Karma!
Hey... you okay, Cos?
Not really.

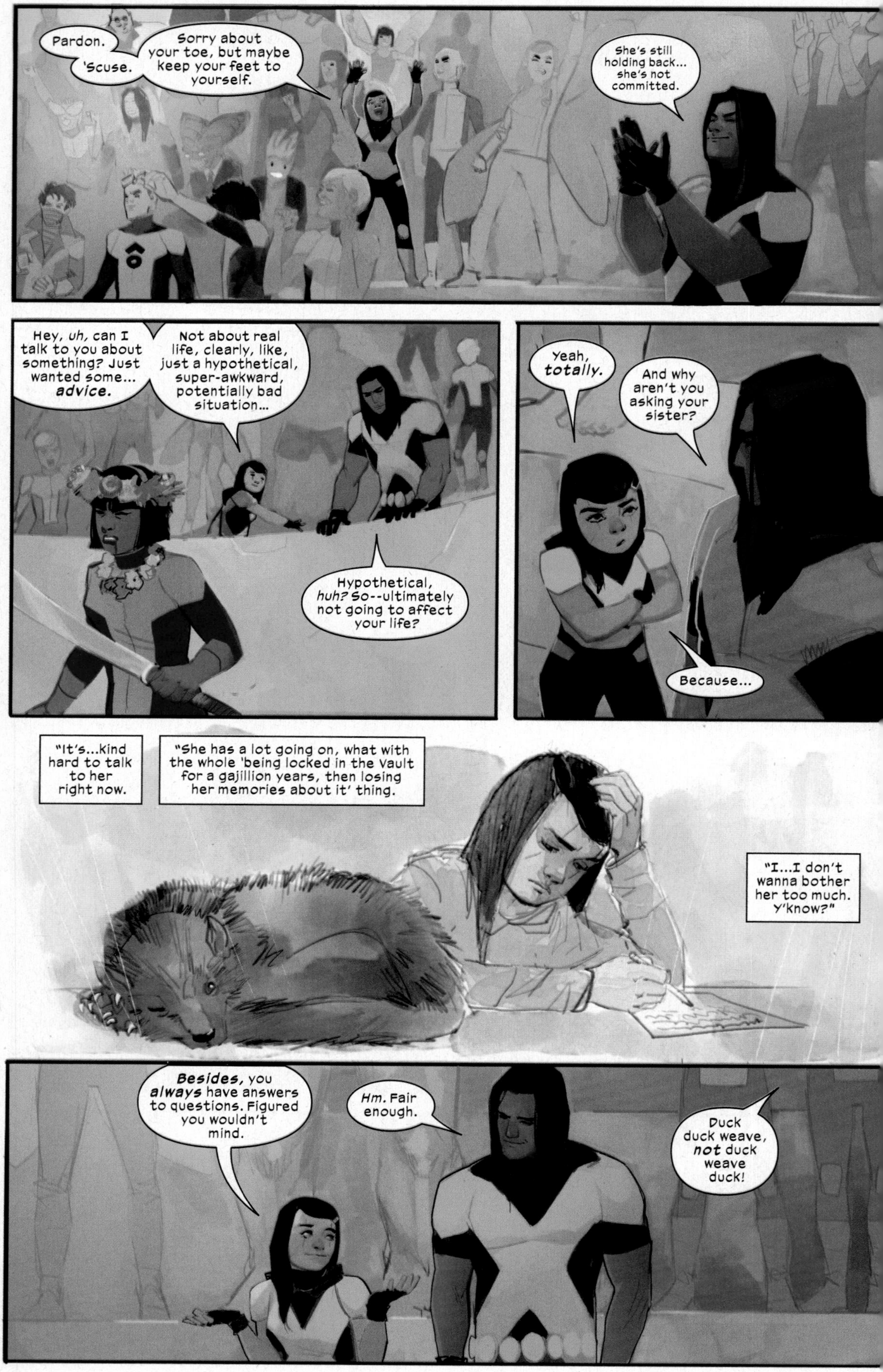
Pardon.
'Scuse.
Sorry about your toe, but maybe keep your feet to yourself.
She's still holding back... she's not committed.
Hey, *uh,* can I talk to you about something? Just wanted some... ***advice.***
Not about real life, clearly, like, just a hypothetical, super-awkward, potentially bad situation...
Hypothetical, *huh?* So--ultimately not going to affect your life?
Yeah, ***totally.***
And why aren't you asking your sister?
Because...
"It's...kind hard to talk to her right now.
"She has a lot going on, what with the whole 'being locked in the Vault for a gajillion years, then losing her memories about it' thing.
"I...I don't wanna bother her too much. Y'know?"
Besides, you ***always*** have answers to questions. Figured you wouldn't mind.
Hm. Fair enough.
Duck duck weave, ***not*** duck weave duck!

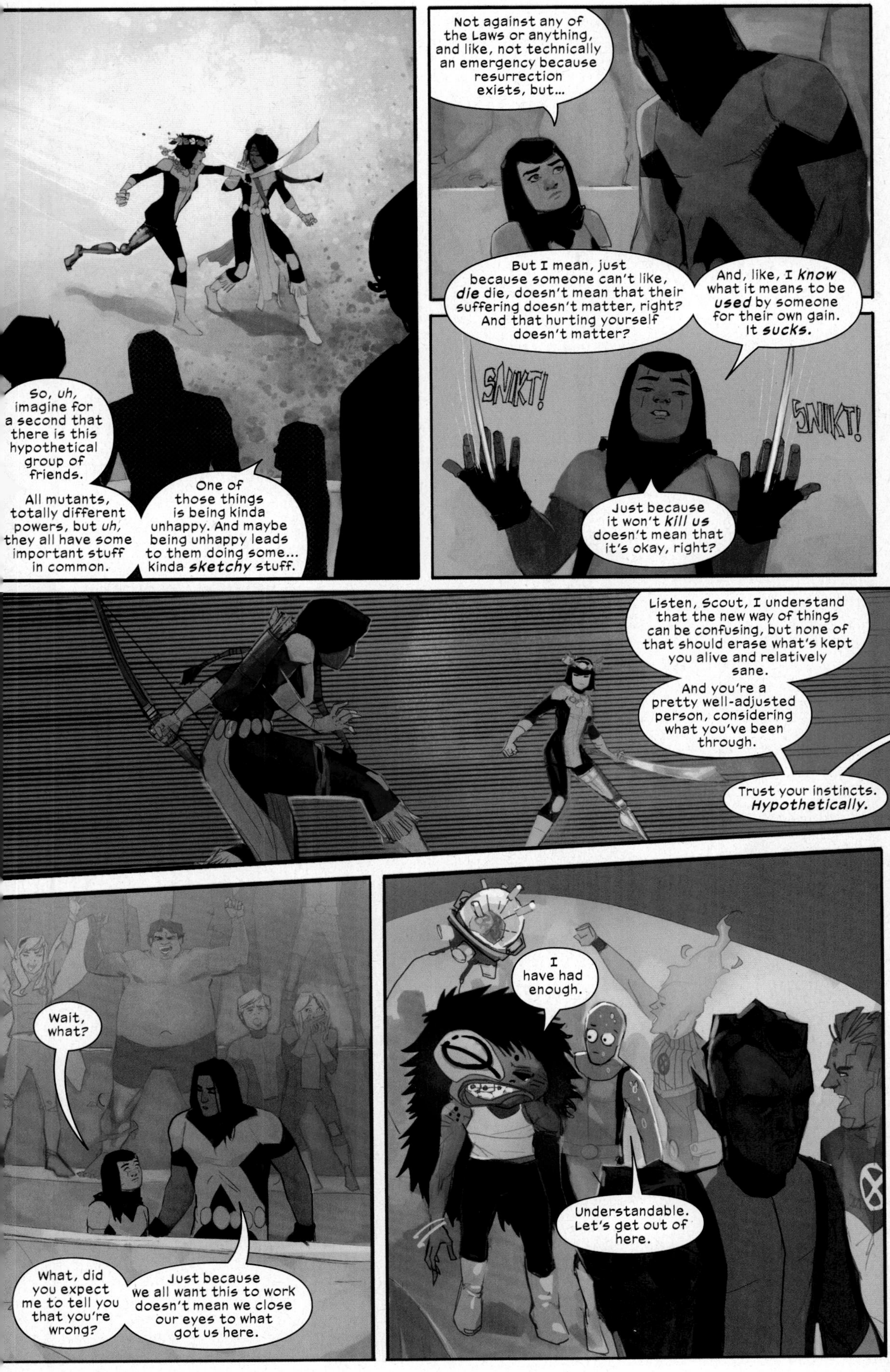

So, uh, imagine for a second that there is this hypothetical group of friends.
All mutants, totally different powers, but uh, they all have some important stuff in common.
One of those things is being kinda unhappy. And maybe being unhappy leads to them doing some... kinda sketchy stuff.
Not against any of the Laws or anything, and like, not technically an emergency because resurrection exists, but...
But I mean, just because someone can't like, die die, doesn't mean that their suffering doesn't matter, right? And that hurting yourself doesn't matter?
And, like, I know what it means to be used by someone for their own gain. It sucks.
SNIKT!
SNIKT!
Just because it won't kill us doesn't mean that it's okay, right?
Listen, Scout, I understand that the new way of things can be confusing, but none of that should erase what's kept you alive and relatively sane.
And you're a pretty well-adjusted person, considering what you've been through.
Trust your instincts. Hypothetically.
Wait, what?
What, did you expect me to tell you that you're wrong?
Just because we all want this to work doesn't mean we close our eyes to what got us here.
I have had enough.
Understandable. Let's get out of here.

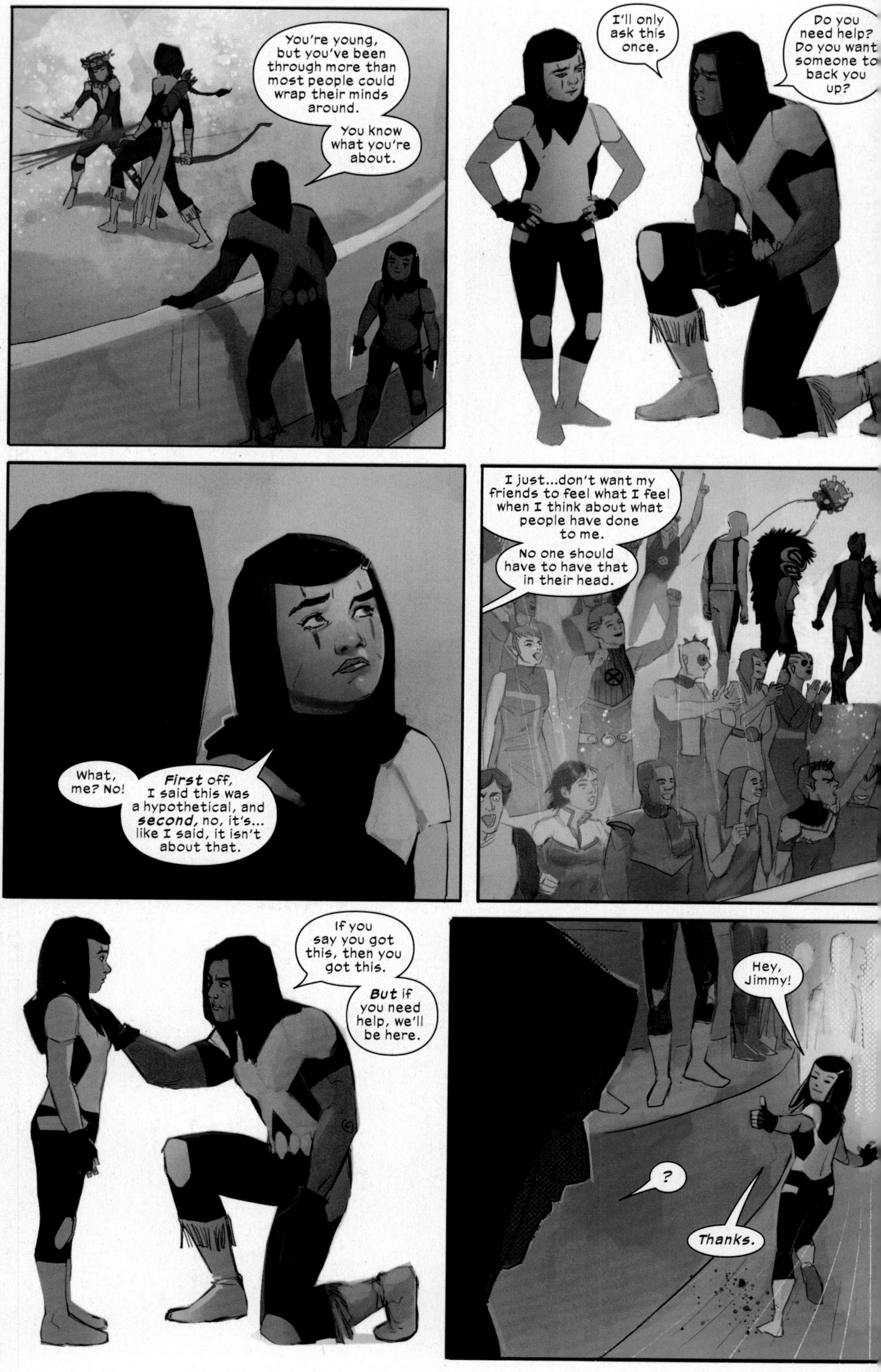
You're young, but you've been through more than most people could wrap their minds around.
You know what you're about.
I'll only ask this once.
Do you need help? Do you want someone to back you up?
What, me? No!
First off, I said this was a hypothetical, and second, no, it's... like I said, it isn't about that.
I just...don't want my friends to feel what I feel when I think about what people have done to me.
No one should have to have that in their head.
If you say you got this, then you got this.
But if you need help, we'll be here.
Hey, Jimmy!
?
Thanks.

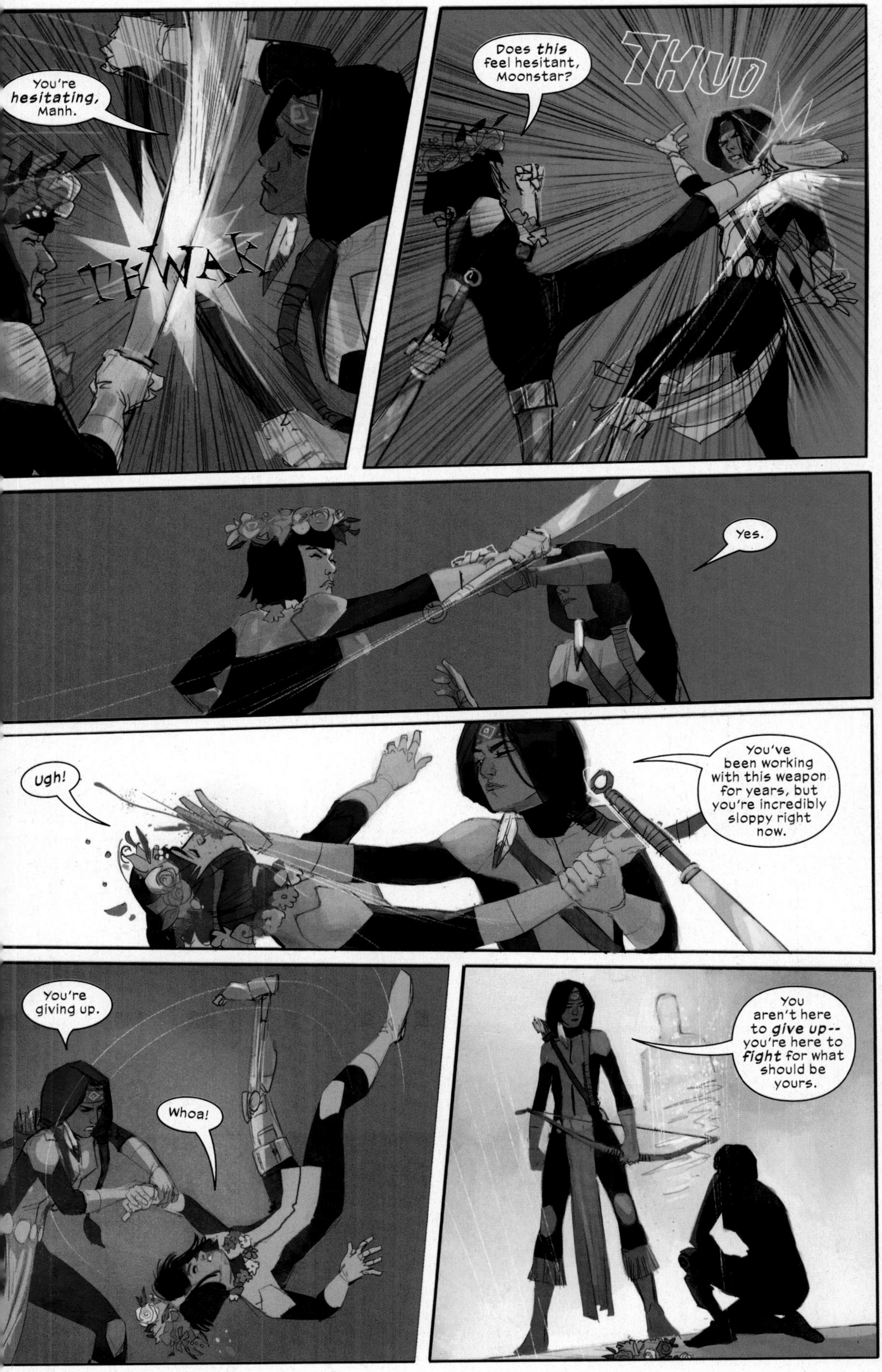
You're *hesitating,* Manh.
THWAK
Does *this* feel hesitant, Moonstar?
THUD
Yes.
Ugh!
You've been working with this weapon for years, but you're incredibly sloppy right now.
You're giving up.
Whoa!
You aren't here to *give up--* you're here to *fight* for what should be yours.

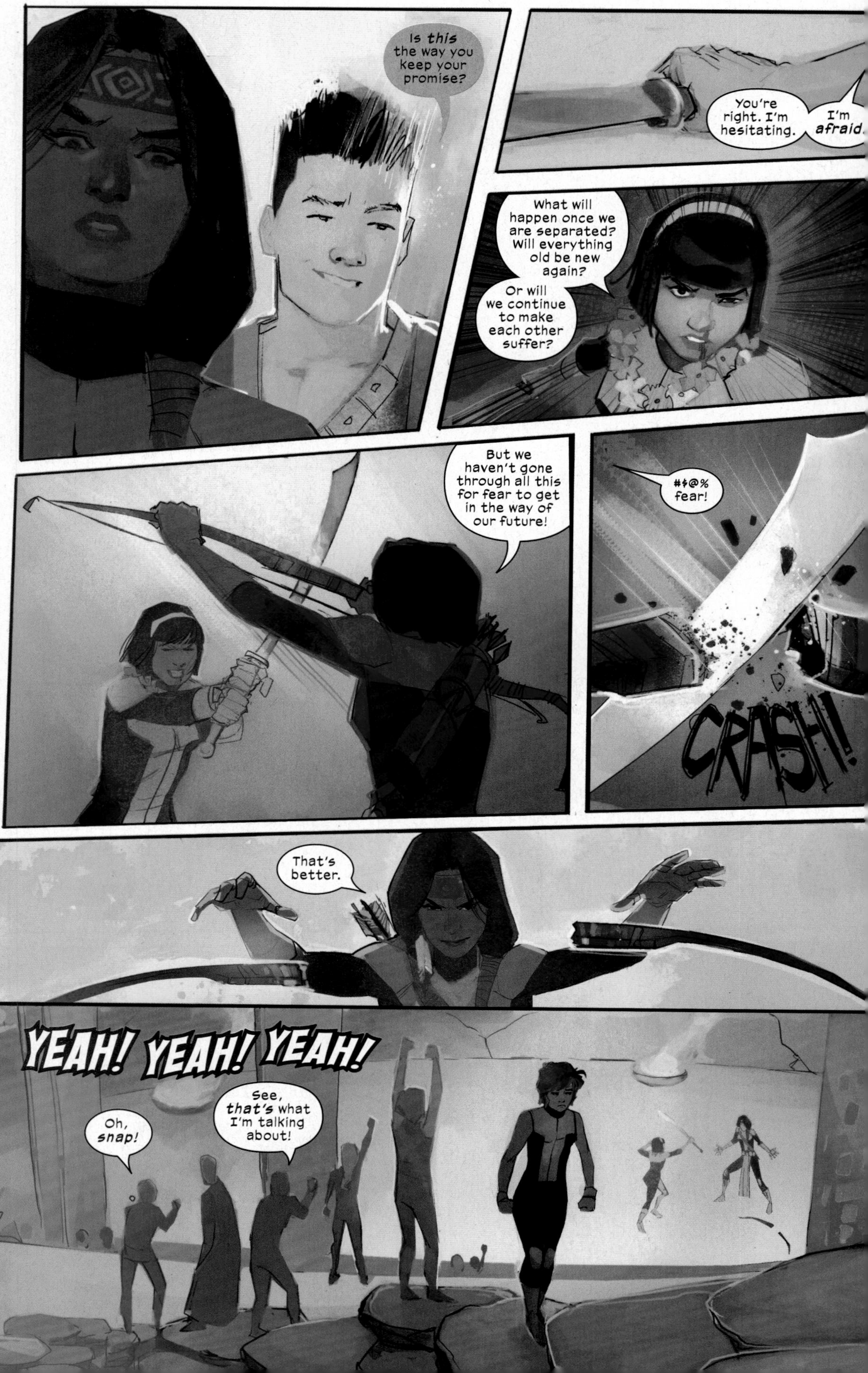

Is this the way you keep your promise?
You're right. I'm hesitating.
I'm afraid.
What will happen once we are separated? Will everything old be new again?
Or will we continue to make each other suffer?
But we haven't gone through all this for fear to get in the way of our future!
#$@% fear!
CRASH!
That's better.
YEAH! YEAH! YEAH!
Oh, snap!
See, that's what I'm talking about!

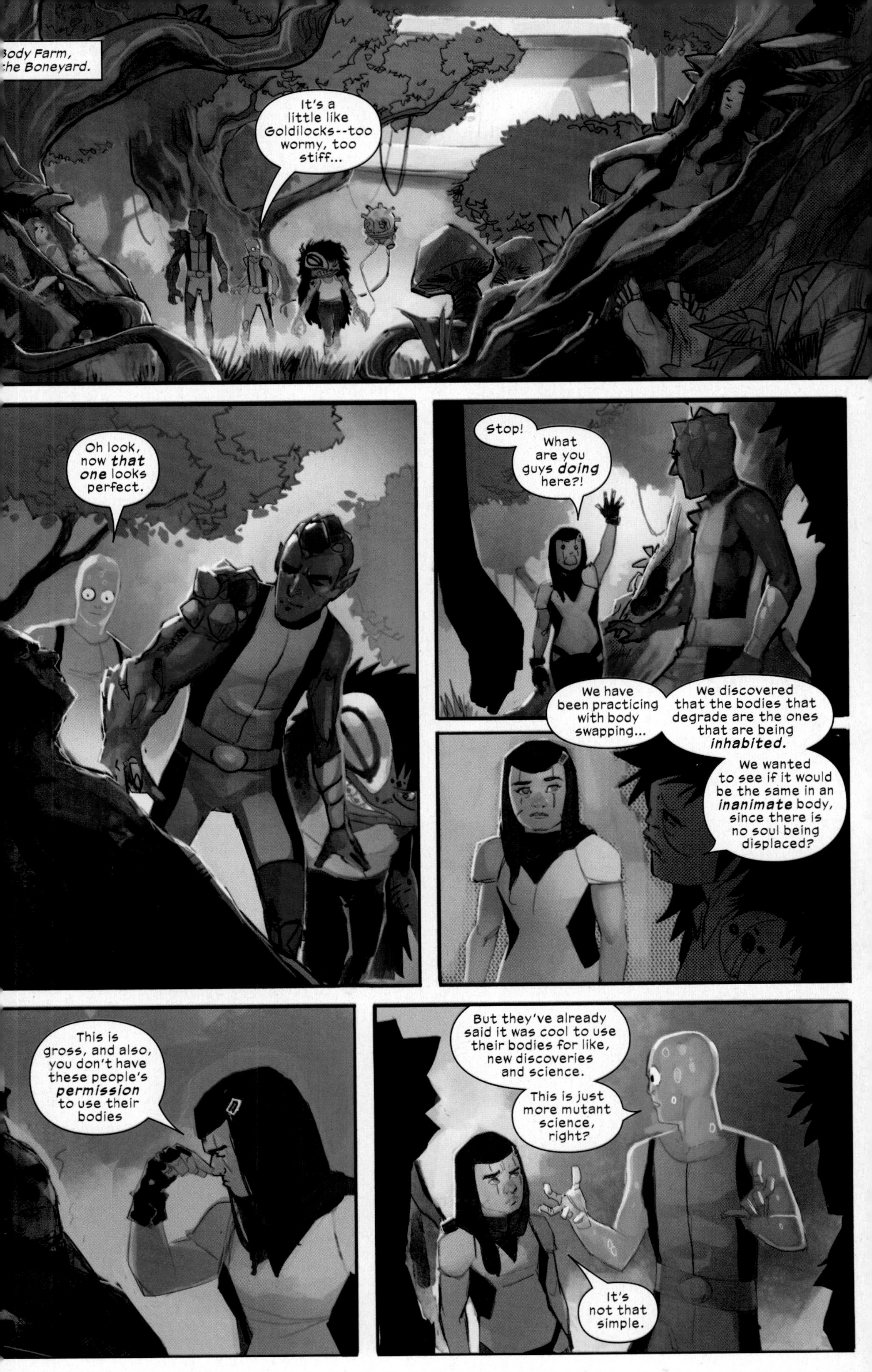
Body Farm, the Boneyard.
It's a little like Goldilocks--too wormy, too stiff...
Oh look, now *that one* looks perfect.
Stop! What are you guys *doing* here?!
We have been practicing with body swapping...
We discovered that the bodies that degrade are the ones that are being *inhabited.*
We wanted to see if it would be the same in an *inanimate* body, since there is no soul being displaced?
This is gross, and also, you don't have these people's *permission* to use their bodies
But they've already said it was cool to use their bodies for like, new discoveries and science.
This is just more mutant science, right?
It's not that simple.

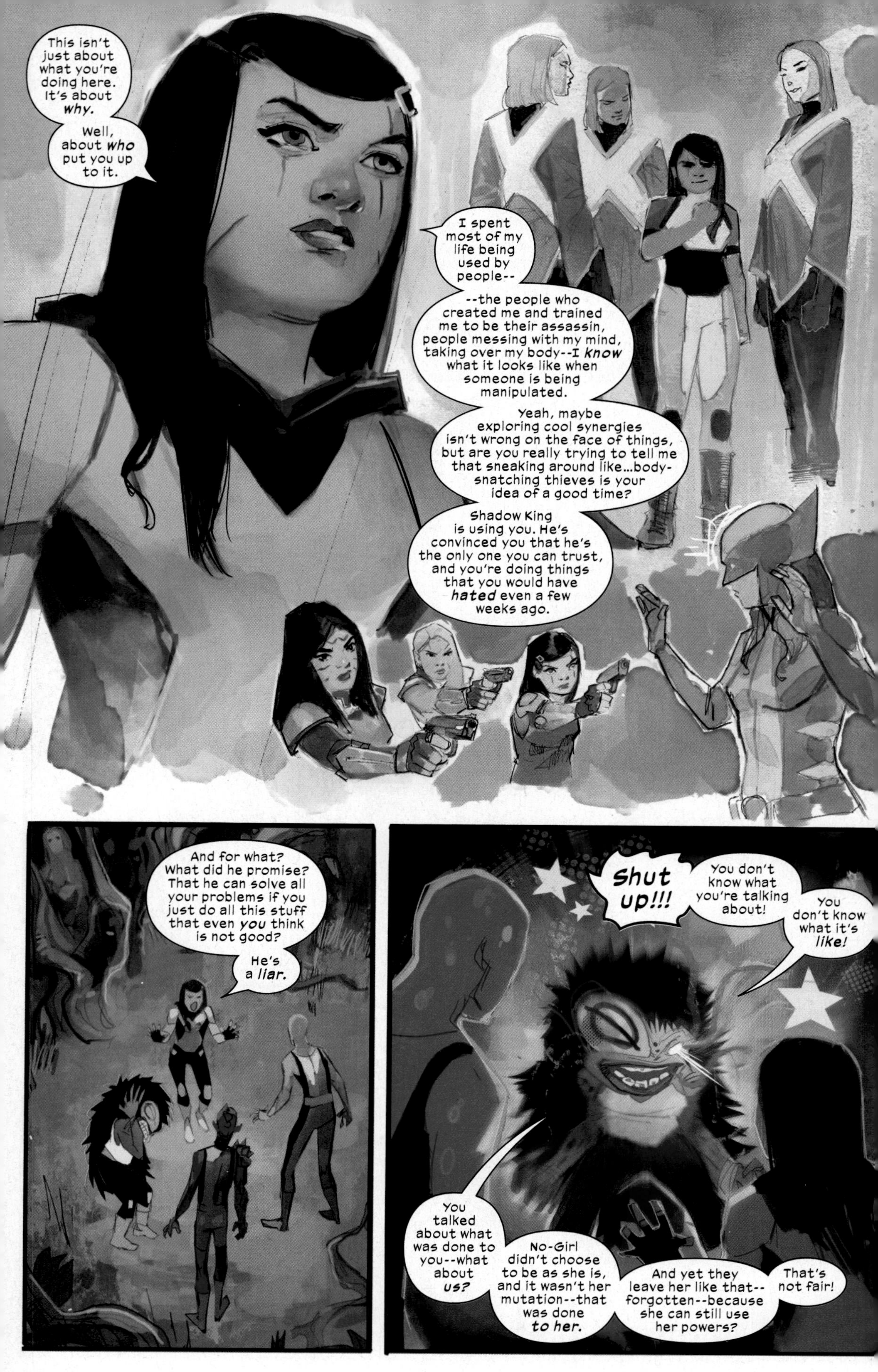
This isn't just about what you're doing here. It's about *why.*
Well, about *who* put you up to it.
I spent most of my life being used by people--
--the people who created me and trained me to be their assassin, people messing with my mind, taking over my body--I *know* what it looks like when someone is being manipulated.
Yeah, maybe exploring cool synergies isn't wrong on the face of things, but are you really trying to tell me that sneaking around like...body-snatching thieves is your idea of a good time?
Shadow King is using you. He's convinced you that he's the only one you can trust, and you're doing things that you would have *hated* even a few weeks ago.
And for what? What did he promise? That he can solve all your problems if you just do all this stuff that even *you* think is not good?
He's a *liar.*
Shut up!!!
You don't know what you're talking about!
You don't know what it's *like!*
You talked about what was done to you--what about *us?*
No-Girl didn't choose to be as she is, and it wasn't her mutation--that was done *to her.*
And yet they leave her like that--forgotten--because she can still use her powers?
That's not fair!

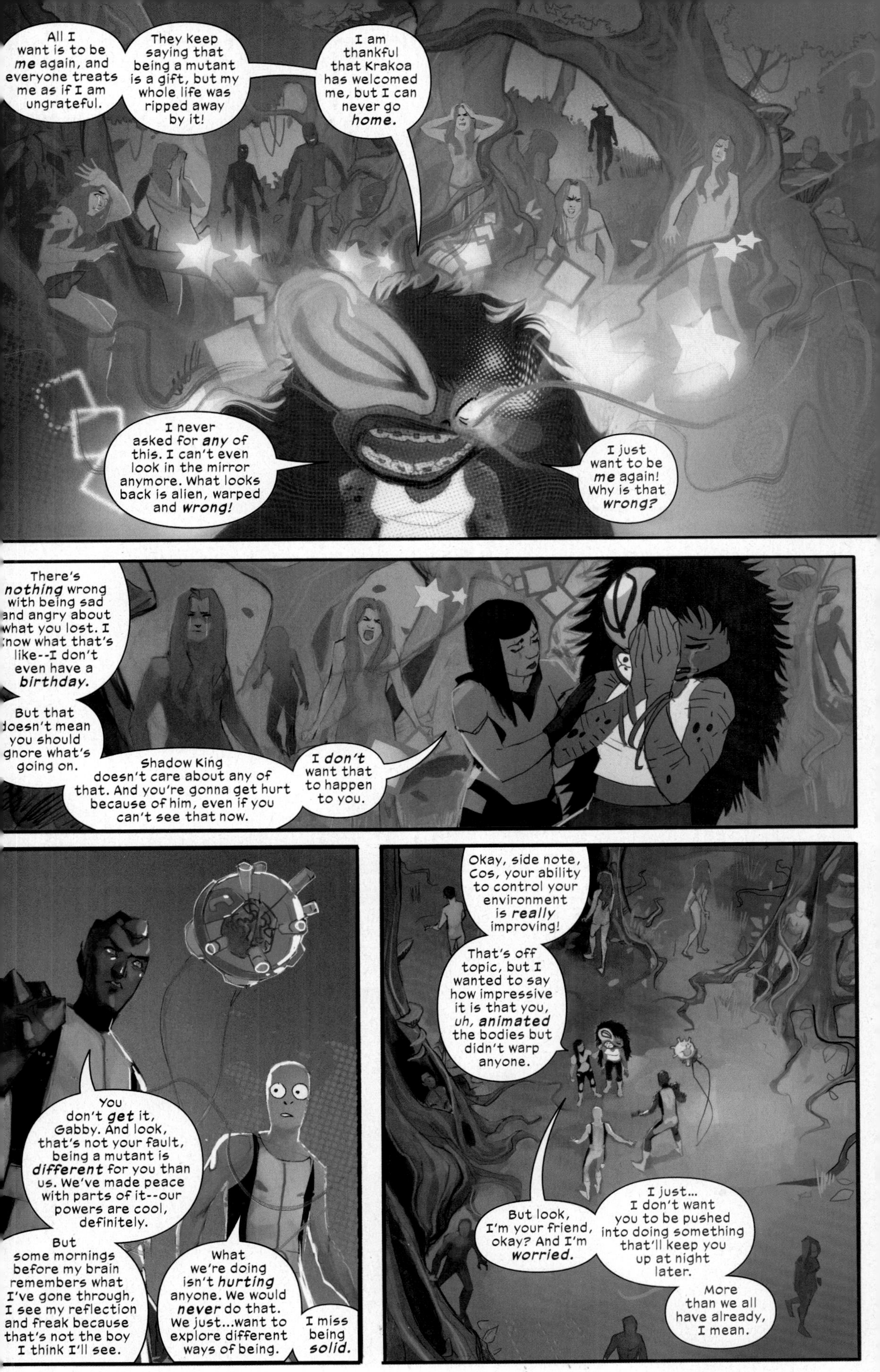
All I want is to be me again, and everyone treats me as if I am ungrateful.
They keep saying that being a mutant is a gift, but my whole life was ripped away by it!
I am thankful that Krakoa has welcomed me, but I can never go home.
I never asked for any of this. I can't even look in the mirror anymore. What looks back is alien, warped and wrong!
I just want to be me again! Why is that wrong?
There's nothing wrong with being sad and angry about what you lost. I know what that's like--I don't even have a birthday.
But that doesn't mean you should ignore what's going on.
Shadow King doesn't care about any of that. And you're gonna get hurt because of him, even if you can't see that now.
I don't want that to happen to you.
You don't get it, Gabby. And look, that's not your fault, being a mutant is different for you than us. We've made peace with parts of it--our powers are cool, definitely.
But some mornings before my brain remembers what I've gone through, I see my reflection and freak because that's not the boy I think I'll see.
What we're doing isn't hurting anyone. We would never do that. We just...want to explore different ways of being.
I miss being solid.
Okay, side note, Cos, your ability to control your environment is really improving!
That's off topic, but I wanted to say how impressive it is that you, uh, animated the bodies but didn't warp anyone.
But look, I'm your friend, okay? And I'm worried.
I just... I don't want you to be pushed into doing something that'll keep you up at night later.
More than we all have already, I mean.

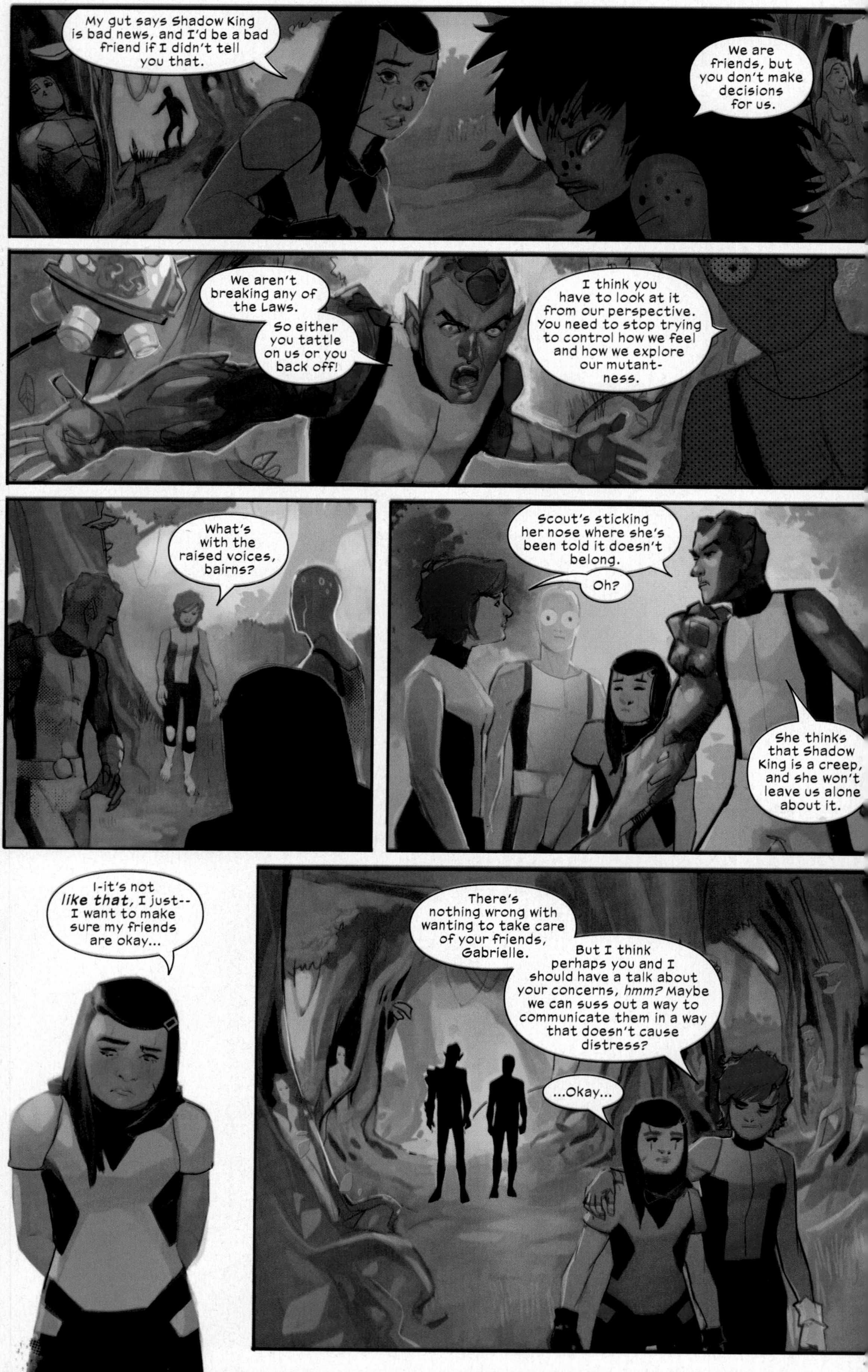
My gut says Shadow King is bad news, and I'd be a bad friend if I didn't tell you that.
We are friends, but you don't make decisions for us.
We aren't breaking any of the Laws.
So either you tattle on us or you back off!
I think you have to look at it from our perspective. You need to stop trying to control how we feel and how we explore our mutant-ness.
What's with the raised voices, bairns?
Scout's sticking her nose where she's been told it doesn't belong.
Oh?
She thinks that Shadow King is a creep, and she won't leave us alone about it.
I-it's not *like that,* I just-- I want to make sure my friends are okay...
There's nothing wrong with wanting to take care of your friends, Gabrielle.
But I think perhaps you and I should have a talk about your concerns, *hmm?* Maybe we can suss out a way to communicate them in a way that doesn't cause distress?
...Okay...

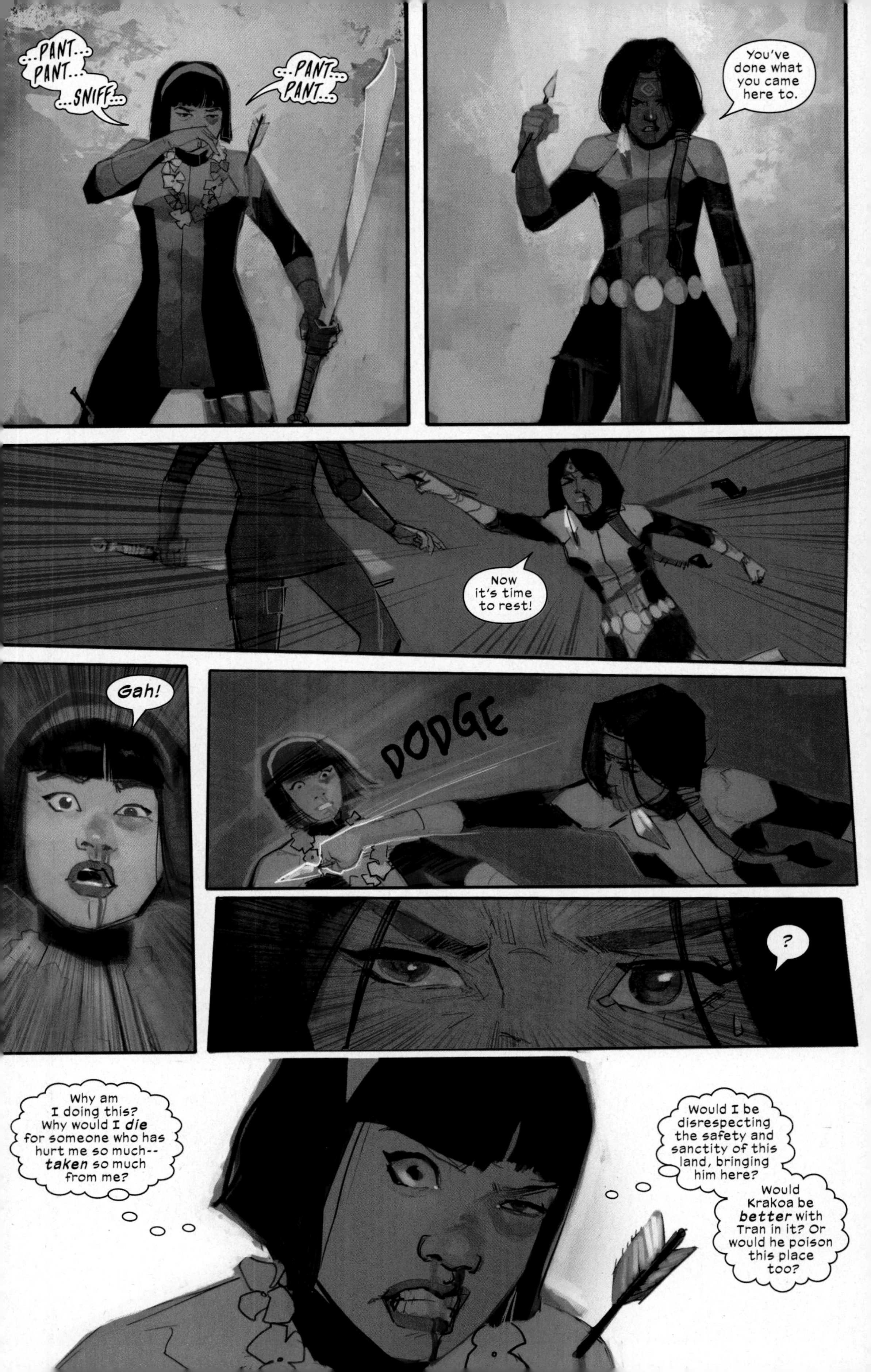
...PANT... PANT... ...SNIFF...
...PANT... PANT...
You've done what you came here to.
Now it's time to rest!
Gah!
DODGE
?
Why am I doing this? Why would I *die* for someone who has hurt me so much-- *taken* so much from me?
Would I be disrespecting the safety and sanctity of this land, bringing him here?
Would Krakoa be *better* with Tran in it? Or would he poison this place too?

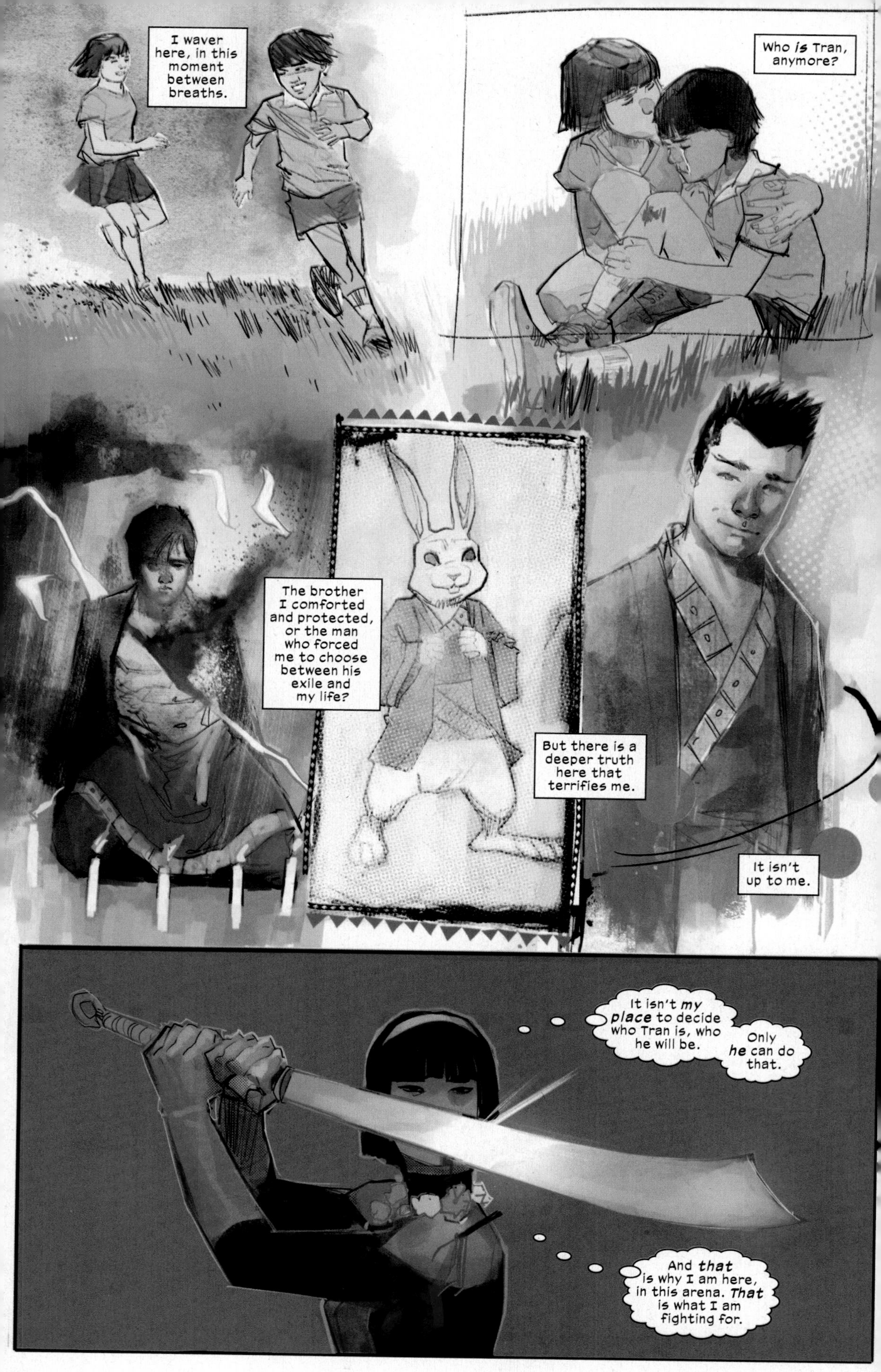
I waver here, in this moment between breaths.
Who *is* Tran, anymore?
The brother I comforted and protected, or the man who forced me to choose between his exile and my life?
But there is a deeper truth here that terrifies me.
It isn't up to me.
It isn't *my place* to decide who Tran is, who he will be.
Only *he* can do that.
And *that* is why I am here, in this arena. *That* is what I am fighting for.

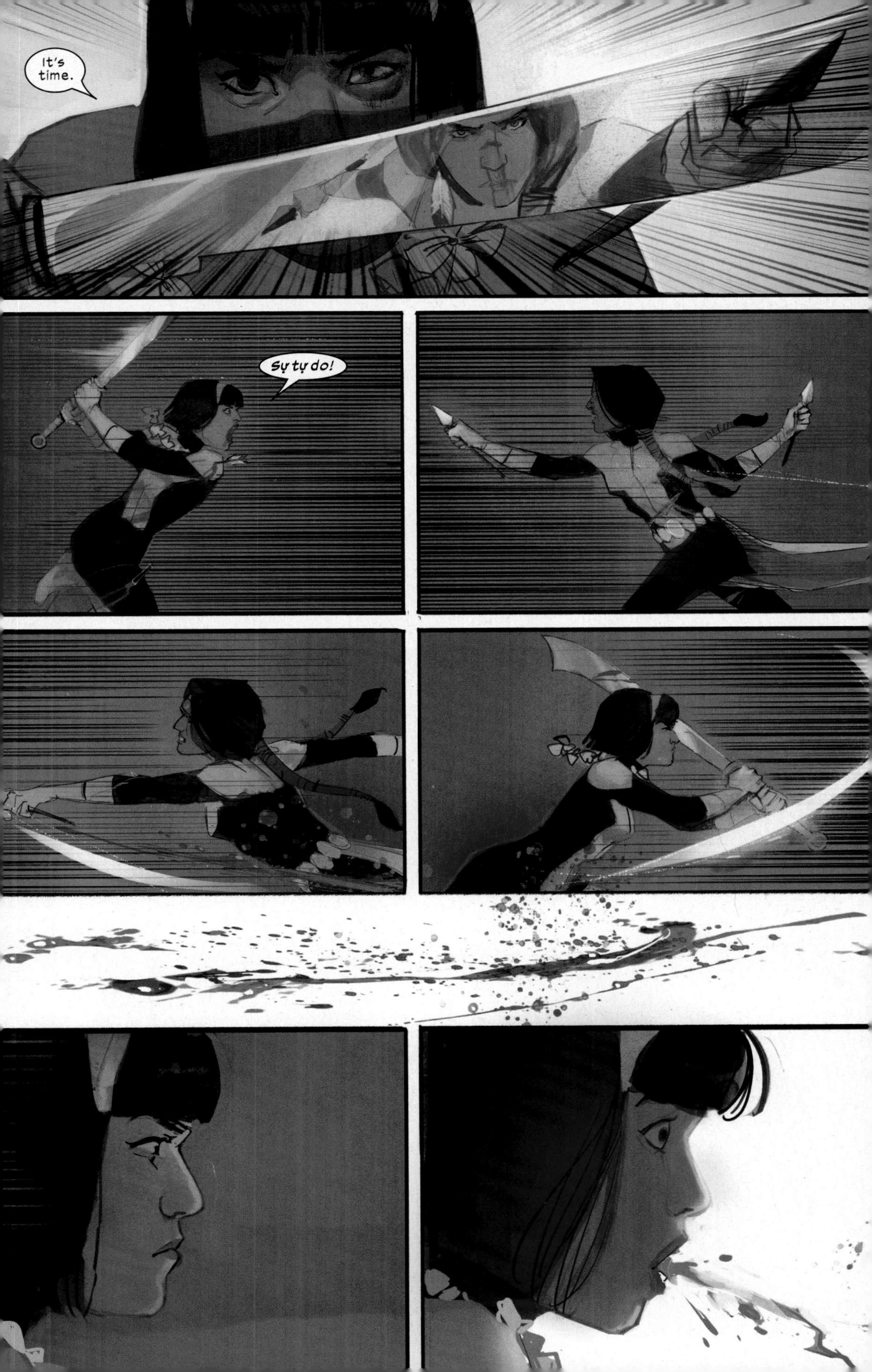
It's time.
Sự tự do!

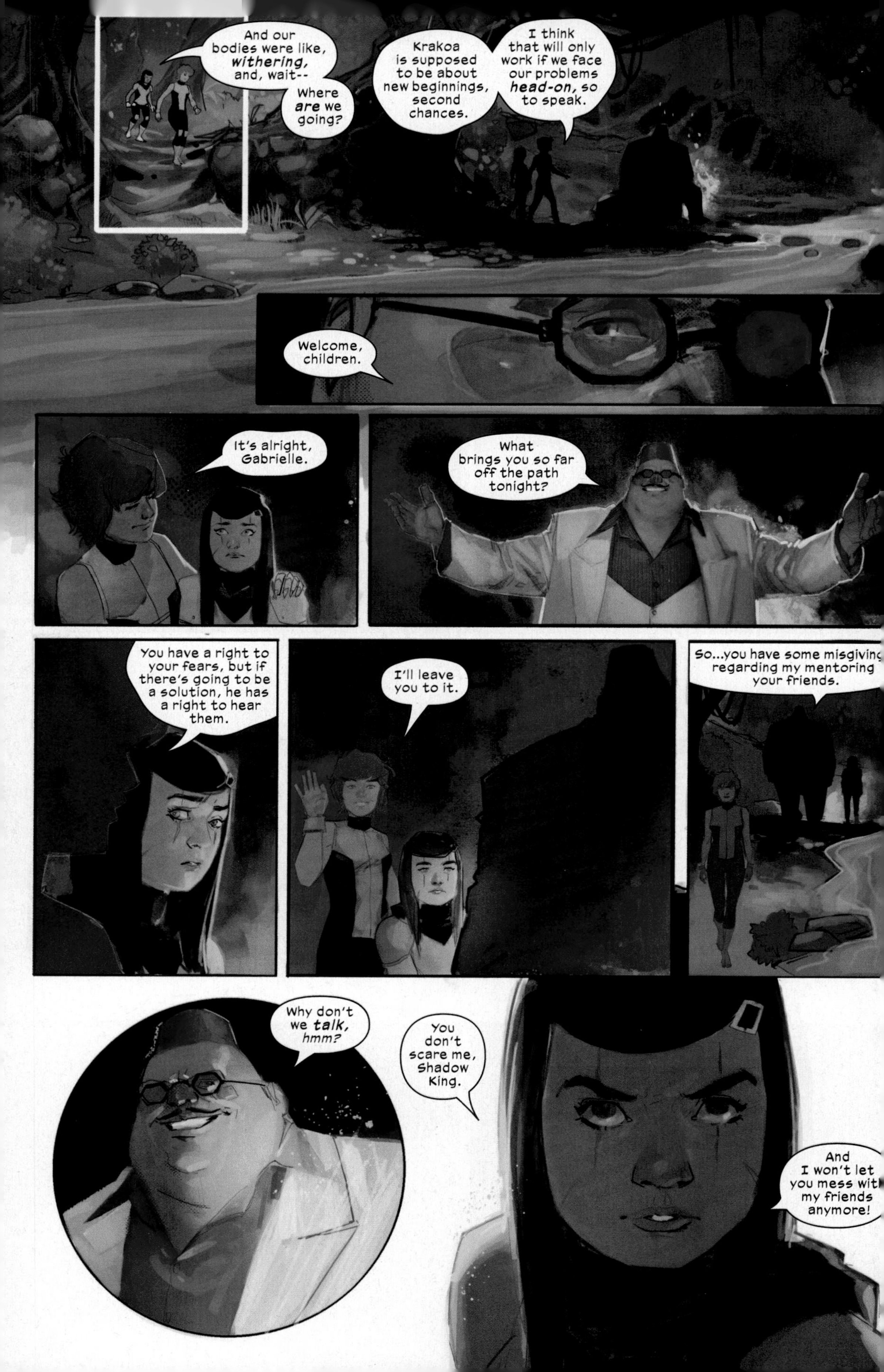
And our bodies were like, *withering,* and, wait--
Where *are* we going?
Krakoa is supposed to be about new beginnings, second chances.
I think that will only work if we face our problems *head-on,* so to speak.
Welcome, children.
It's alright, Gabrielle.
What brings you so far off the path tonight?
You have a right to your fears, but if there's going to be a solution, he has a right to hear them.
I'll leave you to it.
So...you have some misgiving regarding my mentoring your friends.
Why don't we *talk,* hmm?
You don't scare me, Shadow King.
And I won't let you mess wit my friends anymore!

[ACTION....[quietc]_00]
[REPORT....[ouncil]_18]

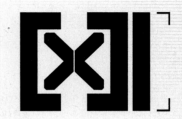

(NON) ACTION REPORT TO THE QUIET COUNCIL

I'll make this quick.

When we came to you with concern about how dangerous the bored mutants running around the island were, you turned it around pretty masterfully and made it our problem to handle. I was ~~butter~~bitter at first, but I'll admit, it turned out to be a smart move--the people on the ground seeing the issue will have a better idea of how to fix it.

But the thing is, we were raised by you. We got our understanding of what it means to be mutants -- of how to deal with the world and each other -- from you. So we ~~appraoched~~ approached the problem like you would.

And we were wrong.

It's not enough to train mutants to "use their powers ~~efficiantgly~~ ~~efficiantly~~ efficiently" and how to fight. These people aren't soldiers or an army, they are supposed to be citizens in a new nation (that already has a pretty well-developed defensive force).

These people (half of them kids) don't need to learn how to kill, they need purpose. They need to feel like they are contributing meaningfully to their new society. They need to feel like a community.

So you're going to start getting requests for more resources, equipment, etc. Jimmy and I are developing a new program, not centered around making child soldiers. Expect some "field trip" requests too.

You ~~gavae~~ gave us this job so that we could do better than you would. So we will.

-- Magik

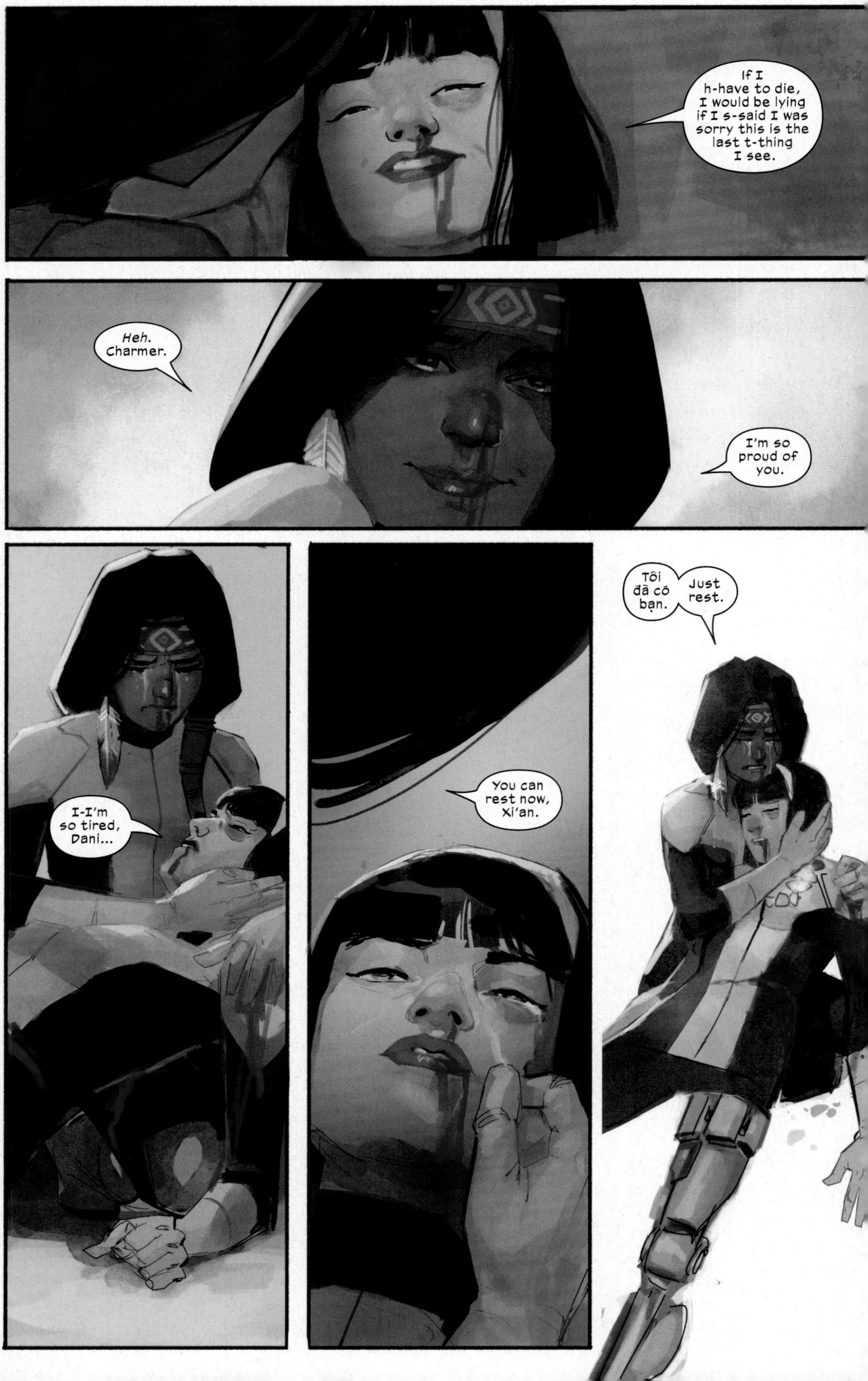
If I h-have to die, I would be lying if I s-said I was sorry this is the last t-thing I see.
Heh. Charmer.
I'm so proud of you.
I-I'm so tired, Dani...
You can rest now, Xi'an.
Tôi đã có bạn.
Just rest.

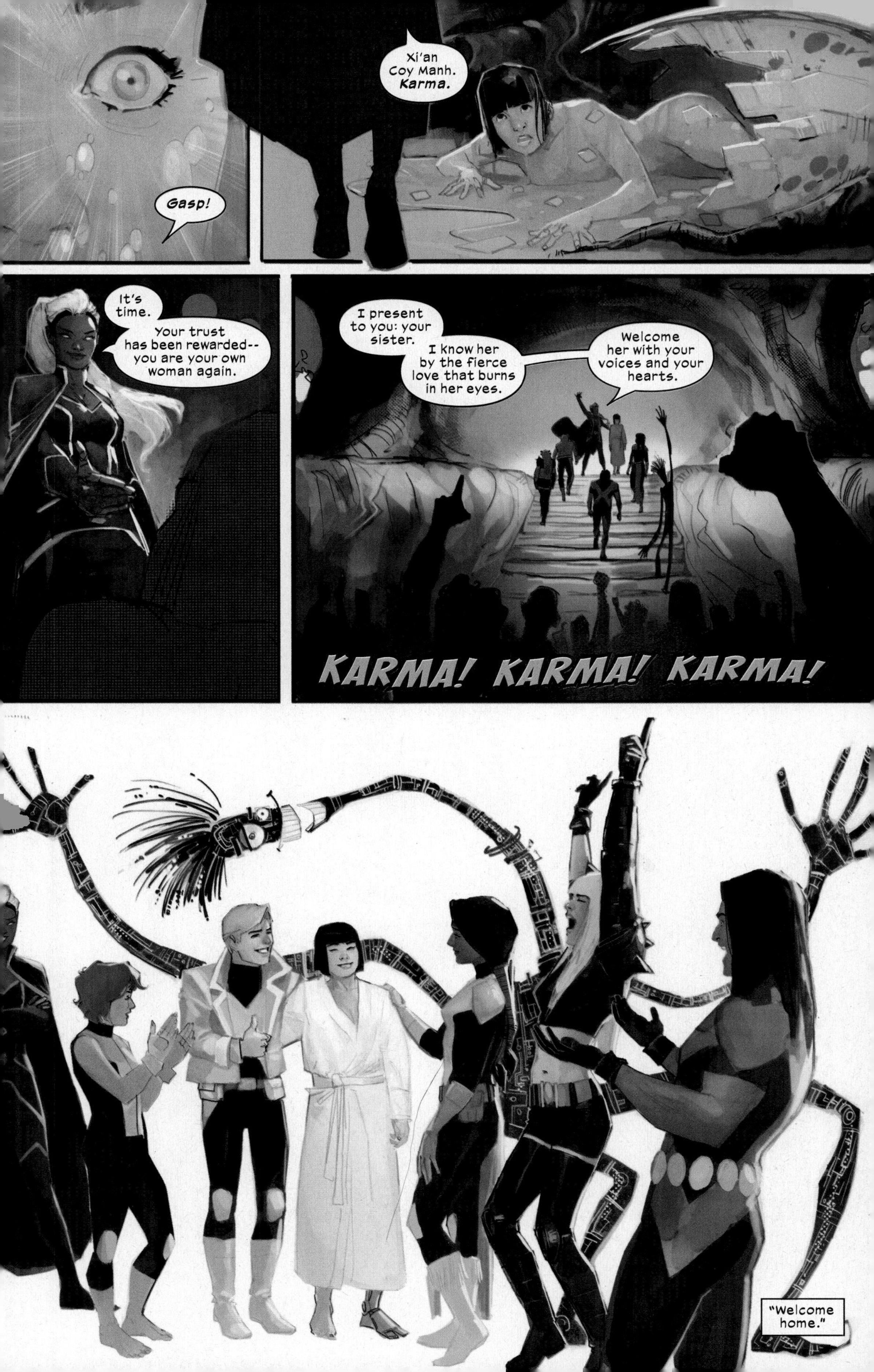
Gasp!
Xi'an Coy Manh. Karma.
It's time.
Your trust has been rewarded-- you are your own woman again.
I present to you: your sister.
I know her by the fierce love that burns in her eyes.
Welcome her with your voices and your hearts.
KARMA! KARMA! KARMA!
"Welcome home."

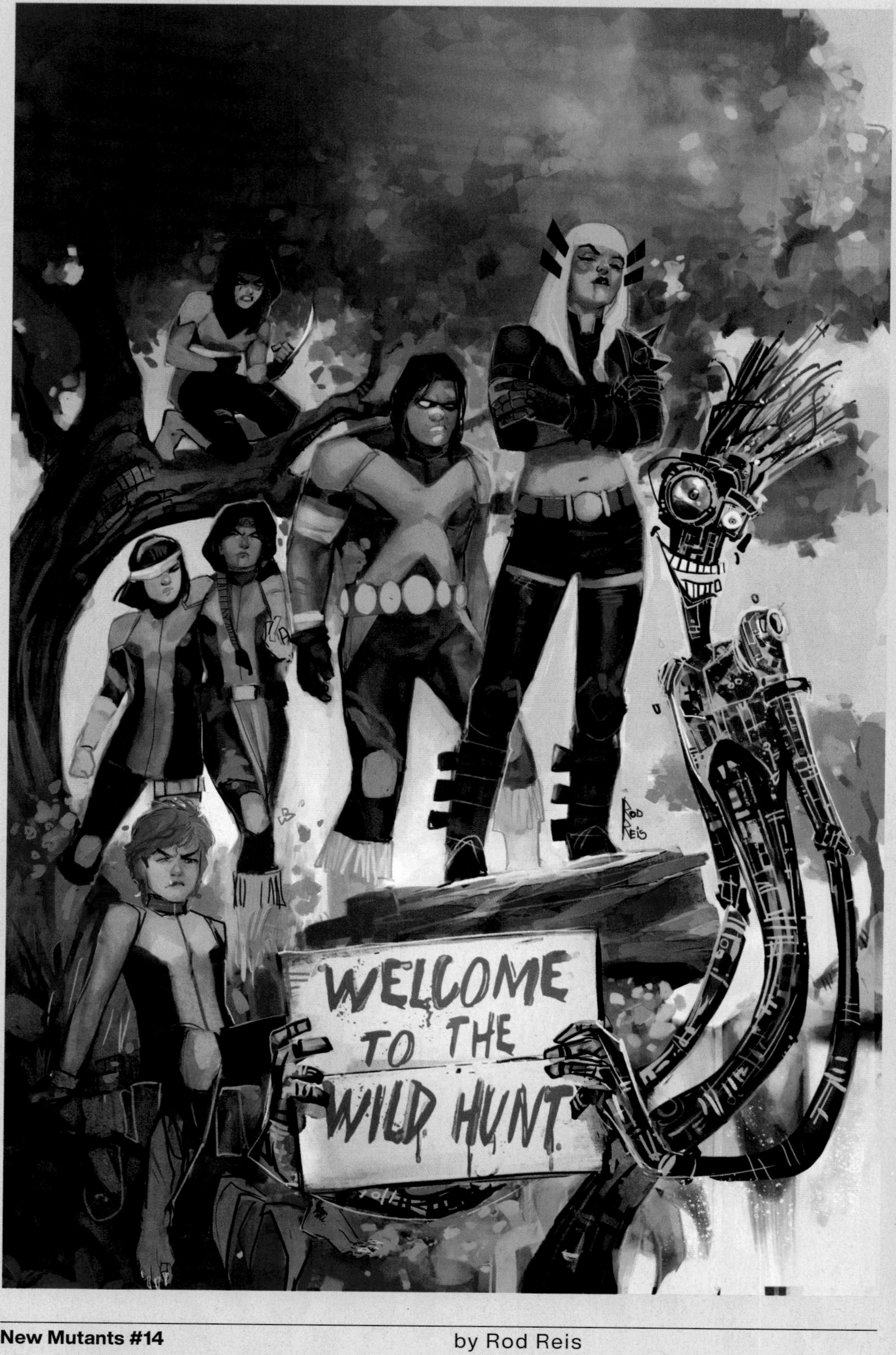
WELCOME TO THE WILD HUNT
ROD REIS

New Mutants #14 by Rod Reis

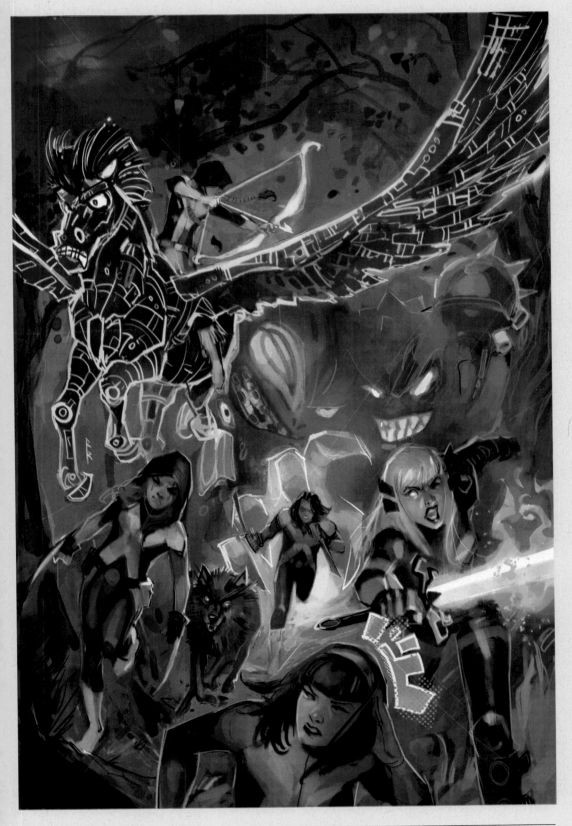

New Mutants #15   by Rod Reis

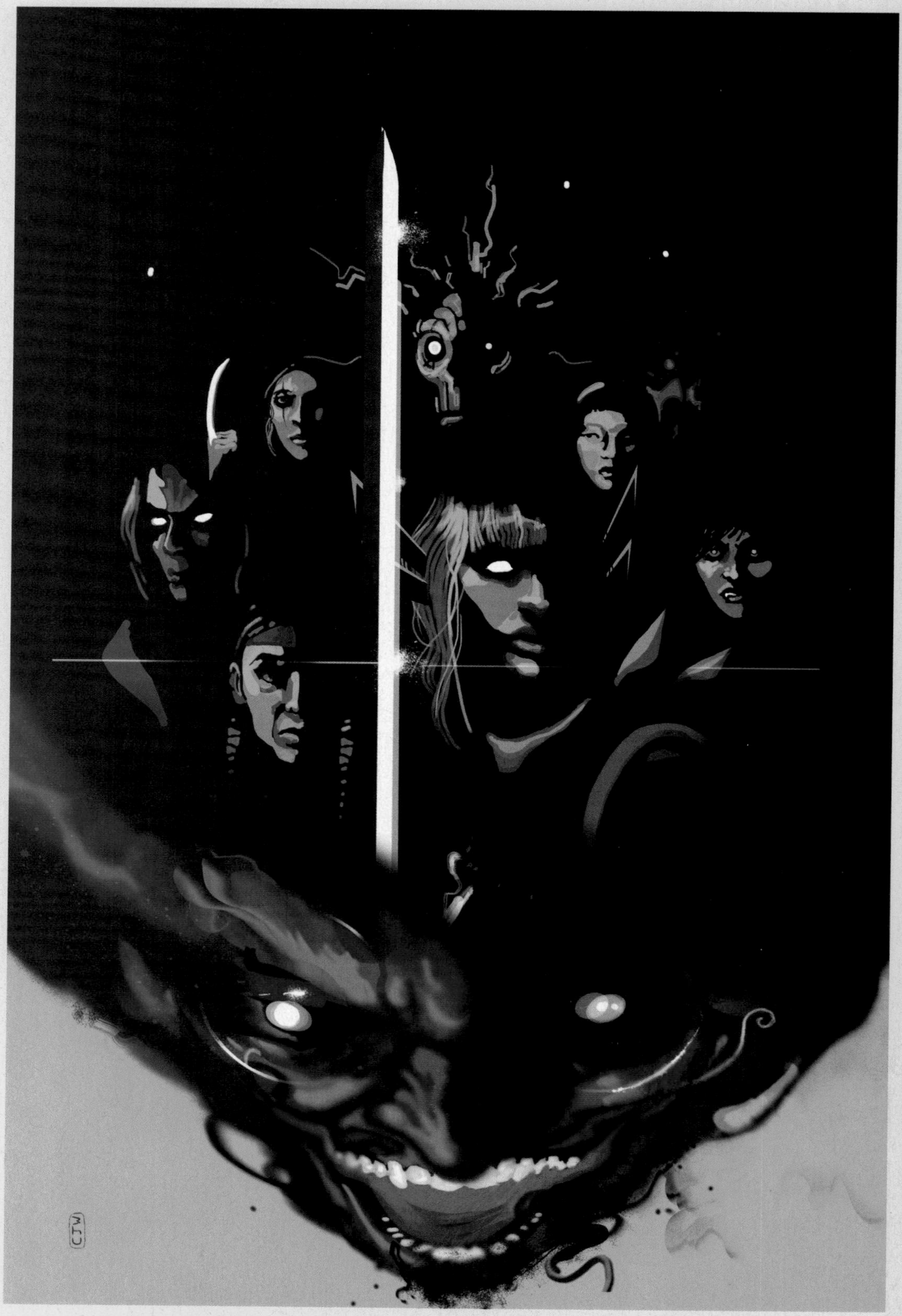

New Mutants #16 by Christian Ward

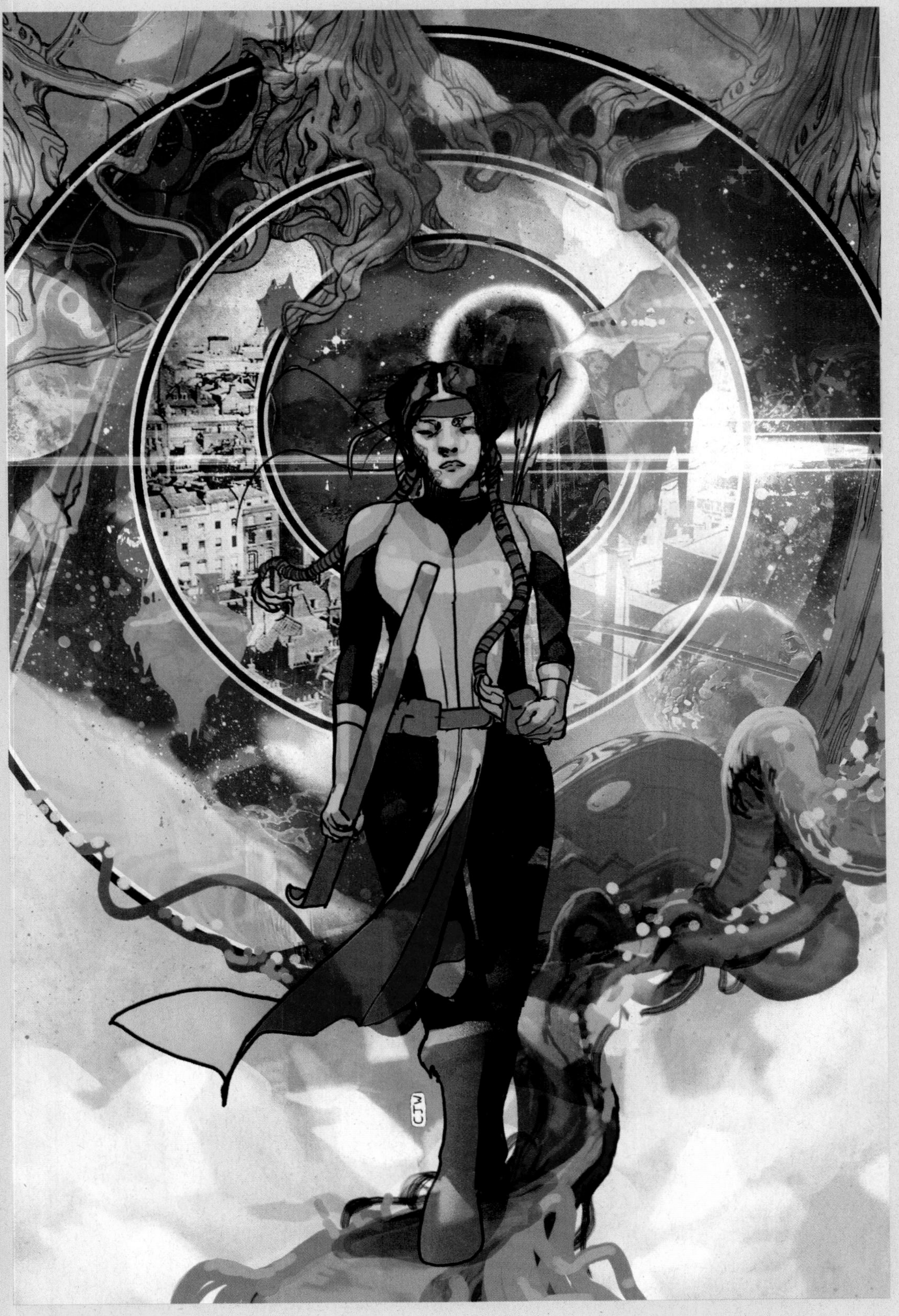
CJW

New Mutants #17 by Christian Ward

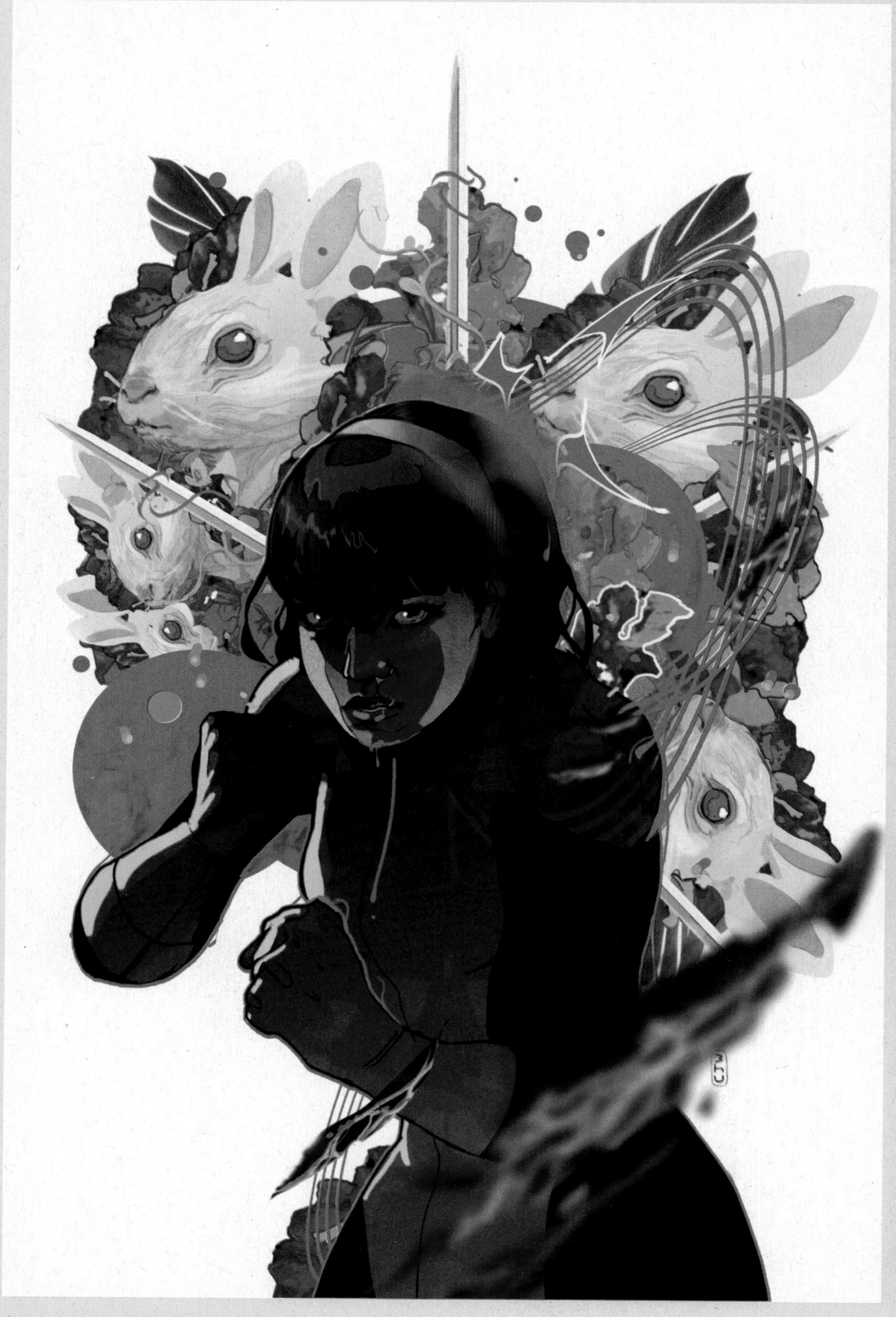

New Mutants #18 by Christian Ward

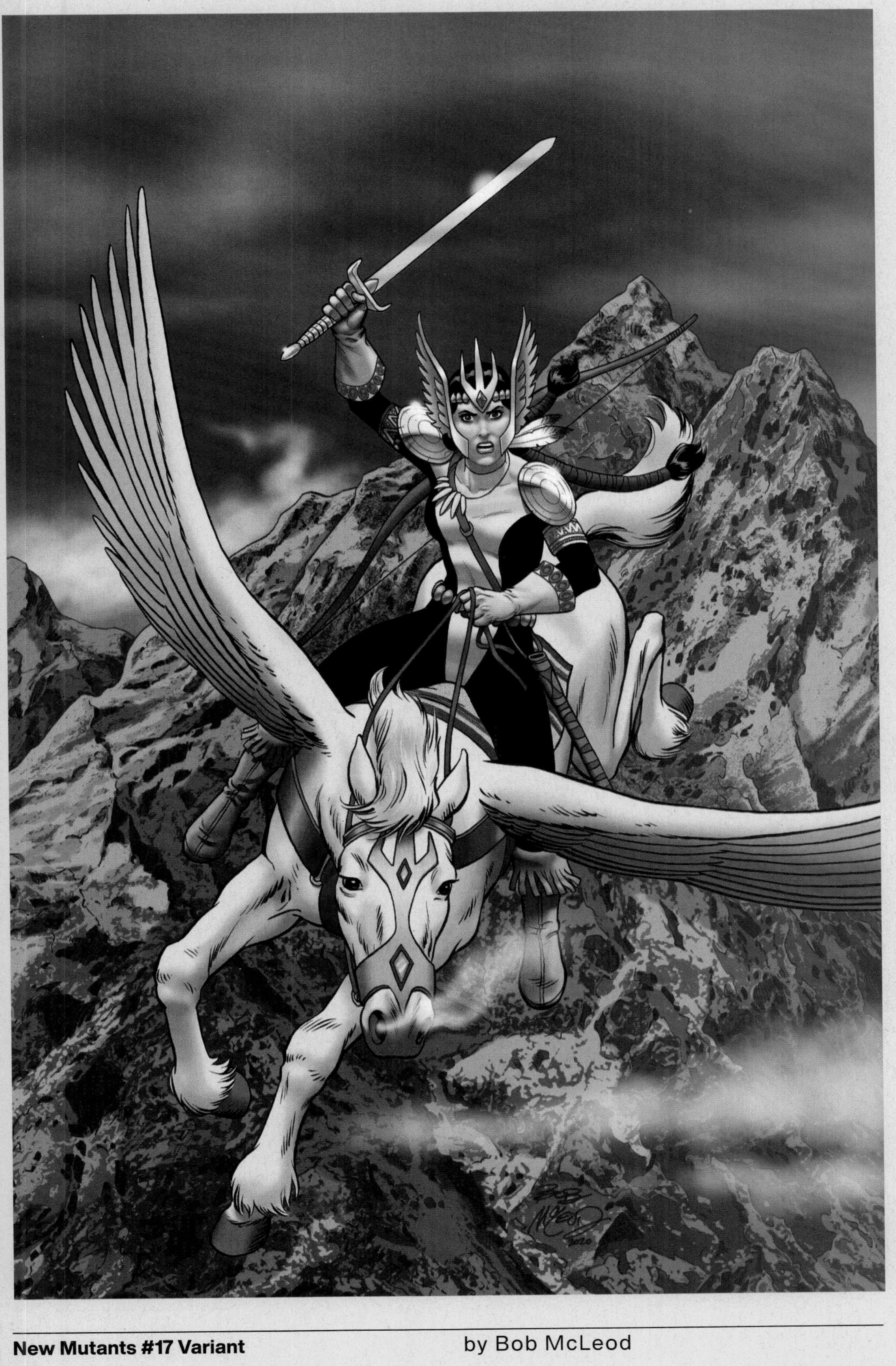

New Mutants #17 Variant by Bob McLeod

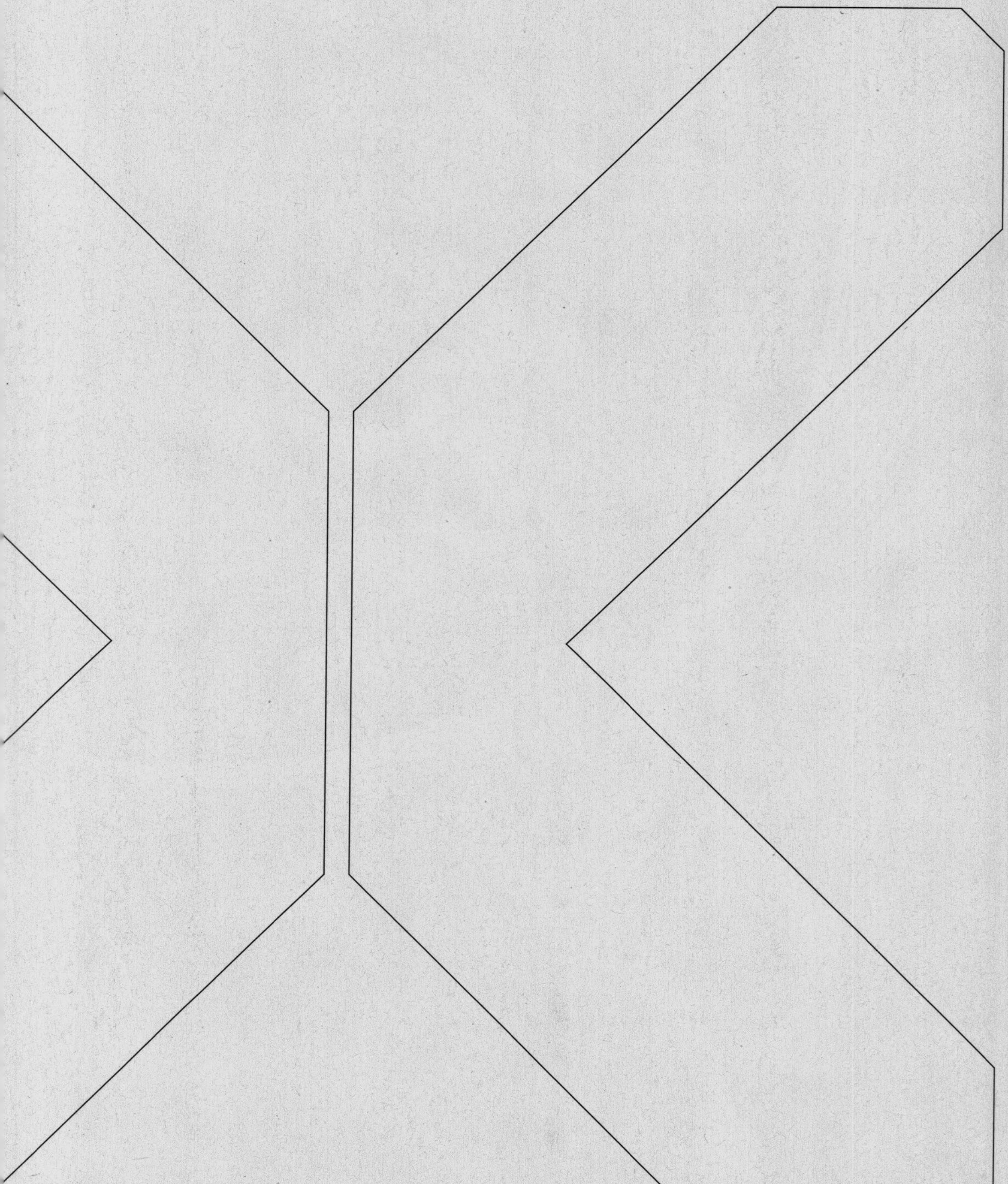